COLLINS COMPUTER SCIENCE 4

PADMAJA SUBHASH

Collins

4

COLLINS COMPUTER SCIENCE

BASED ON WINDOWS 10 & MS OFFICE 2013

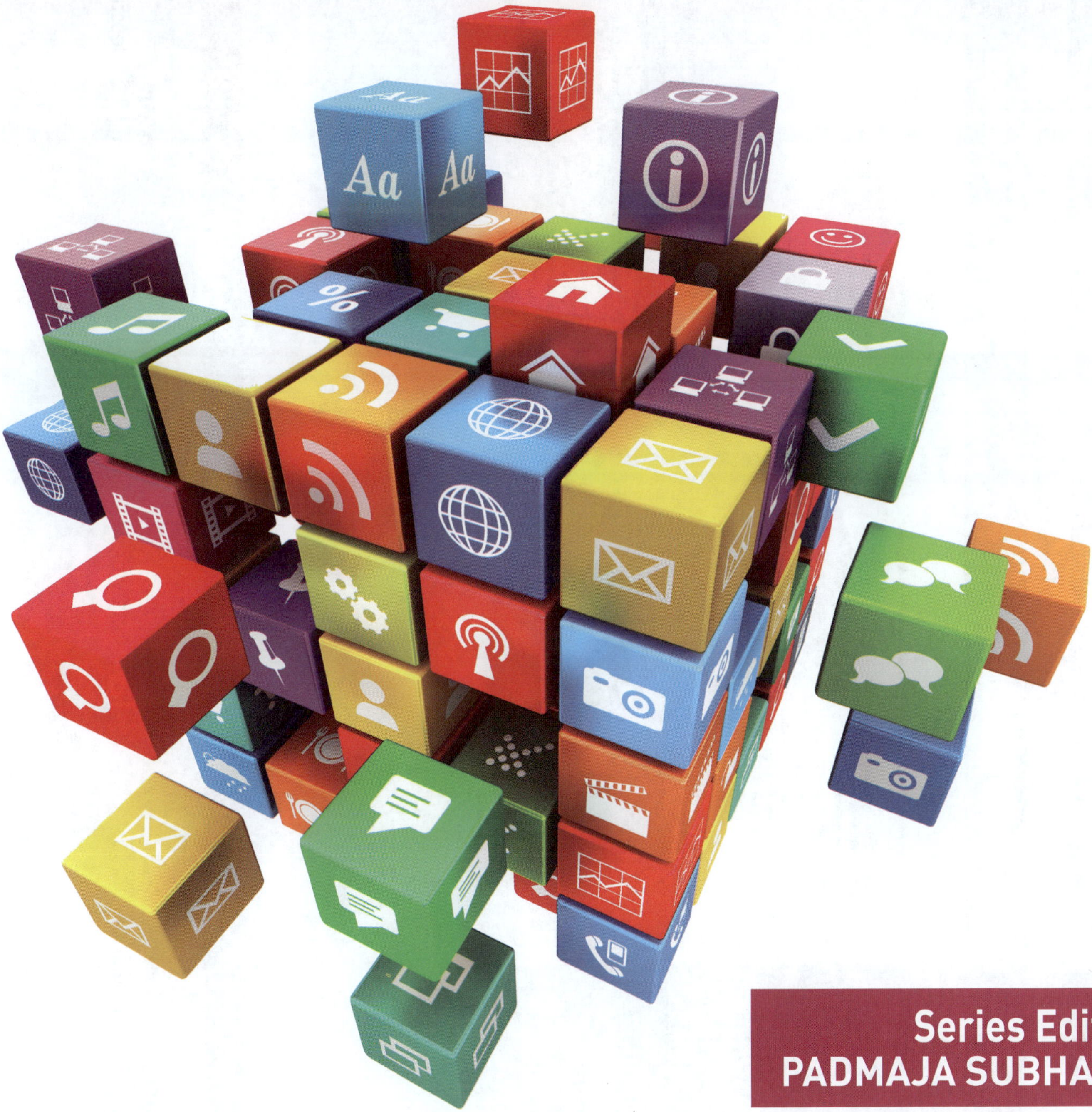

Series Editor
PADMAJA SUBHASH

Student + Teacher

- **a** animations
- **ilt** instructor-led tutorials
- **ia** activities
- **w** worksheets
- audio
- **g** games
- **v** videos

Teacher-only

- **lp** lesson plans
- **w** worksheets
- **tn** teacher's notes
- **ak** answer keys

PREFACE

Collins Computer Science, a series of eight books for Classes 1 to 8, is an interesting amalgamation of the latest technologies powered with interesting and innovative teaching methodologies. This combination ensures that learning outcomes at all the pedagogical levels conforms to the requirements of **National Curriculum Framework** and complies with the syllabus requirements of various boards.

The aim of this series is to create awareness among students about the latest in technological field and at the same time provide them with a strong foundation of the concepts to apply knowledge in real-life scenarios.

The course is based on **Windows 10** and **MS Office 2013** with updates on Open Office and Windows 8. This course also has the **National Cyber Olympiad** paper for students to practice. The concepts are presented in a straight forward manner and the understanding is tested at different levels.

The focus is to introduce computers for primary classes in a simple and lucid manner and extend the course to cover topics like animation, programming, logic building, web-designing in a detailed manner mentioning the steps and supporting it with self-explanatory screenshots. Care has been taken to keep the content updated as on the date of developing the content.

Apart from the basic software applications and operating system like MS Office and Windows, we have introduced the following topics like:

- Scratch Programming
- App Inventor
- Java
- Web 2.0 Education tools
- HTML 5
- Microsoft Visual Studio Code
- Cloud Computing

For creative software applications, we have covered open source software applications like Synfig Studio, OpenShot Video Editor and GIMP so that students can download them easily.

We have covered topics like tablets, electronic readers, smart gadgets, e-commerce and payment gateways so that students stay tuned to the developments in digital arena. Last but not the least, we have given a holistic approach to make the students aware about taking Computers as a career.

The course books are complemented by a comprehensive digital resource, Collins DigiSuite. We also have a detailed Teachers' Manuals for the teachers with suggestive period plan, lesson plan, answers to course book questions, test papers and worksheets with answers. These digital learning and teaching aids strengthen the course offerings empowering the teachers and students in the right way.

We would like to thank all the teachers who have reviewed the series and have ensured that all the pedagogical requirements are met keeping in mind the digital exposure that the student should get. We welcome constructive feedback and suggestions to improve these books further in subsequent editions.

Authors

Key Features

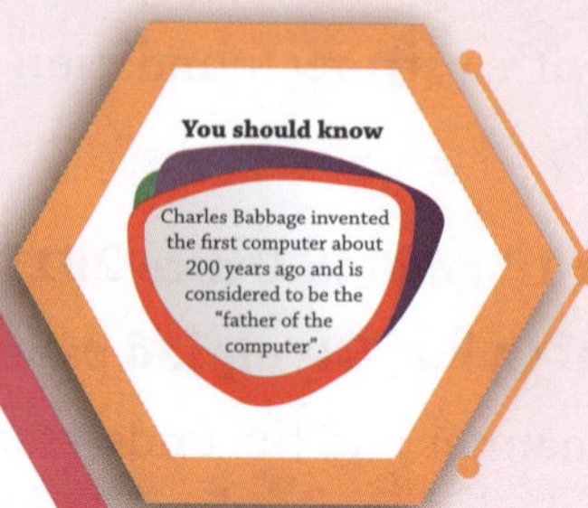

You should know
This feature includes interesting facts about the topic.

Word web
This feature lists the meanings of all the difficult words.

Recall
This feature lists the procedural difference between MS Office 2013 and MS Office 2010.

Digital geek
This feature mentions additional technical information about the topic.

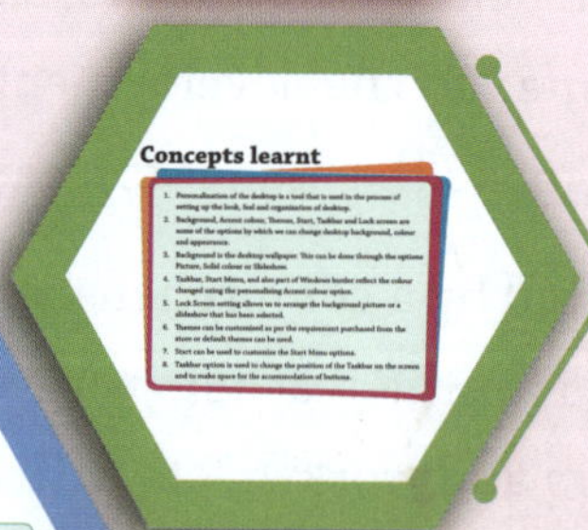

Concepts learnt
This feature recapitulates all the important points covered in the chapter.

Computer is my mentor!
This feature is given to test the practical application of the concept.

Net search
This feature lists the important websites that students can refer to extra information.

Key Features

Hands-on practice
This feature provides solution to hands-on practice questions given after important concepts.

Exercise
This feature is given to reinforce understanding of the concepts covered in each chapter.

Teacher's notes
This feature contains interesting topic-related notes that teacher can take up in class and demonstrate to students.

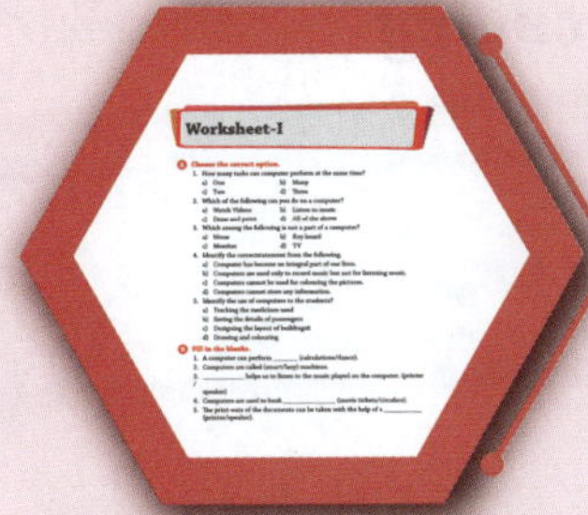

Worksheets
This feature facilitates the students and teachers with additional questions.

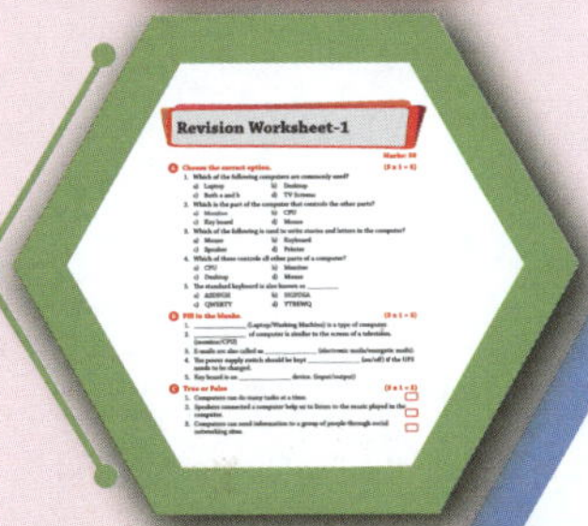

Revision worksheets
This feature adds on to the variety of questions that can be framed for various topics.

National Cyber Olympiad
This features gives the actual Olympiad paper for practice and exposure.

Mastering keyboard
This feature highlights all the keyboard shortcuts for the menu commands.

Contents

1 History of Computers

Learning log

- History of computers
- Five generations of computers

Introduction

List any five uses of a calculator.

1. ....
2. ....
3. ....
4. ....
5. ....

Fig. 1.1: Calculator

Calculator is one of the earliest machines invented by man to simplify mathematical calculations. Computer is a man-made device that processes and stores huge amount of data or information according to a set of instructions. A computer also helps us to perform various kinds of computing calculations.

Word web

computing: activity of using a computer and writing programs for it

The History of Computers

There have been major developments in the field of computers which we use today and, the developments are the outcome of many devices invented by man since the earliest of times for making calculations and storing information.

Milestones in the history of computer

Today we have the power of Internet, mail and entertainment in our smartphones. We need to look back to their evolution from the very basic beginnings. Some of the milestones in the history of computers are listed below:

Name of the device and year of invention	The device	More about the device
Tally stick	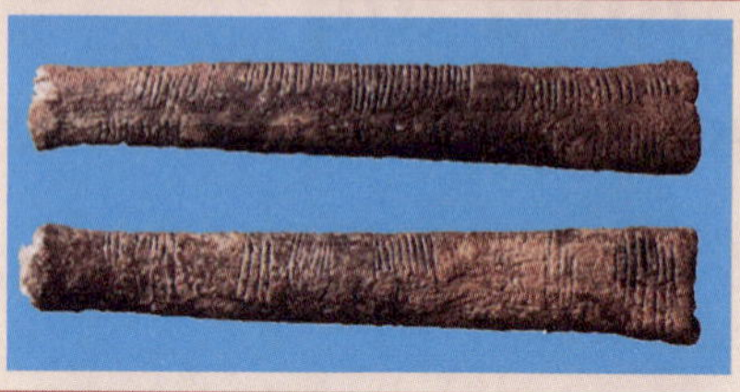	This device was used to record and document data or information which included numbers, words and messages. Tally stick is one of the most ancient memory devices used by man.
Abacus (500 BC)		A mechanical device with beads and strings in a frame called abacus was invented in Babylonia in (300 BC). The form of abacus that we use today for counting and doing mathematical calculation was invented in (500 BC) in China.
Pascaline (1642)	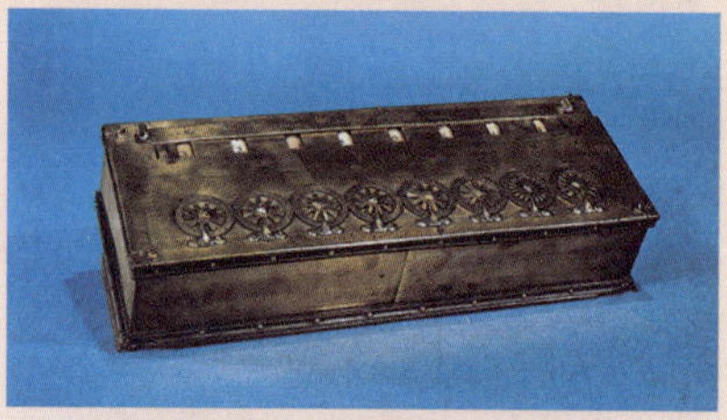	This was invented by Blaise Pascal. The device could do calculations related to addition and subtraction only.
Arithmometer (1820)		This mechanical calculator was invented by Thomas de Colmar. It was used to perform all the four basic mathematical calculations, namely addition, subtraction, multiplication and division. This was the first commercially available calculator.
Difference engine and analytical engine (1822-1840)	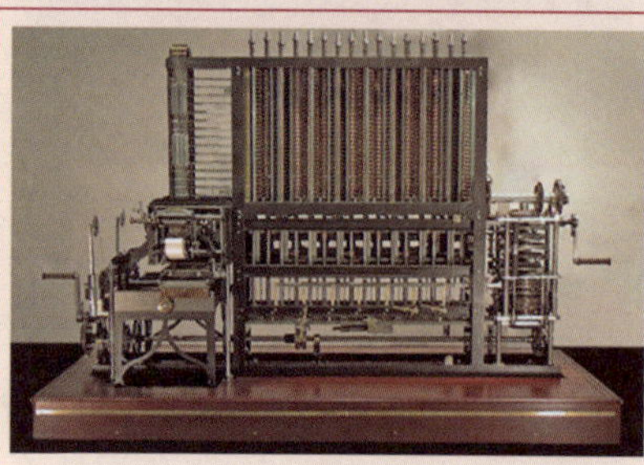	Invented by Charles Babbage, this is considered as the first mechanical computer. This was later improvised by Augusta Ada Byron.

Name of the device and year of invention	The device	More about the device
Z1 (1936–1938)		This was invented by Konrad Zuse. It was the first programmable computer. Inputs and outputs were given using punch tape.
ABC (Atanasoff-Berry Computer) (1939–1942)		Invented by John Atanasoff, it was the first electronic digital computer.
Harvard Mark 1/IBM automatic sequence controlled calculator (IBM ASCC) (1943)		This was invented by Howard H. Aiken and it was the first electro-mechanical computer.
ENIAC (Electronic Numerical Integrator and Computer) (1946)		The first general purpose computer was developed by John Presper Eckert and John W. Mauchly. Later, they developed UNIVAC 1 (UNIVersal Automatic Computer 1), also known as the first commercial computer.
EDVAC (Electronic Discrete Variable Automatic Computer) (1952)		The first stored program computer was developed by Von Neumann. This had the memory to store program as well as data.
Osborne 1 (1981)		Developed by Osborne Computer Corporation, this was the first portable computer.

The Five Generations of Computers

During the last 50 years, tremendous changes have taken place in the make up of computers. However, the computer as we find it today has come through five distinct generations. Each generation has distinct hardware and software, on which it is run.

There are distinct periods to which the development of each of the five generations of computer can be divided into. They are:

1. First-generation: (1946–1958)
2. Second-generation: (1959–1964)
3. Third-generation: (1965–1970)
4. Fourth-generation: (1971–2010)
5. Fifth-generation: (2011–onwards)

Word web

computer hardware: the physical parts of a computer

computer software: a set of instructions the computer runs on

First-generation of computers

The first-generation computers used to have a vacuum tube to run and magnetic drums to store information. The vacuum tube, a device used in radio, transmitters, television, apart from computers was the only available computing electronic device in those days. These first-generation computers used large space and were limited to solving one problem at a time. They also used a great amount of electricity and were expensive to run. The input was made through punched cards and the outputs came out through prints.

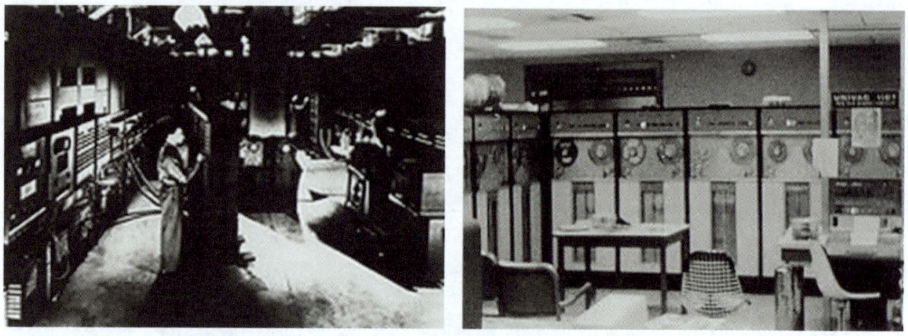

Fig. 1.2: First-generation computer

Second-generation of computers

The electric transistor replaced the heavy vacuum tubes by 1955. These transistors occupied lesser space and had higher operating speed. Magnetic core technology was used to store instructions into their memory, a change from magnetic drums. The input

Fig. 1.3: Second-generation computer

and output remained the same as in the first-generation computers. The transistors did not consist of a filament like the vacuum tubes. Thus, size and cost of the second-generation computers were reduced to a great extent.

Third-generation of computers

In third-generation computers, many transistors, resistors and capacitors were integrated into a single circuit called the integrated circuit. The integrated circuits were invented in the year 1964. This generation of computers was much smaller and cheaper when compared to the previous generation computers. They were fast and accurate in generating outputs. The keyboard was used as an input device. The Central Processing Unit (CPU) was used to run multiple instructions at a time and a monitor was used to display the output.

Fig. 1.4: Third-generation computer

Fourth-generation of computers

The computers we use today were invented around 1975. These are much smaller in size and cheaper than their previous forms. The fourth-generation computers use large scale integrated circuits (LSIC), built on a single chip called a **microprocessor**. The heavy processing unit of the previous generations was replaced by the microprocessor. Very large scale integrated (VLSI) circuits have replaced the LSIC. These are generally called personal computers or PC. These computers can be connected to form a network using LSIC and VLSI technology, and they are connected

Fig. 1.5: Fourth-generation computers

Word web

resistors: resist the flow of current in an electronic circuit
capacitators: tiny batteries which store electric charge and release it when required
integrated circuit: an electronic circuit material that can transfer information
silicon: it is a semi-conductive element which can transfer information through it and is the basic material of chips

on a small silicon chip. This global networking ultimately led to the development of the global communication system, the Internet. Mouse and other handheld devices like joystick, microphone and web camera were invented during this period.

Fifth-generation of computers

The use of optic fibres has revolutionized the world of computers. These have a very high processing speed and are highly reliable. Fifth-generation computers imitate intelligent human behaviour and are hence called **artificially intelligent**. Such computers respond to human language as input. They are capable of self-learning and self-organizing. Voice recognition applications used in our day-to-day life, where speech is converted to text, is an example.

Fig. 1.6: Fifth-generation computer

Word web

network: a set of computers connected to each other to share some information
internet: a set of computers connected globally to share information
optic fiber: a flexible, transparent fiber associated with the transmission of information from one place to another

Concepts learnt

1. Calculator was the first man-made device or machine used to simplify mathematical calculations.
2. Later they began to be used for storing information. The origin of computer goes back to the earliest efforts of man to calculate and memorize. Computers are grouped into different generations based on the hardware and software used in them.
3. There are five generations of computers.
4. The first-generation computers used vacuum tubes, the second-generation computers used transistors, the third-generation computers used integrated circuits, fourth-generation computers used LSIC and VLSI and the fifth-generation computers used optic fibres.
5. The fifth-generation computers are further being improvised using science and technology.

Exercise

A Fill in the blanks.

1. The beads and string device used for mathematical calculation is _______________ (abacus/tally stick).
2. Blaise Pascal invented the device called _______________ (Arithmometer/ Pascaline).
3. The first programmable computer is also known as _______________ (IBM ASCC/Z1).
4. The vacuum tube device belongs to the _______________ (first/third) generation of computers.
5. The second-generation computers were using _______________ (electric processors/electric transistors).

B Write T for True or F for False.

1. The Pascaline device was able to do all the four basic mathematical calculations. ☐
2. The difference and analytical engine was invented by Charles Babbage. ☐
3. ABC was the first electronic digital computer. ☐
4. The Electronic Controls Company was developed by UNIVAC 1. ☐
5. The fourth-generation computers used to occupy large space. ☐

C Choose the correct option.

1. Which of the following refers to the first basic calculating device?
   - (a) A person with maths skills
   - (b) Abacus
   - (c) UNIVAC
   - (d) ENIAC
2. Which generation used magnetic core technology ?
   - (a) First-generation
   - (b) Second-generation
   - (c) Third-generation
   - (d) Fourth-generation
3. Which of the following generations of computer could form a network?
   - (a) Fourth-generation
   - (b) First-generation
   - (c) Second-generation
   - (d) Third-generation

Exercise

4. What allows a computer to imitate human behaviour?
   (a) Power supply (b) Input devices
   (c) Artificial intelligence (d) Output devices
5. Which of the following generations of computer continues to evolve?
   (a) Second-generation (b) Third-generation
   (c) Fourth-generation (d) Fifth-generation

D Answer these questions briefly.

1. Name the first computer that could perform all the four mathematical calculations.
2. Which is the first portable computer?
3. Explain punched cards.
4. What is meant by generation of computers? How many generations of computers exist?
5. In which generation of computers were hand held devices used?

E Answer these questions in detail.

1. State one difference between first and second-generation computers.
2. Which invention do you think helped the computers to give faster outputs?
3. Which generation computers were fast and accurate in generating outputs? What were their circuit boards made up of?
4. Fifth-generation computers are called artificially intelligent computers. Justify the statement.
5. How did fourth-generation computers help people to share information globally?

Computer is my mentor!

1. Demonstrate the basic working of a desktop, laptop and a smartphone.
2. Discuss their advantages based on cost and usefulness.

2 Personalizing the Desktop

Learning log

- How to change Personalization settings
  - Desktop background
  - Lock screen
  - Start
  - Accent colour
  - Themes
  - Taskbar

Introduction

We all have our personal preferences for the way things around us should look, be it people, clothes, cutlery, bed or places. We even change the appearance or features of things to suit our own tastes. This choice is different for each of us. When we personalize something, we like to have it or see it in our own way. The choice of colours that we make for our study room is different from others. The clothes that we choose is different for every individual. This is a way of personalizing things in our day-to-day life. Likewise, our computer screens can also be personalized in the way they are displayed.

Personalization is the process by which the user can design the appearance of the computer screen. Desktop personalization improves the user's comfort level. It also gives a glimpse into our creativity.

Personalizing the desktop includes a variety of applications by which the user can change the desktop background, the theme which includes sound, colour and appearance of the windows border and lock the screen according to his or her interest. Certain operating systems hold additional features based on their versions.

Changing personalization settings

Here are two methods to change personalization settings in Windows 10:

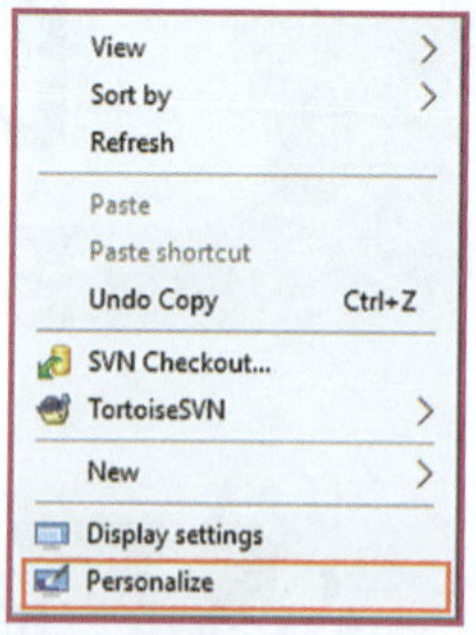

Fig. 2.1: Changing personalization settings using the right click option

Method I

1. Right-click on the open desktop.
2. From the drop-down menu, left-click on the Personalize option.

Method II

1. Left-click on Windows button from the Taskbar.
2. Left-click on Settings from the list.
3. Left-click on the Personalization tab from the Settings home page.

Personalization settings have a set of options that can be used to customize the appearance of the desktop. Following are the tabs available under Personalization.

1. Background
2. Color
3. Lock screen
4. Themes
5. Start
6. Taskbar

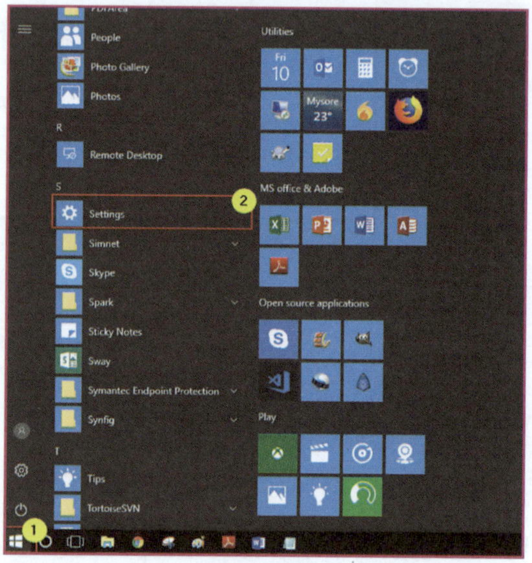

Fig. 2.2 (a): Alternate steps to start personalization from Windows Settings option

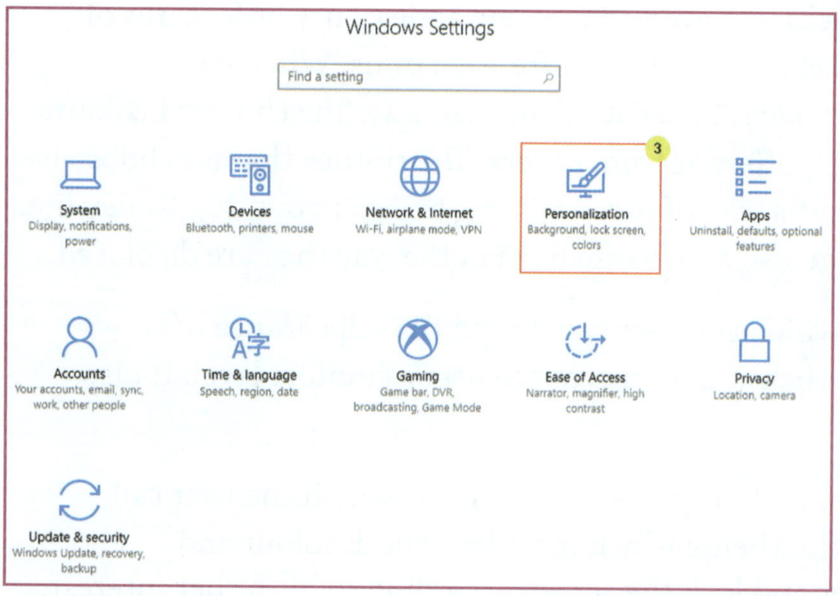

Fig. 2.2 (b): Alternate steps to start personalization from Windows Settings option

Background

Background refers to the desktop's wallpaper. A wallpaper of our choice marks the desktop as our own. The wallpaper can be selected in this tab. The Background menu offers three choices as shown in Figure 2.3.

> **Word web**
>
> **customize:** to make changes to suit an individual's requirements

1. **Picture:** One of the photos that is provided by Windows or a digital image of your own can be used as a static or fixed background.
2. **Solid Colour:** To keep a very simple desktop background, one can choose a plain Solid colour for the background. The colour can be chosen from a palette of 24 colours.
3. **Slideshow:** With this option, one can change the background image frequently to avoid the boredom of gazing at one thing for long time. Images for this need to be added in a folder and the same can be used as a slideshow.

While displaying a picture or a slideshow as your desktop background, the position of the image can be specified. Through the Choose a fit menu any of the following options may be chosen:

- **Fill:** The image fills every inch of the desktop.
- **Fit:** The entire image appears without cropping but black bars appear on the sides or at the two ends if the image is too large.
- **Stretch:** It stretches the picture either horizontally or vertically to fit the screen.
- **Tile:** This repeats the photo over and over until many images fill the monitor vertically or horizontally.
- **Center:** This places your photo in the centre surrounded by blank spaces, if the picture is smaller than the background and chops off the edges, if the picture is larger.

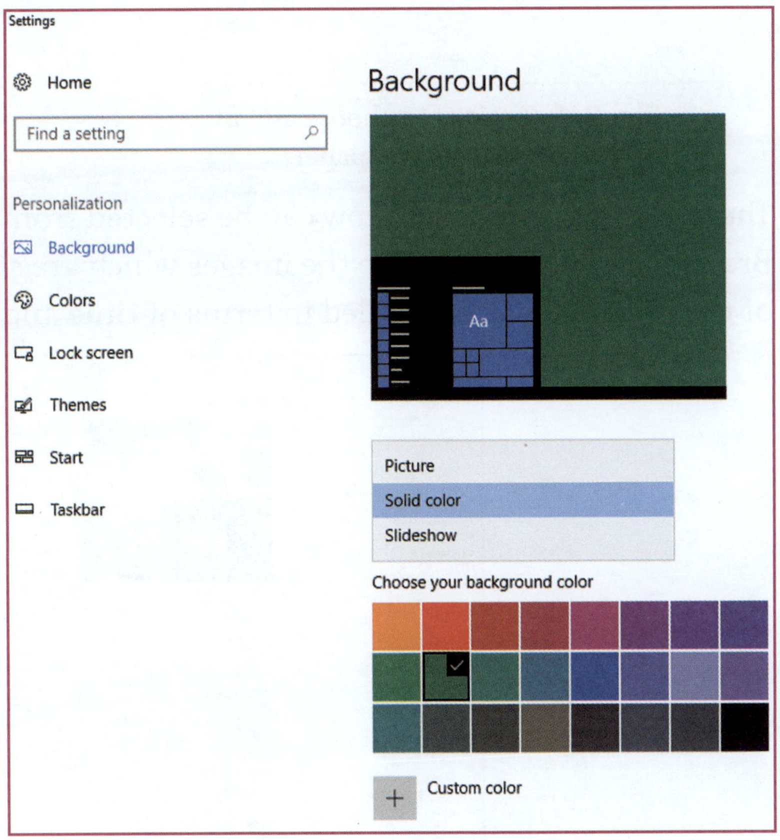

Fig. 2.3: Options to change the Background

- **Span:** This works well for multiple monitors and allows fitting one photo across multiple displays.

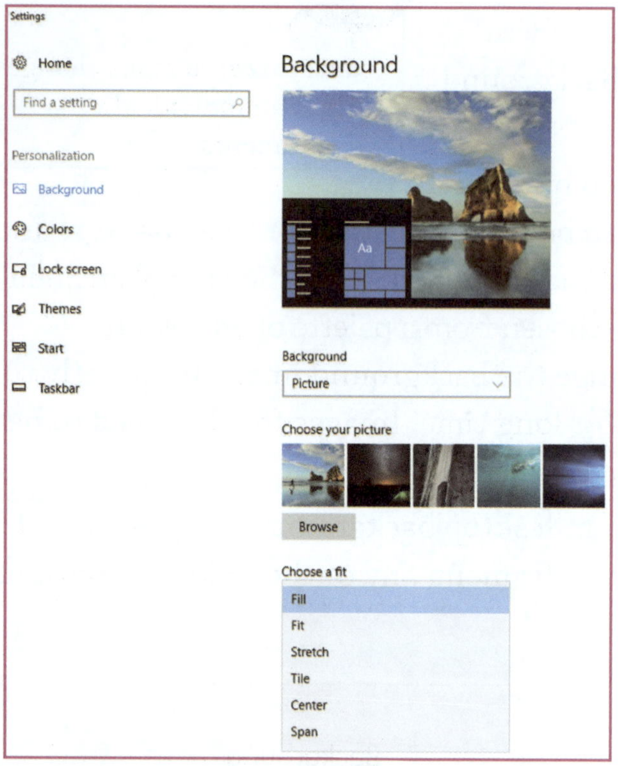

Fig. 2.4: Options to choose and fit an image as Wallpaper

You should know

Background Personalization page in Settings remembers the last five images that have been used previously.

The pictures for the slideshow can be selected from any album of your choice. The Browse tab helps us browse the images which are stored in the system. The appearance of the image can be scheduled in terms of time and shuffling.

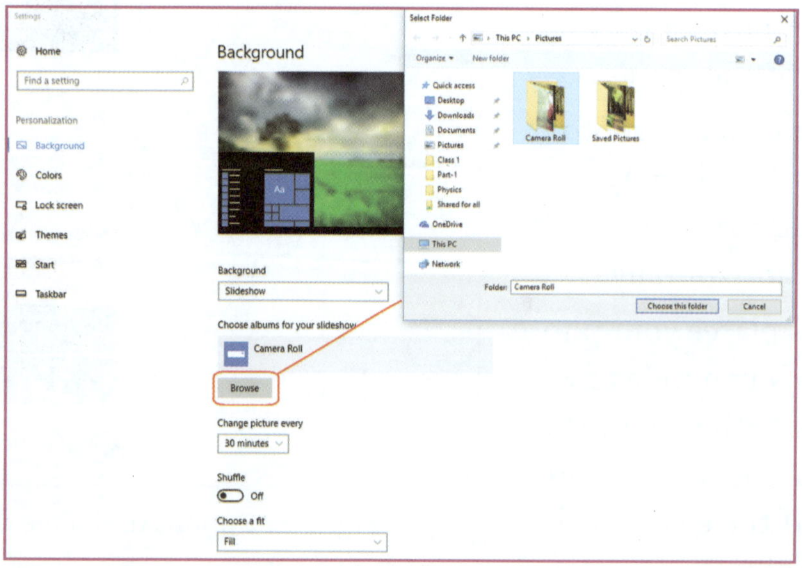

Fig. 2.5: Options to browse and add images to the Wallpaper slideshow

Accent colour

The colours displayed on the Start screen, Taskbar and Window of any application are controlled by the Colors settings. This option is just below the Background option.

On checking the option **Automatically pick an accent color from my background**, the computer automatically extracts the primary colour that matches with the background. These colours can be seen on the Taskbar, Start menu and Action Center.

The new dark theme is introduced by the technical preview phase which appears in the Taskbar, Start menu and Action Center. This will be the default theme when the Show accent colour on Start, taskbar, action center and Title bars option is disabled. When the option is enabled, colours flow from the Custom color selection or primary color, depending on the background image.

Options like Make Start, Taskbar and action center transparent are introduced to enable or disable transparency for Start menu but they can control transparency for Taskbar and action center as well.

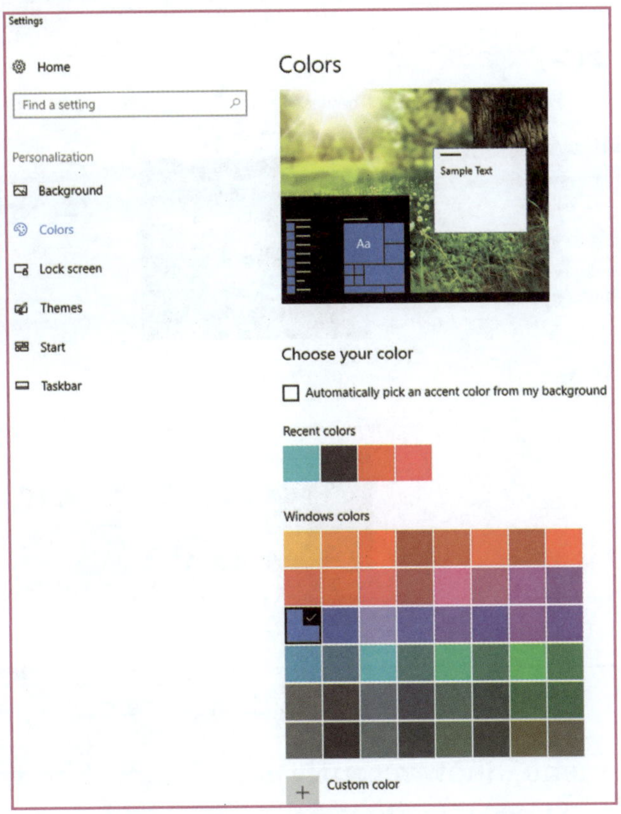

Fig. 2.6: Options to change Color

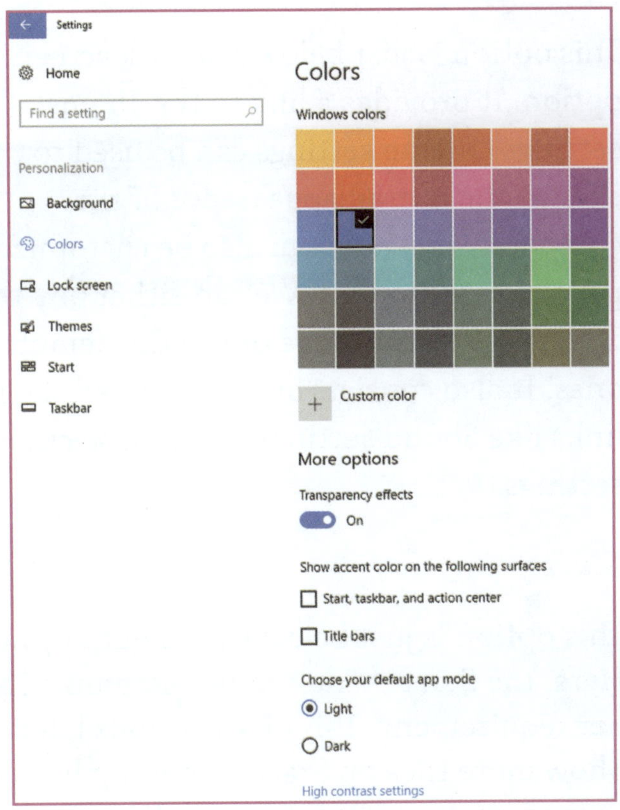

Fig. 2.7: More options to change Color

Lock screen

The Lock screen option appears just below the Colors option. Lock screen settings allows us to arrange or change the picture or add a slideshow. This appears when the computer screen is locked. It also has an option to pull down random background from the Internet called **Windows spotlight**.

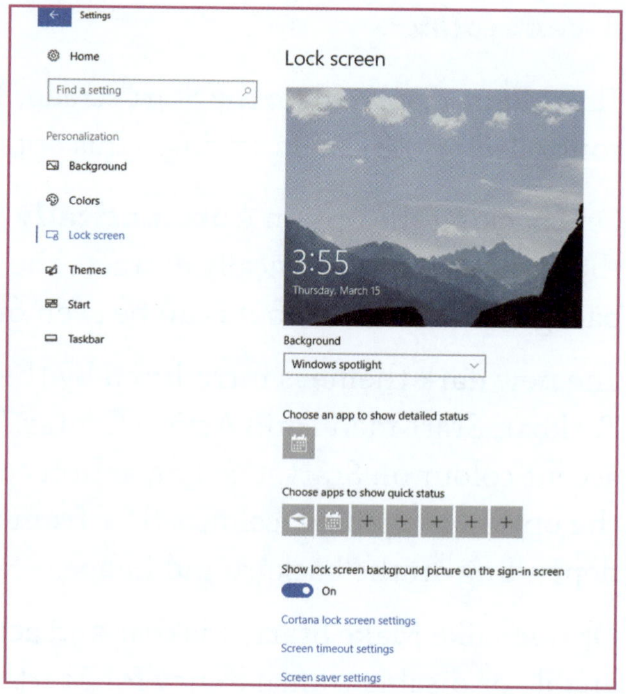

Fig. 2.8: Options to change Lock Screen

On the Lock screen option, features like clock, calendar, mail, weather, xbox, etc., can also be added to check their quick status. It also provides advanced options like Cortana lock screen settings, Screen timeout and Screen saver settings.

Themes

This option is just below the Lock screen option. It provides a link to the Theme settings. Theme settings can be used to change the overall appearance of the computer screen. It can also be customized as per the requirement. We can either buy the Themes from the Store or use the default ones. It also consists of a few related settings links like Sound settings and Mouse cursor settings.

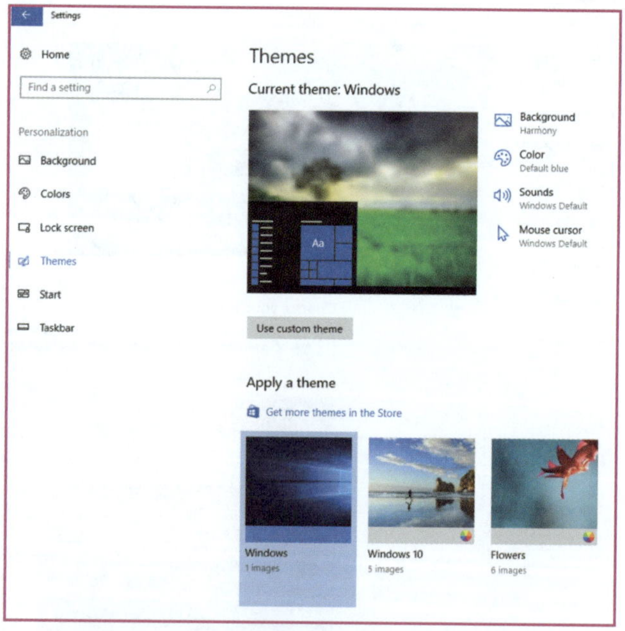

Fig. 2.9: Options to change Themes

Start

This option is just below the Themes option. Here, the Start menu can be customized as per requirement. This gives options like: Show more tiles on Start, Show app list in Start menu, Show recently added apps, Show most used apps, Occasionally show suggestions in Start, Use Start full screen and also Show recently opened items in Jump Lists on Start or the taskbar.

Under advanced options it also gives options to choose the folders that appear on Start. Folders like Documents, Download, File Explorer, Music, etc., can be added to the Start.

Digital geek

Desktop background image history can be deleted by typing 'Regedit' in Run command and then typing WIN+R.

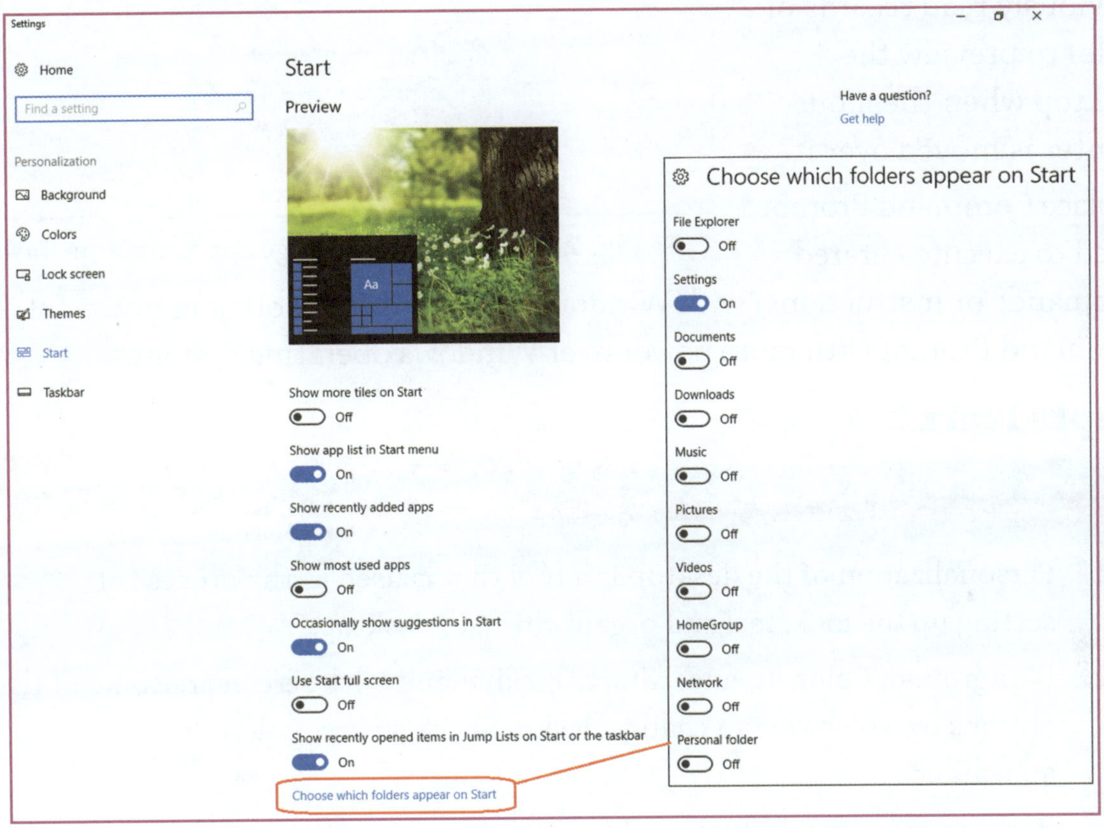

Fig. 2.10: Options to change appearance and features in Start

Taskbar

This option is just below the Start option. It provides access to move the Taskbar from its default location to any other edge of the screen. Regardless of the Taskbar location, the height or the width of the Taskbar can be changed to accommodate more buttons. Switch on Use small taskbar buttons which provides more space to accommodate the buttons.

Some of the other changes that can be made are:

- Differentiation of active app buttons by a coloured bar.
- Hiding the taskbar.
- Using Peek function (a tool that allows us to peek into previously read records of a table) to preview the desktop when the mouse pointer is moved over it.
- Replace Command Prompt (used to execute entered commands or instructions) with Windows PowerShell, a tool more powerful than Command Prompt with more power over Windows operating system.

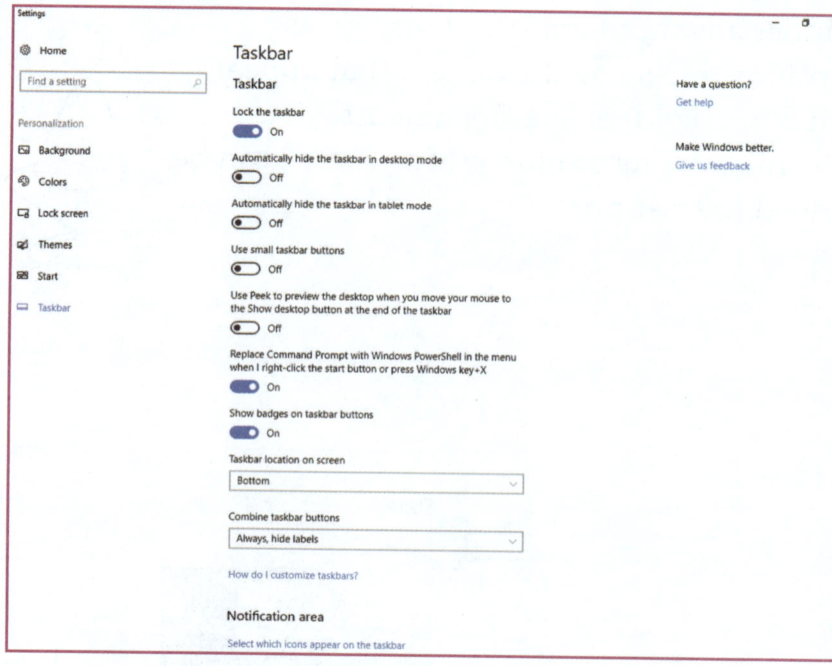

Fig. 2.11: Options to change appearance on Taskbar

Concepts learnt

1. Personalization of the desktop is a tool that is used in the process of setting up the look, feel and organization of desktop.
2. Background, Color, Themes, Start, Taskbar and Lock screen are some of the options by which we can change desktop background, colour and appearance.
3. Background is the desktop wallpaper. This can be set through the options Picture, Solid color or Slideshow.
4. Taskbar, Start Menu, and also part of Windows border reflect the colour changed using the personalizing Color option.
5. Lock Screen setting allows us to arrange the background picture or a slideshow that has been selected.
6. Themes can be customized as per the requirement purchased from the store or default themes can be used.

Hands-on practice

With the premission of your teacher, change the Personalization settings of a computer in school lab. Try to give a slideshow of the pictures of your school's Annual Day in the background. Also, move the taskbar to the right-edge of the compuer screen. Write the steps you followed in the space given below.

Exercise

A Fill in the blanks.

1. ________________ (Personalization/Slideshow) is to design the appearance of the computer screen to meet an individual's requirement.
2. ________________ (Slideshow/Display) option needs to be selected to display images from a folder as wallpaper.
3. Automatically pick an accent colour from my background enables systems to automatically extract ________________ (primary/secondary) colours in background.
4. ________________ (Color/Theme) settings can be used to change the overall appearance of the computer screen.
5. Choose which folder appears on Start is an advanced option that appears in ________________ (Start/Color) option.

B Write T for True or F for False.

1. Desktop personalization improves user comfort level. ☐
2. Choose a fit is available on Background setting screen. ☐
3. Mouse cursor setting is available on Theme setting screen. ☐
4. Windows Spotlight, Picture and Slideshow are available on Lock Screen settings. ☐
5. The new dark theme is introduced by technical preview phase which appears in the Taskbar. ☐

C Choose the correct option.

1. Changing the settings of desktop background themes to user comfort level is called ________________.

   (a) user accounts (b) system

   (c) personalization (d) program and features

2. Which one of the following is not a part of Personalization settings?

   (a) Background (b) Taskbar

   (c) Lock screen (d) Address bar

3. Which of the following words also means the background of your desktop?
   (a) Wallpaper (b) Screen saver
   (c) Main screen (d) Lock screen
4. Which of the following features is not available for Lock Screen?
   (a) Solid color (b) A picture
   (c) Slideshow (d) Windows spotlight
5. Which of these options from Personalization setting provides quick status check of the weather report?
   (a) Background (b) Lock screen
   (c) Theme (d) Start

D Answer these questions briefly.

1. What is meant by personalizing the desktop?
2. How do you set a new background in your desktop? What are the options available to change the background?
3. What are the settings available in the Colors option from the Personalization settings?
4. Explain the uses of Lock screen options in Personalization settings?
5. What are the options available in the Start option of Personalization settings?

E Answer these questions in detail.

1. Smith wants to change the appearance of his computer screen. What should he do to change the settings?
2. Henry wanted to have a slideshow of images as his wallpaper. What should he do to get the same?
3. Emily keeps her computer monitor locked for long hours. During this time she fails to check the new mails she gets. She is usually late in replying to her mails. What option from the personalization setting can she use to overcome this issue?

Computer is my mentor!

Personalize your destop wallpaper with slideshow.

3 Organizing Files and Folders in Windows 10

Learning log

- The meaning of File, Folder and Sub-folder
- Windows 10 File Explorer
- Components of File Explorer

Introduction

You may have noticed that in supermarkets, similar things are grouped separately in various sections like fruits, vegetables, cosmetic items so that we can pick them up quickly without searching much. Similarly, in a cloth shop or in a library, the clothes or the books are arranged in a systematic way.

Fig. 3.1 (a): Arranging files

In the same manner, every file or folder on the computer is represented by an icon so that we can recognize them easily. But that is not enough. When we work on a computer, it is essential to save and organize the information in a systematic way to locate it easily. Let us learn about the organization of information that is saved in the form of files and folders in Windows 10 in detail in this chapter.

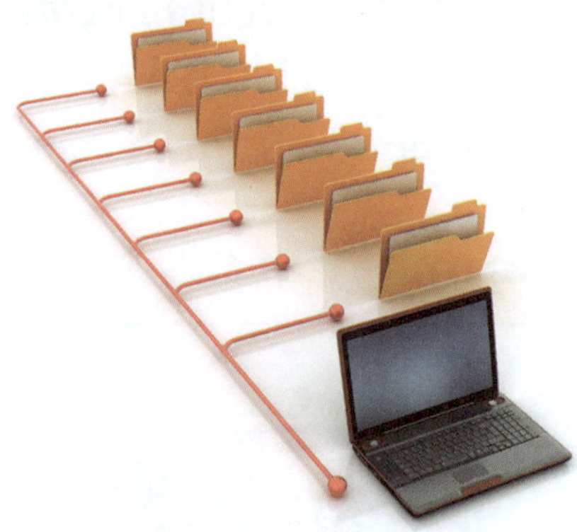

Fig. 3.1 (b): Sorting files

File Explorer

File Explorer is used to explore files and folders on a computer system.

File

Almost all information that is stored in a computer such as text, image, audio, video, and programs must be in a file. Different kinds of files store different kinds of information. For instance, PowerPoint Presentation and Word Document are two different kinds of files. Fig. 3.2 shows icons of different types of files. The name of a file helps us to identify it. We can rename a file whenever we want. Files are represented by icons to locate them easily.

Fig. 3.2: Different files and their icons

Folder

The place where a file is saved is known as a folder. Fig. 3.3 represents an icon of a folder. Name of the folders provide clue about their content and they can be changed just like file names. Folders help us to locate files easily on a computer.

Fig. 3.3: Folder icon

Sub-folder

The folder within a folder is called a sub-folder. Icon of a sub-folder is same as icon of a folder as in Fig. 3.3. Users can create any number of files and sub-folders in a folder.

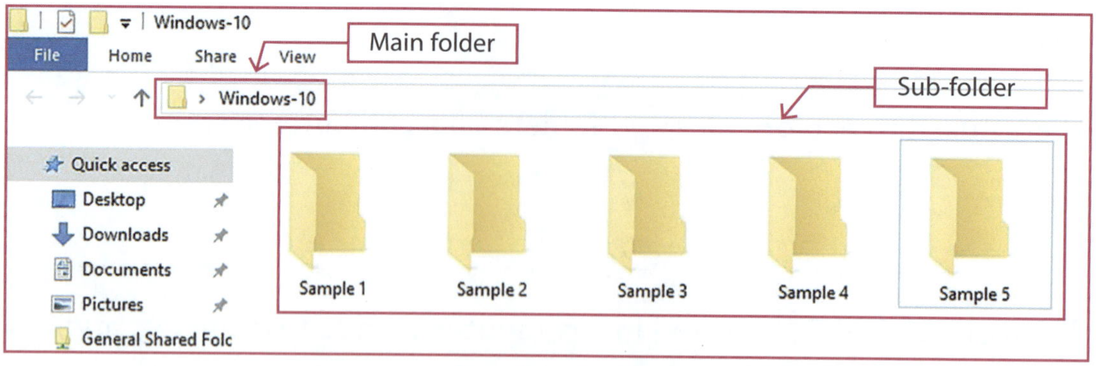

Fig. 3.4: Sub-folders within a folder

Windows 10 File Explorer

We can create, view and organize the files and folders using File Explorer in Windows 10.

1 Click on the Start button and select the File Explorer to start it.

2 A new File Explorer window will appear by double-clicking on any of the folders on the desktop.

Recall

In Windows 7 and in earlier versions, it was called as Windows Explorer.

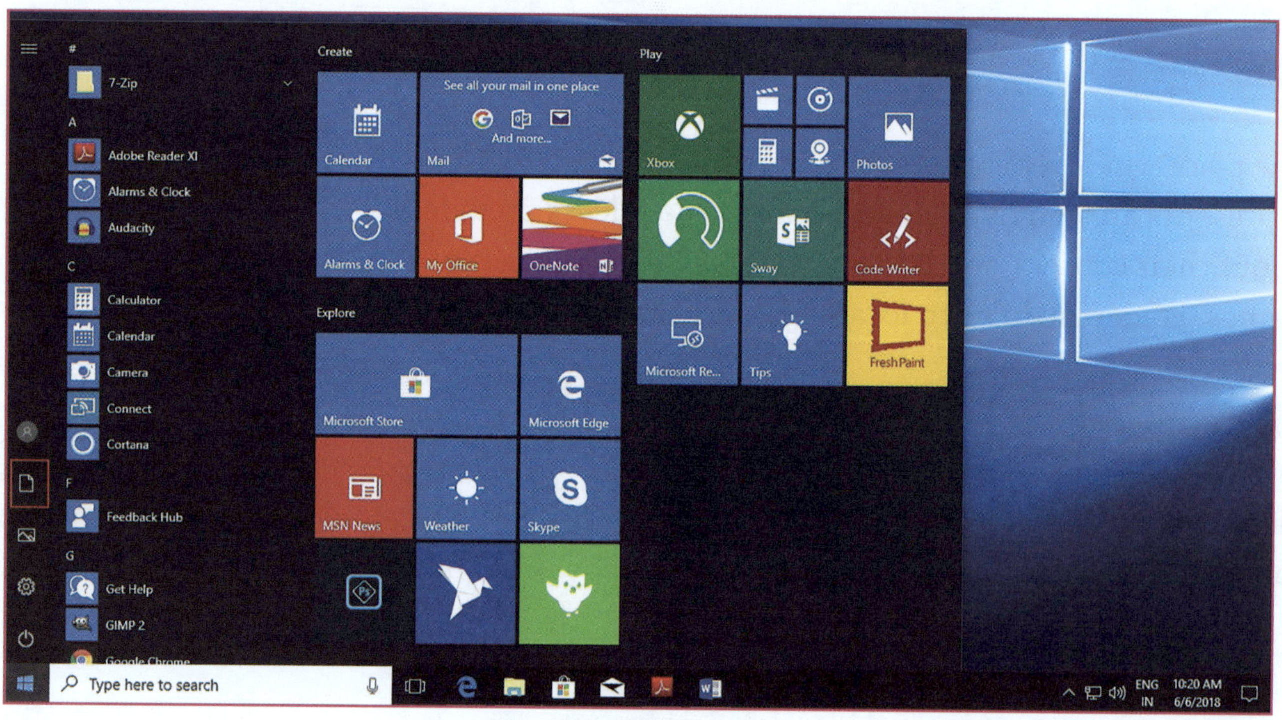

Fig. 3.5: File Explorer

Components of File Explorer

The various tabs of Windows 10 File Explorer and their uses are given below:

Left pane

Left pane is used to see different locations and drives of the system.

Quick access toolbar

The folders that the users commonly access can be pinned to Quick Access Toolbar.

Ribbon

Ribbon appears when a user selects a file or folder. It displays the options for the users to rename, copy, change the view, move and delete.

Navigation bar

Navigation bar is used to move forward and backward between folders.

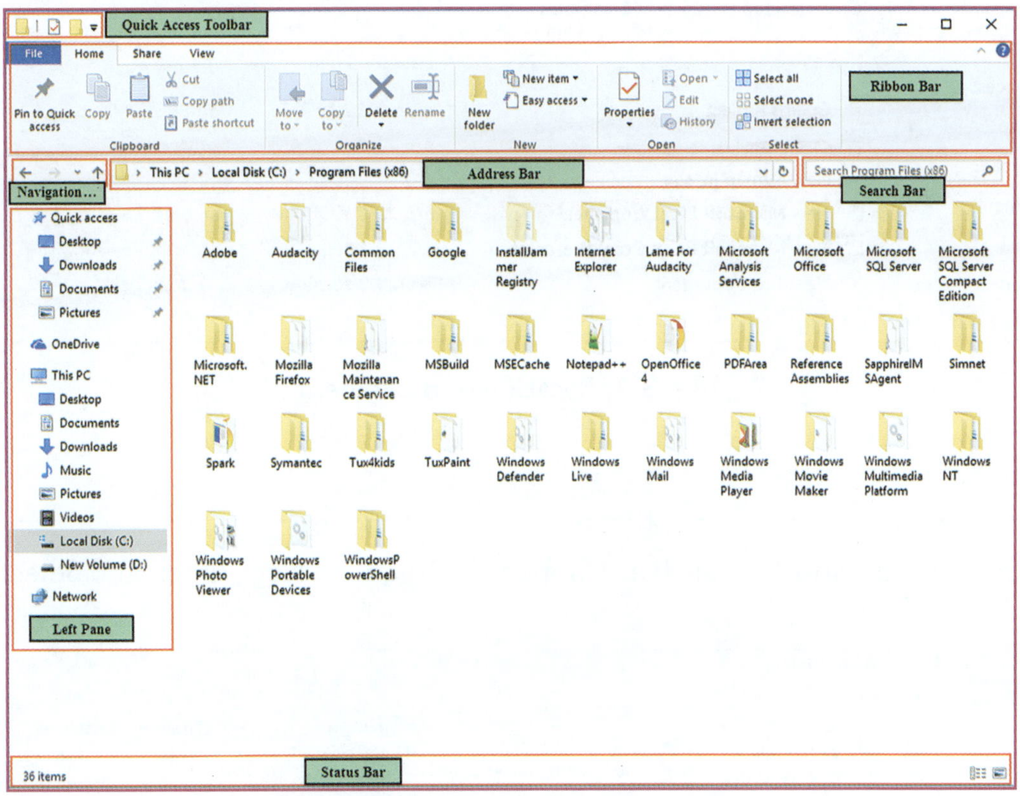

Fig. 3.6: Components of File Explorer

Address bar

Address bar is the field that helps us to locate the website.

Search box

Search box is used to locate the files that are stored in the selected folder.

Status bar

Status bar provides information about the size and the number of files that are stored in the window.

How to know the location of the folder?

The location of the folder can be seen in the Address bar situated at the top of the window. Refer to Fig. 3.7.

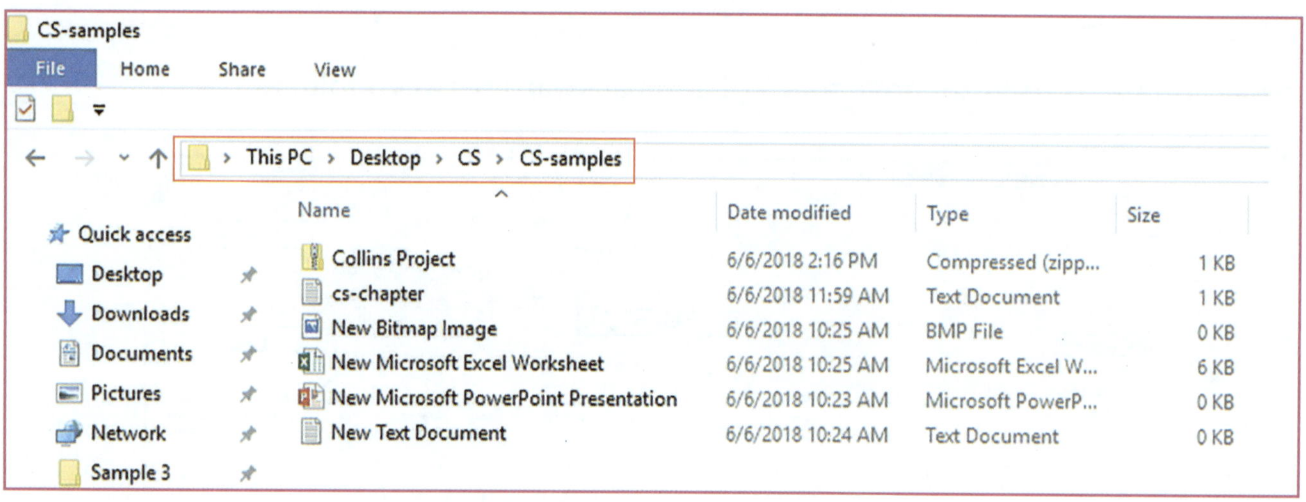

Fig. 3.7: Location of the folders

Home tab

The Home tab contains sub-tabs such as Clipboard, Organize, New, Open and Select as shown in Fig. 3.8.

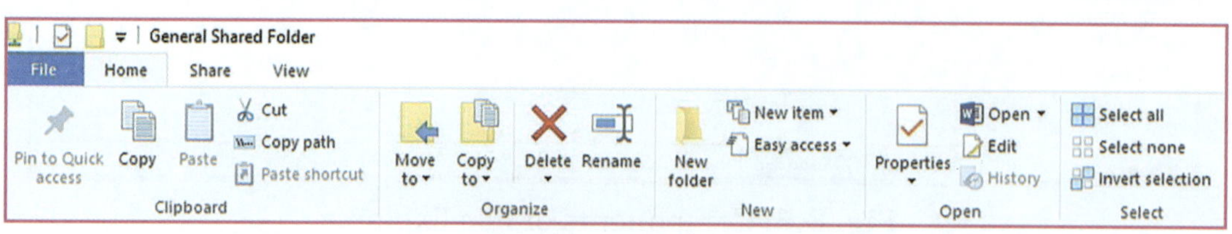

Fig. 3.8: Home tab

Creating a new folder

The steps to create a new folder are as follows:

1 In the File Explorer, select a location where the folder needs to be created as in Fig. 3.9 (a).

2 Identify the New folder icon and click on the icon as in Fig. 3.9 (b).

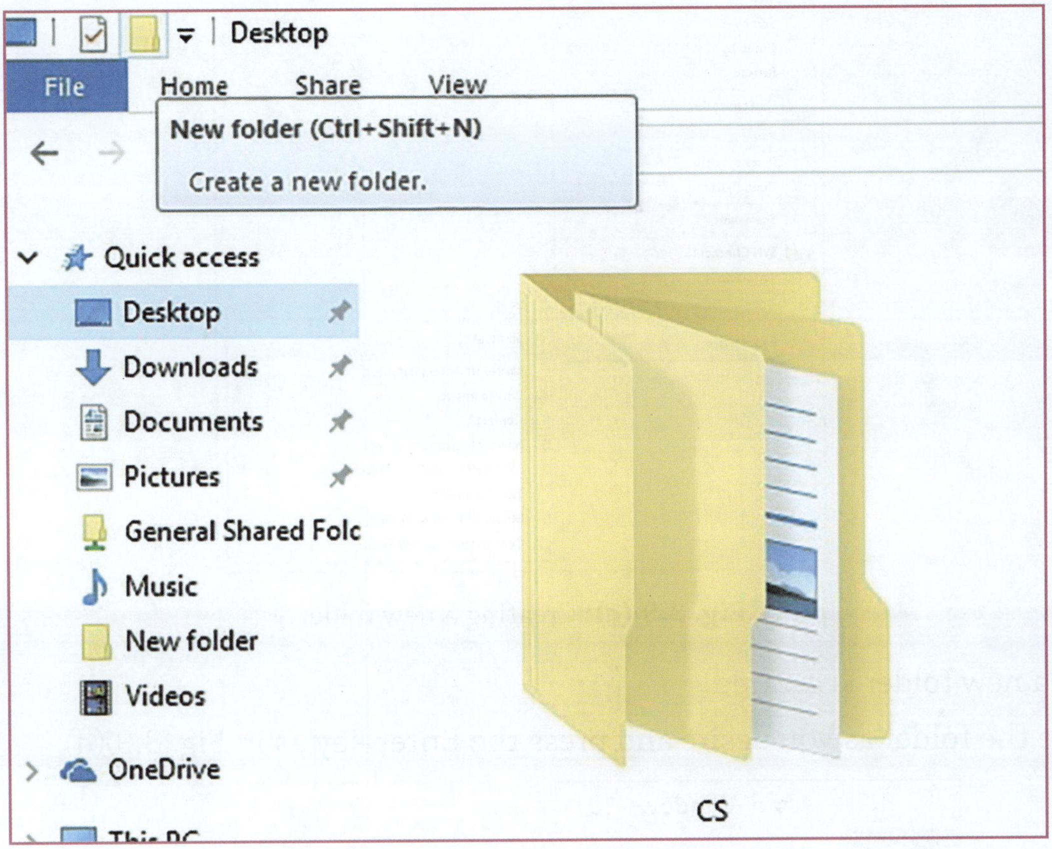

Fig. 3.9 (a): Selecting location for new folder

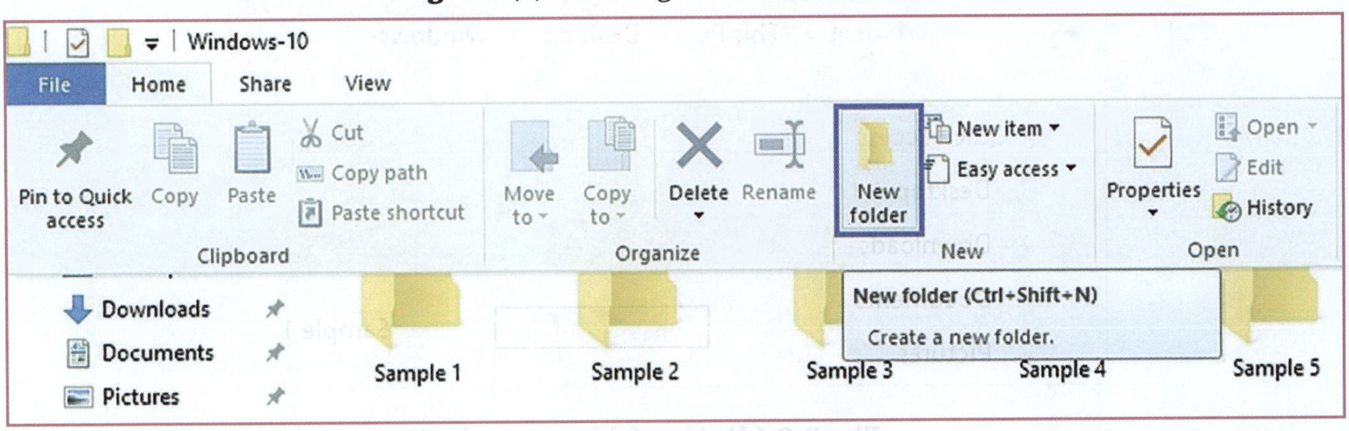

Fig. 3.9 (b): Creating new folder

(Or)

3 Right-click on the blank space where you desire to create a folder. A drop-down of menu will be displayed.

4 Choose the option New from the drop-down menu and again select the Folder option and click on it. Refer to Fig. 3.9 (c).

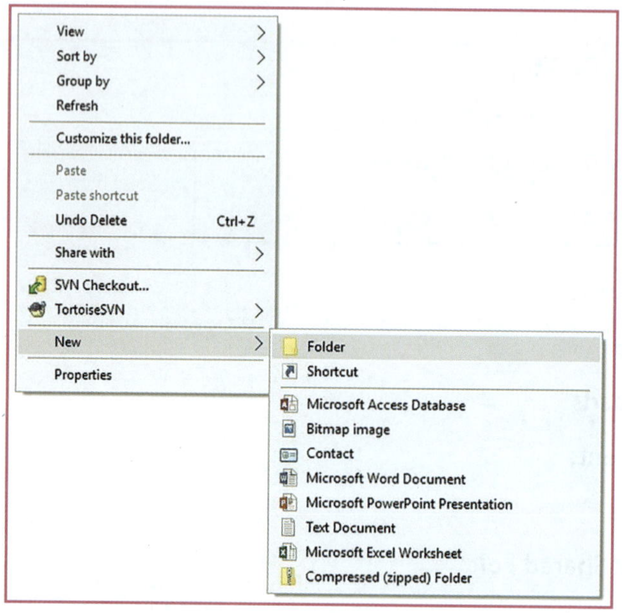

Fig. 3.9 (c): Creating a new folder

5 Now a new folder is created.

6 Name the folder as you desire and press the Enter key as in Fig. 3.9 (d).

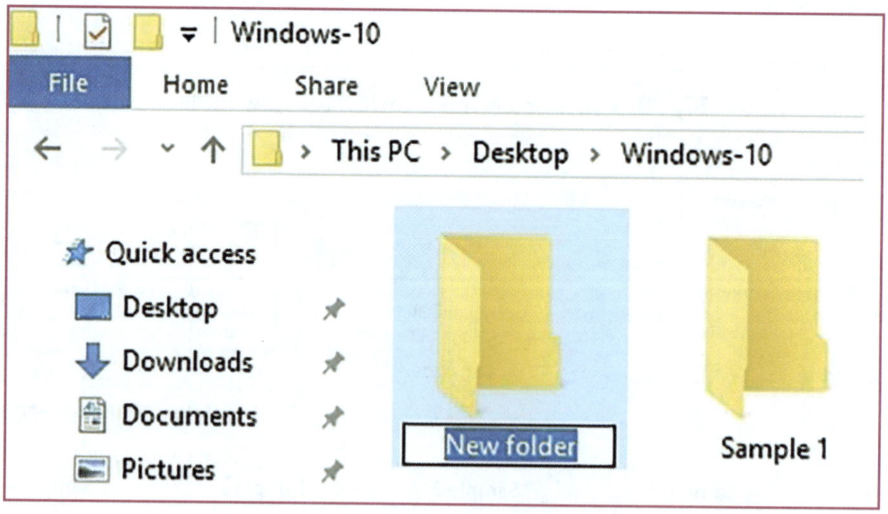

Fig. 3.9 (d): New folder created

7 The files can be moved now into the new folder.

Creating a new item

The steps to create a new item are as follows:

1 Click on the tab New item situated in the Home tab; a drop-down menu pops up on the screen. Refer to Fig. 3.10.

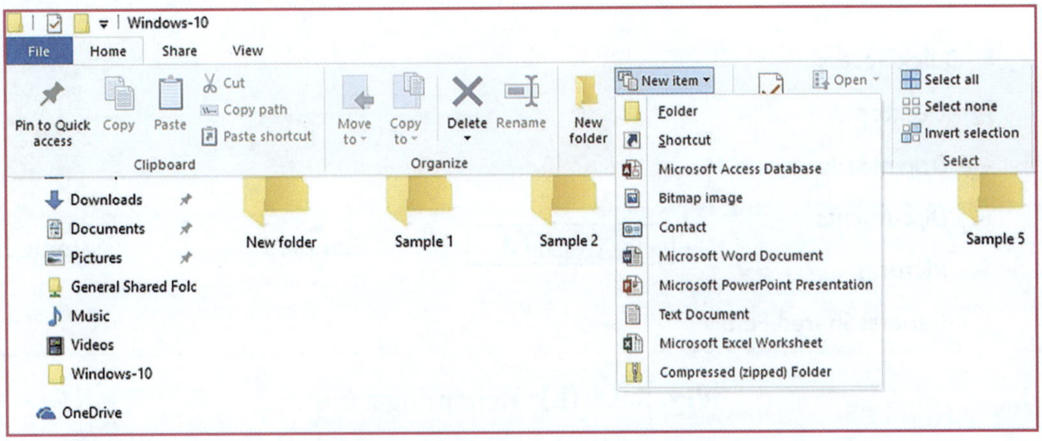

Fig. 3.10: Creating a new item

2 Choose the type of file that you need to create and click on it.

3 Now a new type of file that you chose is created.

Renaming a file or a folder

Providing a unique name for the files and folders that are stored in computers help to locate them easily and to know the type of content saved in them.

The steps to rename the files are as follows:

1 Right-click on a file or a folder that you desire to rename.

2 Select the option Rename from the drop-down menu. Refer to Fig. 3.11 (a).

(Or)

3 Click on the file or a folder that you desire to rename, wait for a second and click on that file or folder again.

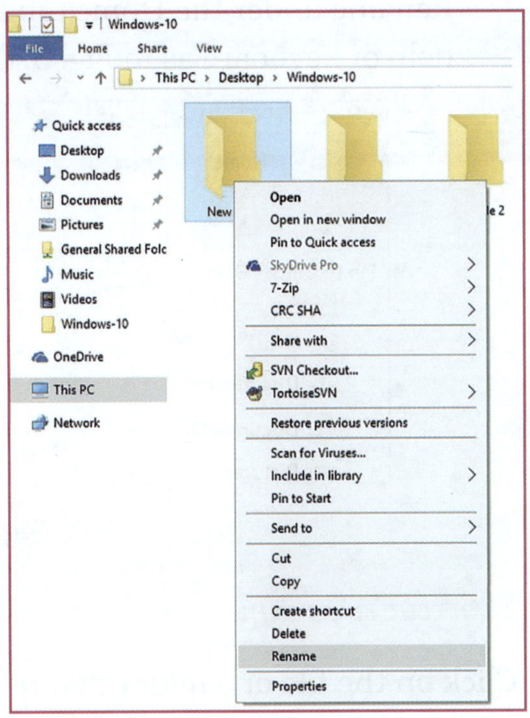

Fig: 3.11 (a): Renaming a file

4 Now a highlighted editable text field will appear as shown in Fig. 3.11(b).

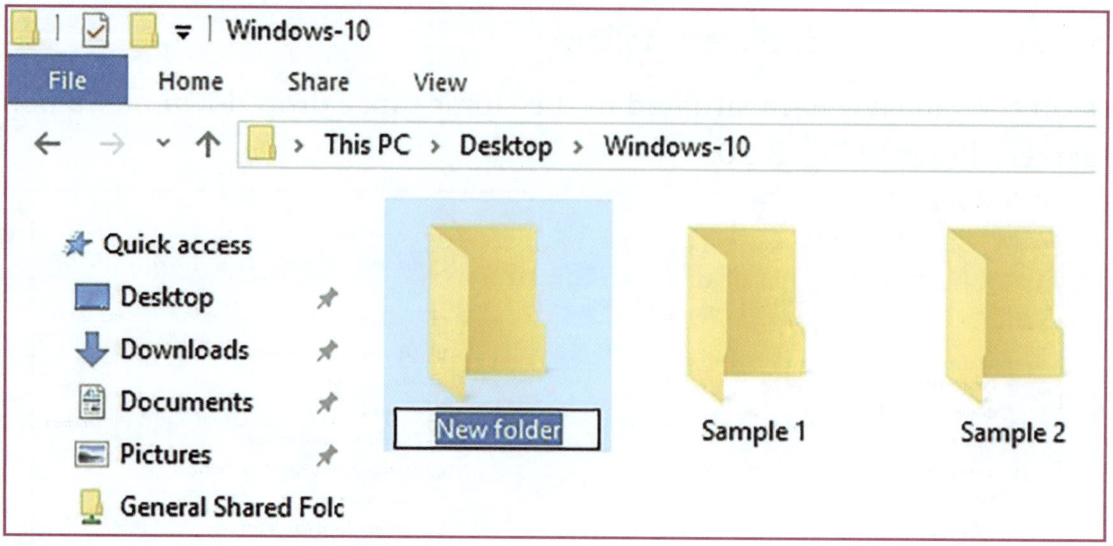

Fig. 3.11 (b): Renaming a file

5 Type the name that you desire and press the Enter key.

6 The name of the file or folder is changed now.

Or

7 To rename the files easily without leaving the current location, select the option Rename under the Home tab and write the name that you desire by typing with the help of keyboard as in Fig. 3.11 (c).

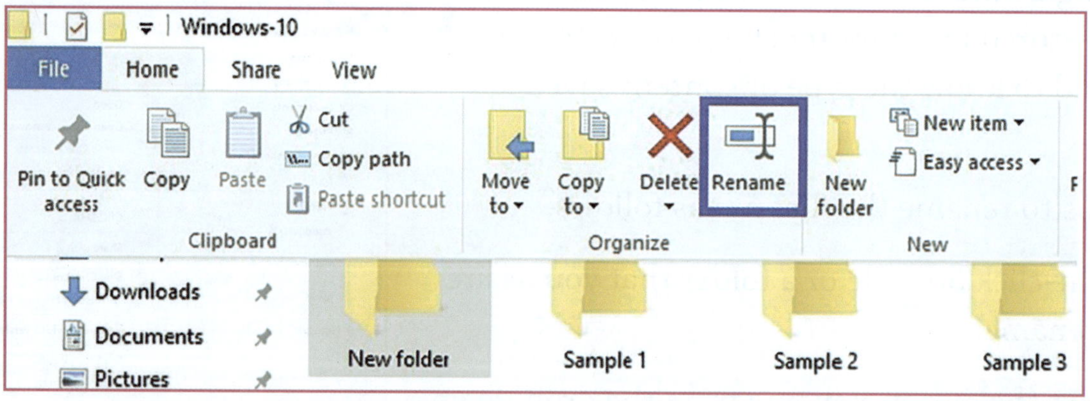

Fig. 3.11 (c): Renaming a file

Shortcut to rename

Click on the file or a folder that needs to be renamed and then press **F2** key on the keyboard. Type the desired name in the highlighted portion and press Enter key.

File naming convention

While naming the files and folders, make sure that the following characters are not used as these characters are not supported.

< (less than)	> (greater than)	: (colon)
" (double quote)	/ (forward slash)	\ (backslash)
| (vertical bar or pipe)	? (question mark)	* (asterisk)

Copying and pasting a file or a folder

When users want to take a copy of files or folders to a new location as well as retain them in their original location, the option of Copy is used.

The steps to copy a file or a folder are as follows:

1 Click on the file or folder that you want to copy. Refer to Fig. 3.12 (a).

2 Select the Copy option under the Home tab.

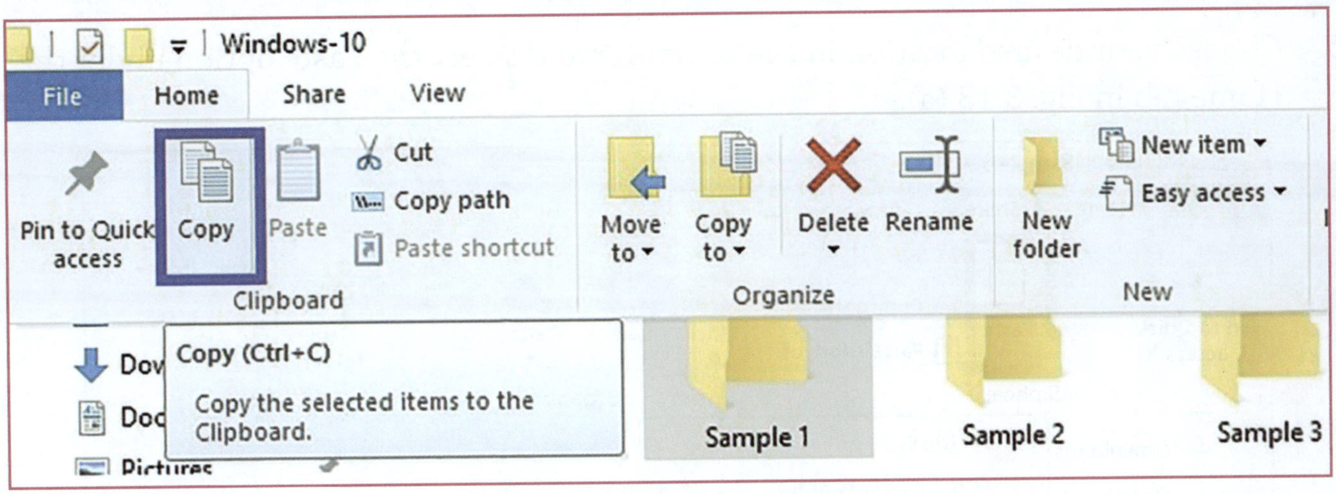

Fig. 3.12 (a): Copying a file

(Or)

3 Right-click on a file or a folder that you wish to copy. Refer to Fig. 3.12 (b).

4 Select the option Copy from the drop-down menu.

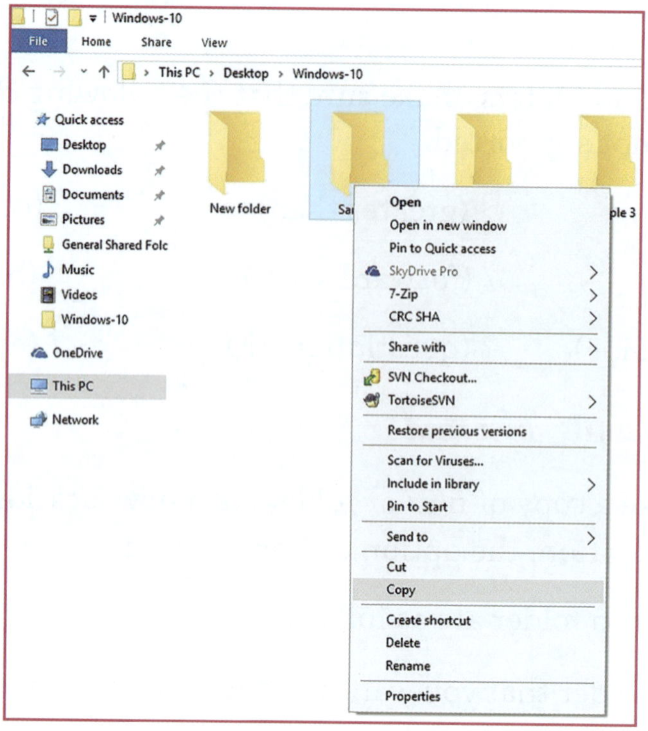

Fig. 3.12 (b): Copying a file

5 Choose your desired location in the computer and select the Paste option under the Home tab in Fig. 3.13 (a).

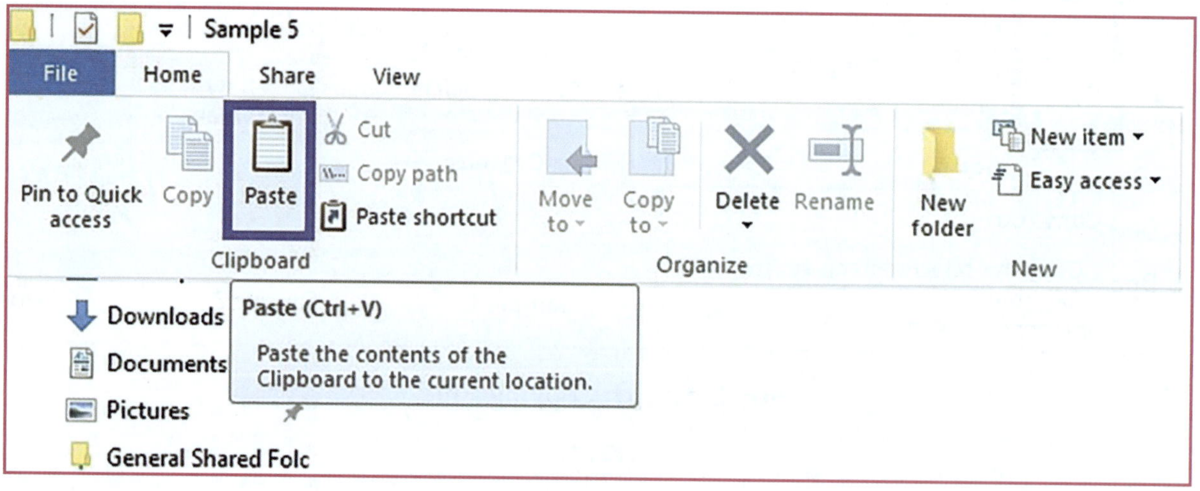

Fig. 3.13 (a): Pasting a file

6 Now the files get pasted in the new location.

(Or)

7 To copy the files easily without leaving the current location, select the option Copy to under the Home tab and choose the location to which you want these files or folders copied to. Refer to Fig. 3.13 (b).

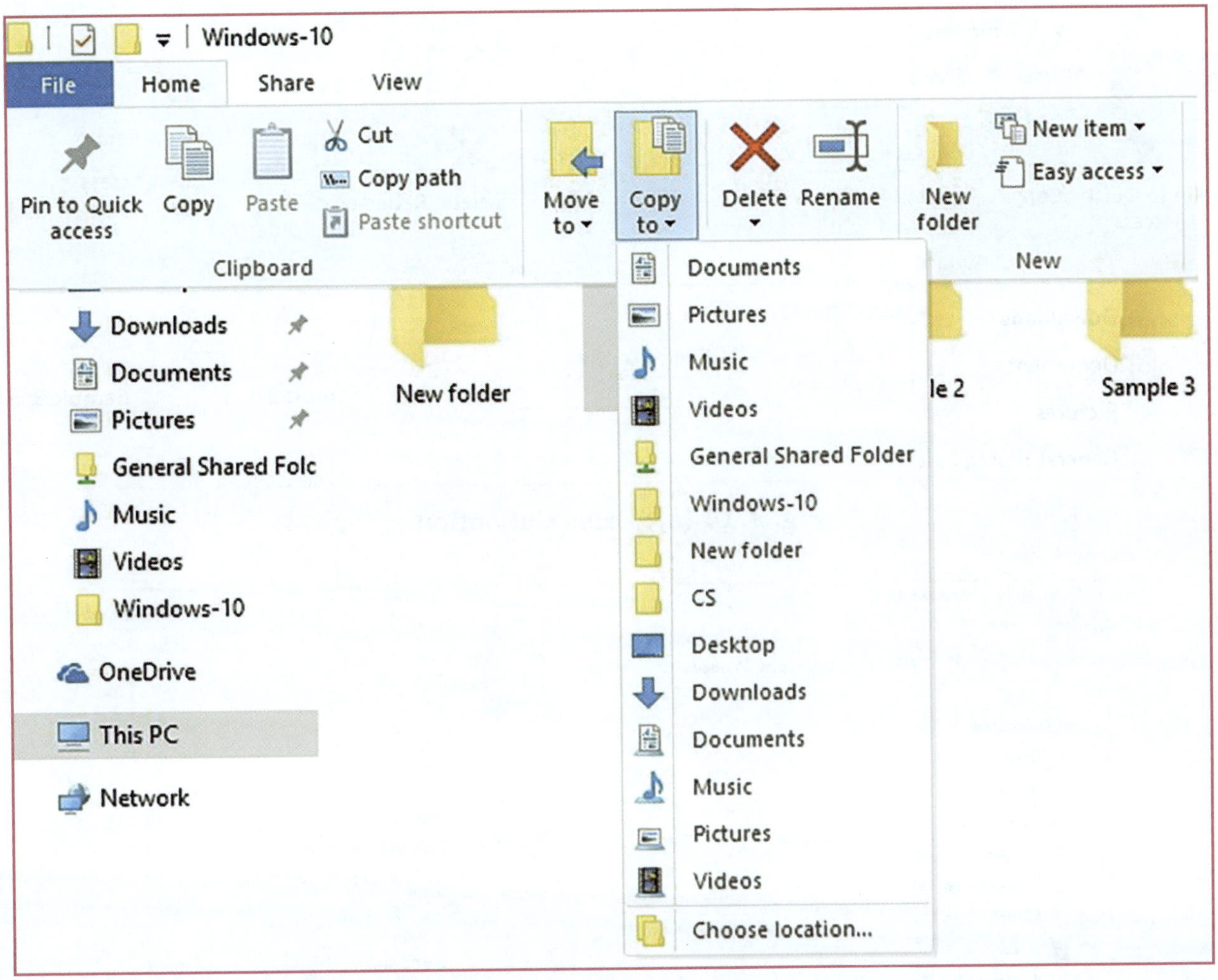

Fig. 3.13 (b): Pasting without leaving current location

Cutting and pasting a file or a folder

- When users want to take a copy of files or folders to a new location by deleting it from the original location, the option of Cut in the Home tab is used as in Fig. 3.14 (a).

(*Or*)

- Right-click on a file or a folder that you desire to move. Refer to Fig. 3.14 (b).
- Select the option Cut from the drop-down menu.

Moving a file or a folder

When users want to transfer files or folders to a new location in the computer from its original location, the option of Move is used.

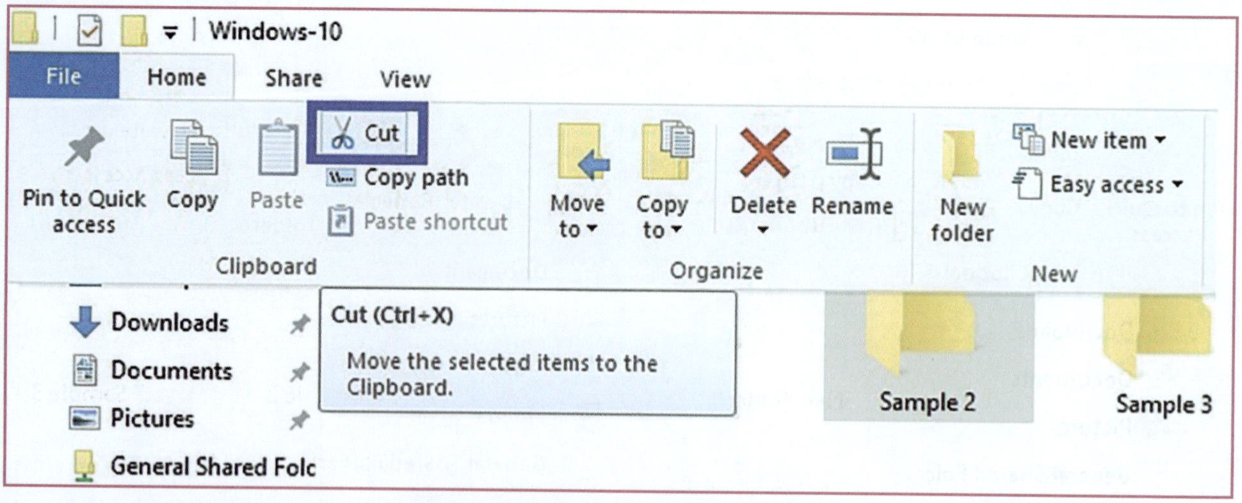

Fig. 3.14 (a): Using Cut option

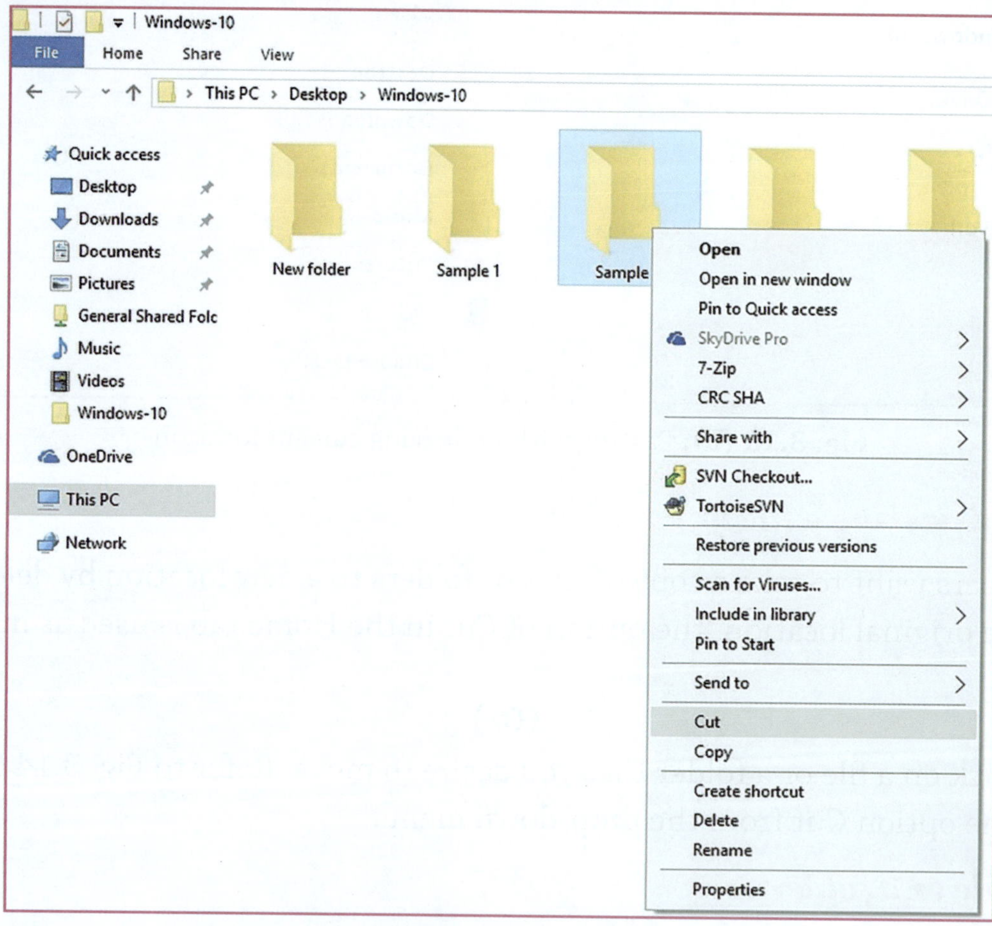

Fig. 3.14 (b): Using Cut option

The steps to move a file or a folder are as follows:

- Click on the file or folder and drag them to the desired location (Fig. 3.15).

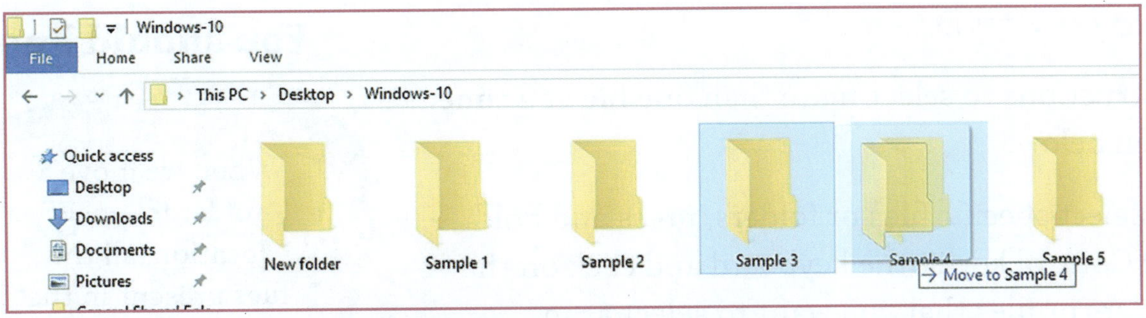

Fig. 3.15: Moving a file or a folder

- Release the mouse. You can see the file or folder in the new location.

(Or)

- To move the files easily without leaving the current location, select the option Move to under the Home tab and choose the location to which you want these files or a folder to get moved to. Refer to Fig. 3.16.

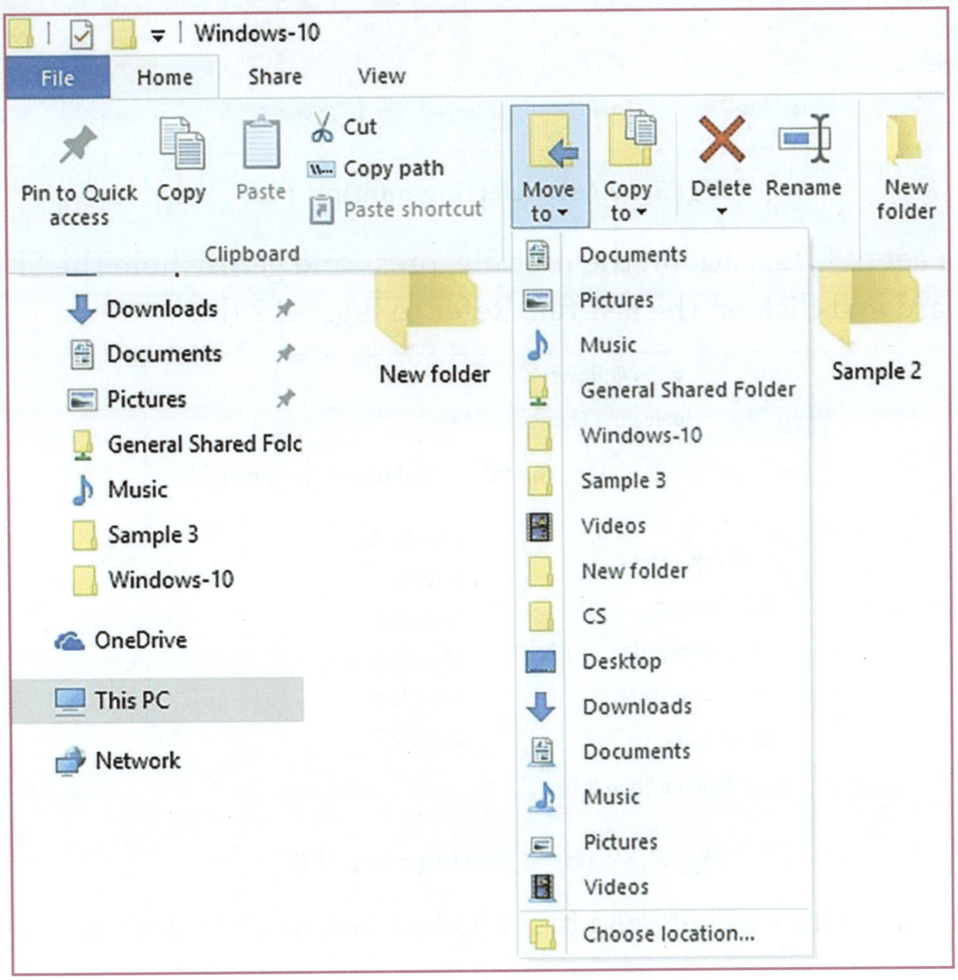

Fig. 3.16: Moving a file or a folder without leaving the current location

Selecting multiple files

The instructions to select more than one file at a time are given below:

- To select specific files or folders, press and hold the Control key of the keyboard and click on the folders or files that you want to select as in Fig. 3.17 (a).

You should know

When we move a folder to a new location, all the files present in the folder will also move.

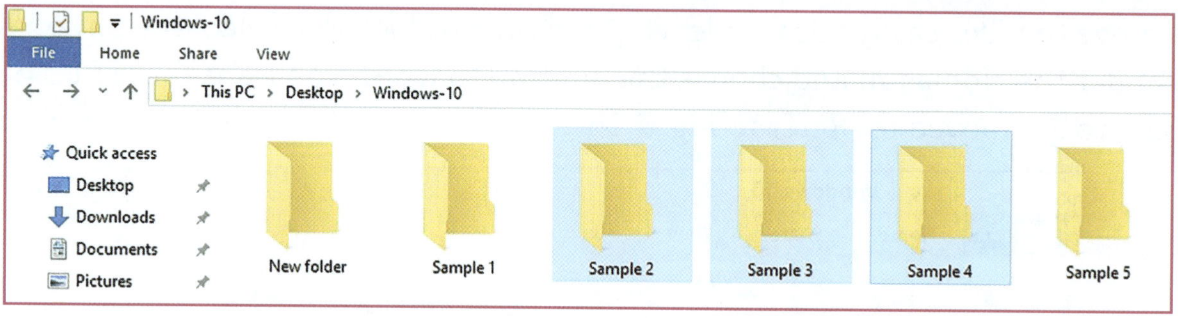

Fig. 3.17 (a): Selecting multiple files

- To select a set of files, click on the first file, press and gently hold the Shift key of the keyboard and click on the last file. Refer to Fig. 3.17 (b).

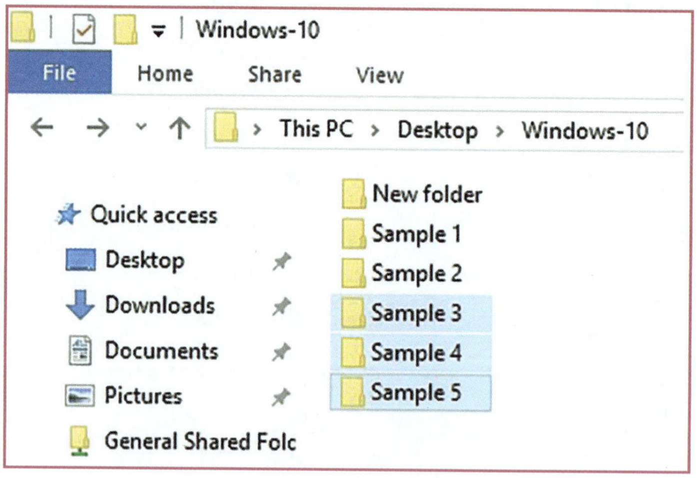

Fig. 3.17 (b): Selecting a set of files

- Now all the files situated between first and last one will be selected.

(Or)

- Click on the file. Drag the mouse slowly to draw a box around the selected files and release the mouse as in Fig. 3.17 (c).

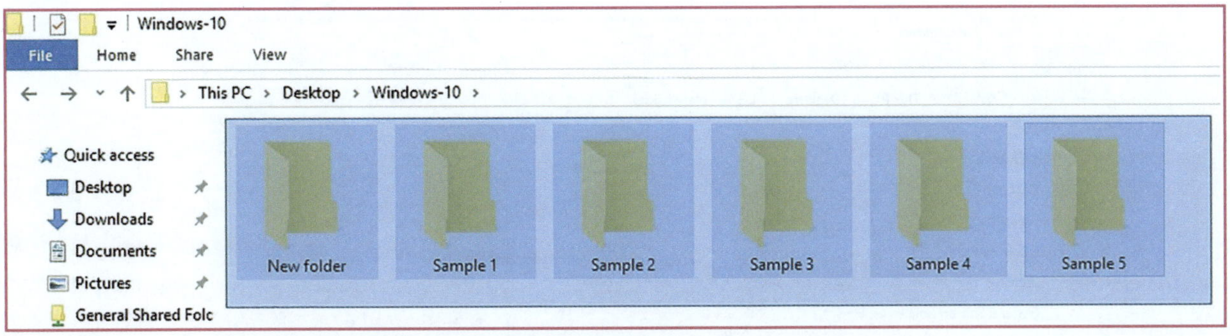

Fig. 3.17 (c): Selecting using a mouse

- Now these selected multiple files can be copied or moved or deleted at the same time.
- When you are done, release the mouse; the files will be selected. You can now move, copy, or delete all these files at the same time.

(Or)

- Go to Home tab and click on the tab Select all. All the files or folders present in the window get selected at the same time. Refer to Fig. 3.17 (d).

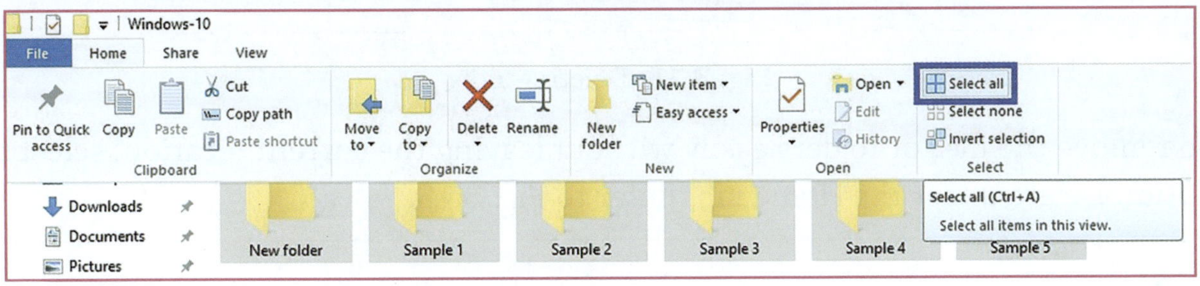

Fig. 3.17 (d): Selecting all files at a time

Deleting a file or a folder

When users want to remove files from the computer that they feel are of no use, the option Delete is used. The steps to delete a file or a folder are as follows:

- Click on the file or folder that you want to delete.
- Press the Delete key on your keyboard.

(Or)

- Right-click on a folder or a file that you want to remove. Refer to Fig. 3.18.
- Select the option Delete from the drop-down menu.

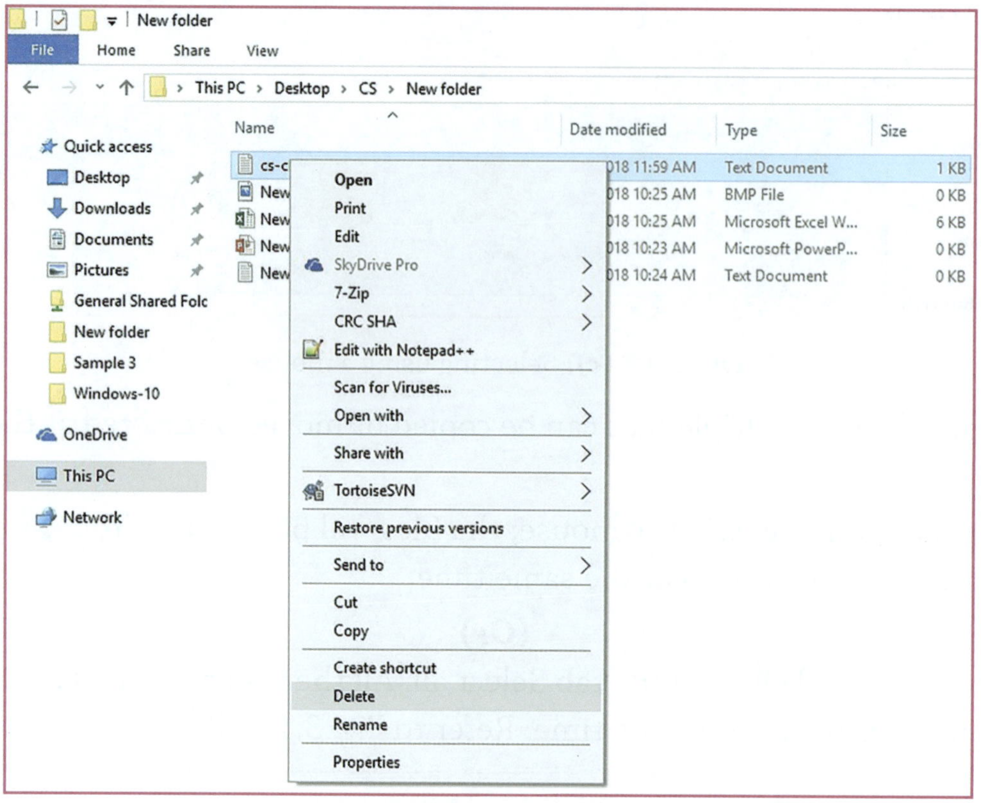

Fig. 3.18: Deleting a file

- To remove the files or folders easily without leaving the current location, select the option Delete under the Home tab. Refer to Fig. 3.19.

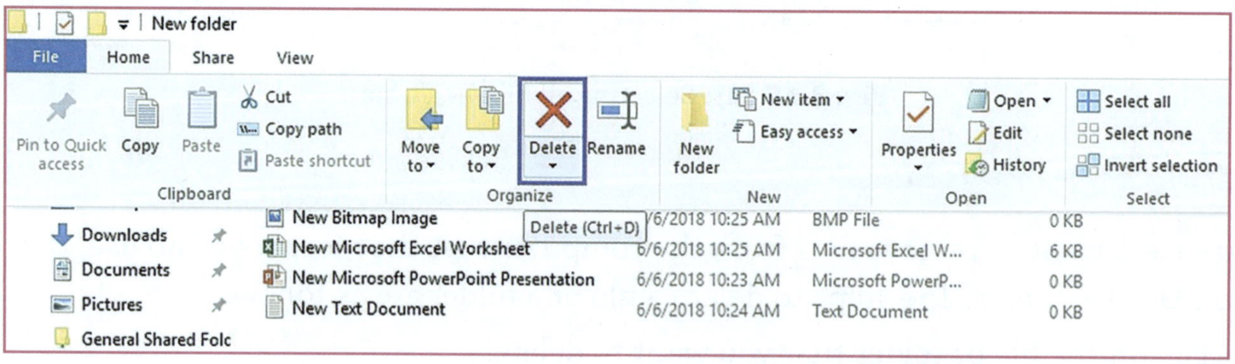

Fig. 3.19: Deleting without leaving the current location

- A dialog box appears on the screen for the confirmation as shown in Fig. 3.20.

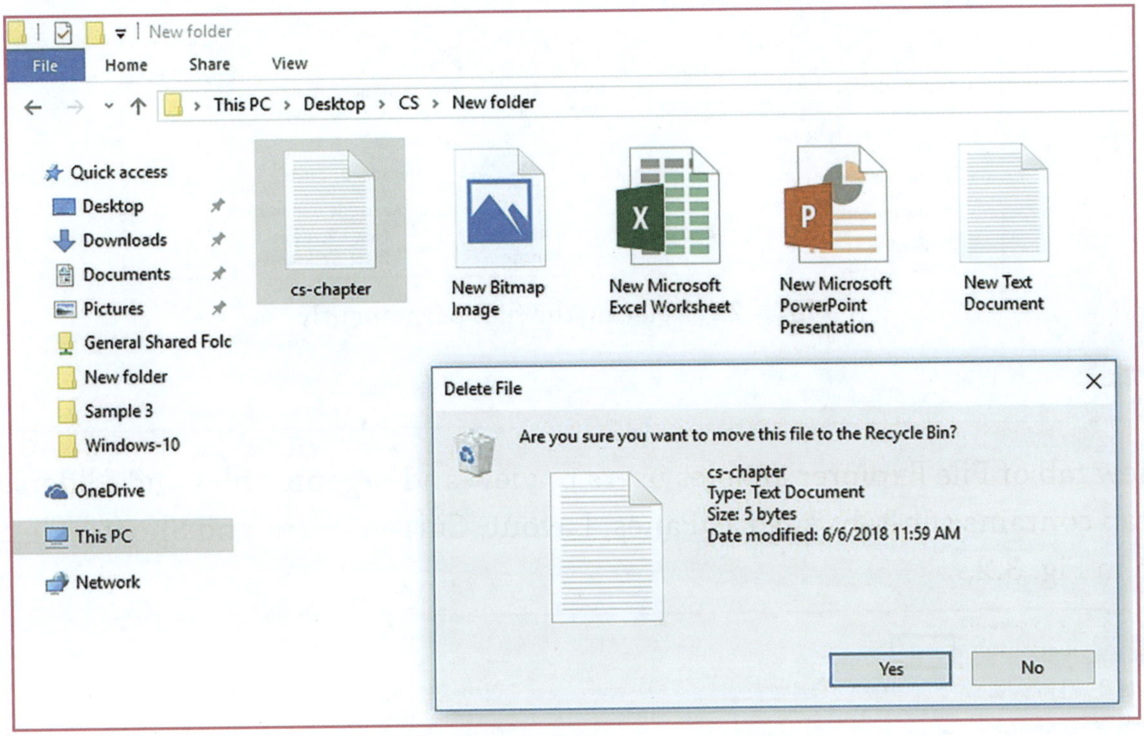

Fig. 3.20: Delete file dialog box

- Click on the Yes button for deleting the files.

(Or)

- Click on the file or folder to be deleted and select the option Recycle under the Delete tab. Refer to Fig. 3.21.

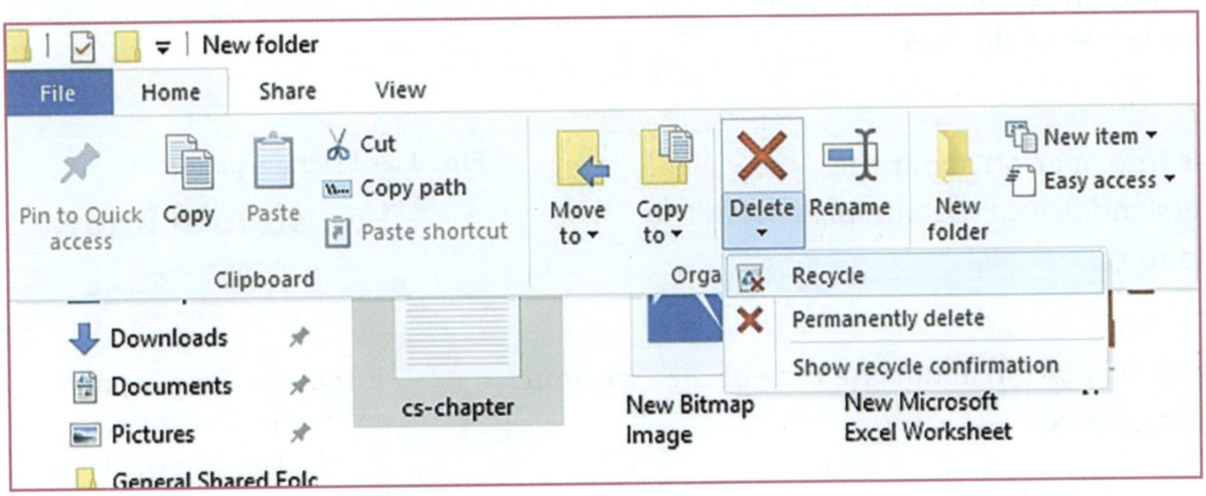

Fig. 3.21: Moving the files to Recycle Bin

- If you wish to remove the files permanently, click on the file or folder and select the option Permanently delete under Delete tab as in Fig. 3.22.

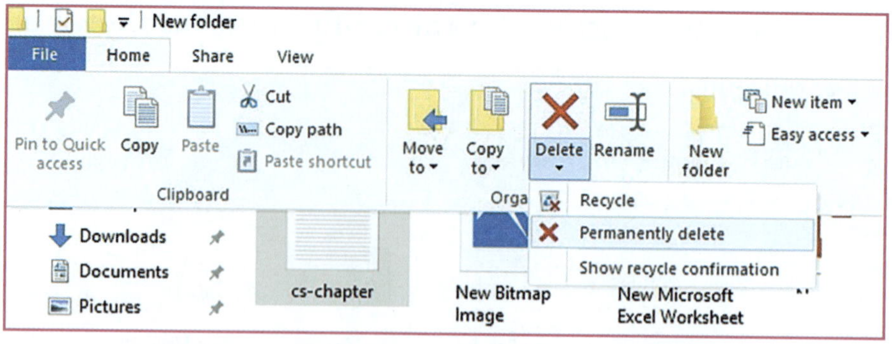

Fig. 3.22: Deleting the files permanently

View tab

The View tab of File Explorer enables users to view and organize files and folders. The View tab contains sub-tabs such as Panes, Layout, Current view, and Show/hide as shown in Fig. 3.23.

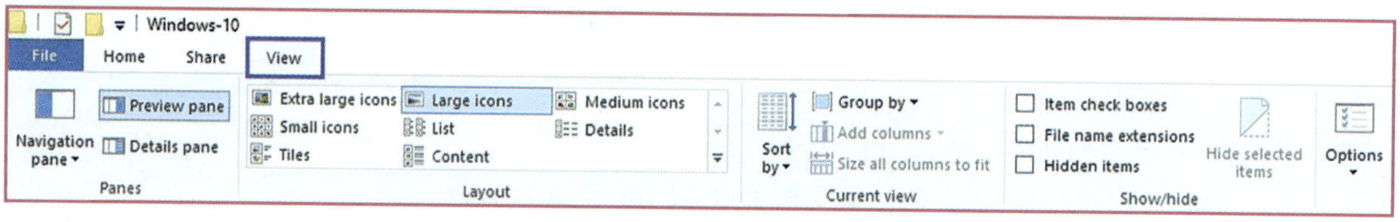

Fig. 3.23: View tab

Different panes in File Explorer

The option of various panes in the File Explorer enables users to preview information about the files and folders as in Fig. 3.24.

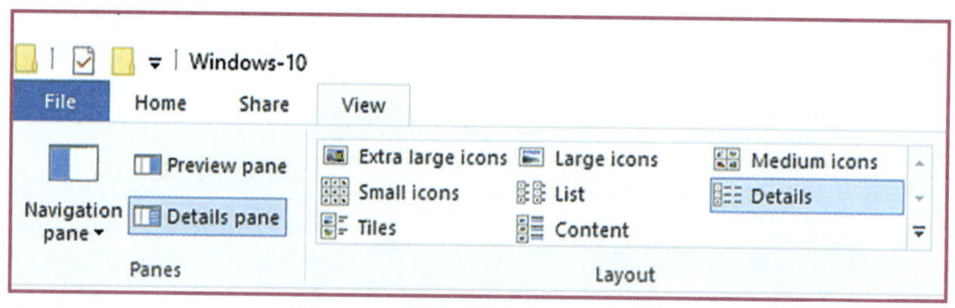

Fig. 3.24: Details pane

Navigation pane

Gives information about the folders and drives that are present in the computer.

Preview pane

Gives information about the type of files without opening them.

Details pane

Gives information about the files and folders such as size of the file, name of the file and the last modified date.

You should know

Either the Details pane or the Preview pane can be displayed in the File Explorer. Both cannot be displayed at the same time.

Layout

The Layout option enables the user to view the files in different modes as shown in Fig. 3.25.

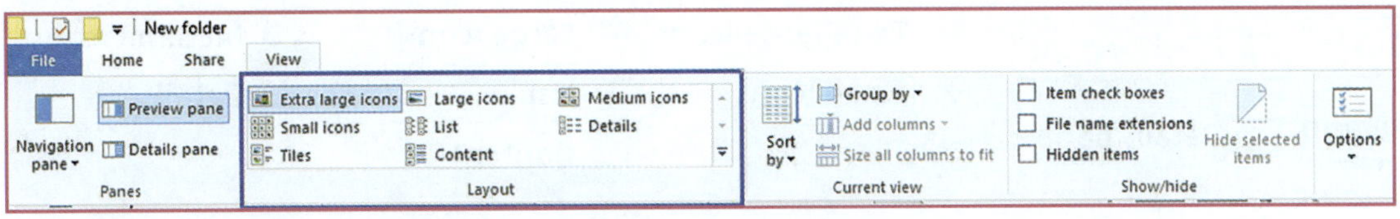

Fig. 3.25: Options in Layout

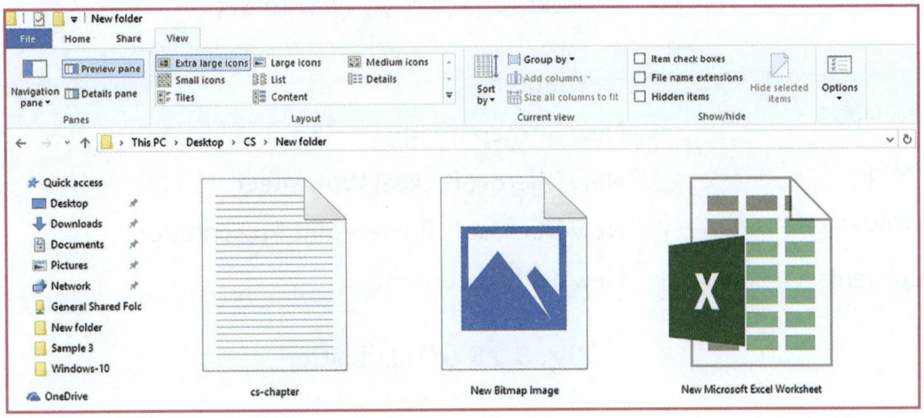

Fig. 3.25 (a): Extra large icons

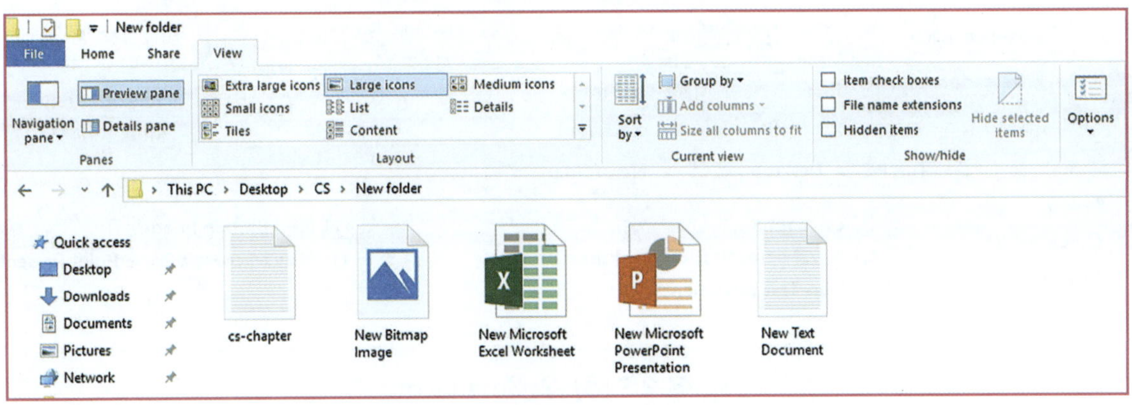

Fig. 3.25 (b): Large icons

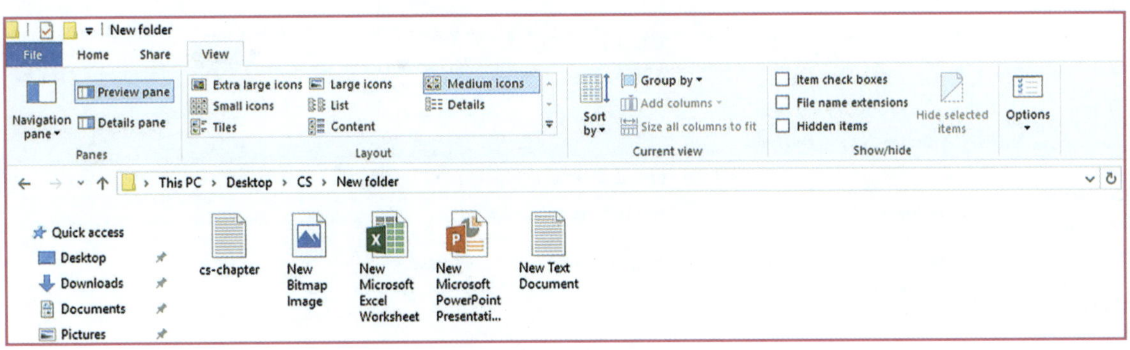

Fig. 3.25 (c): Medium icons

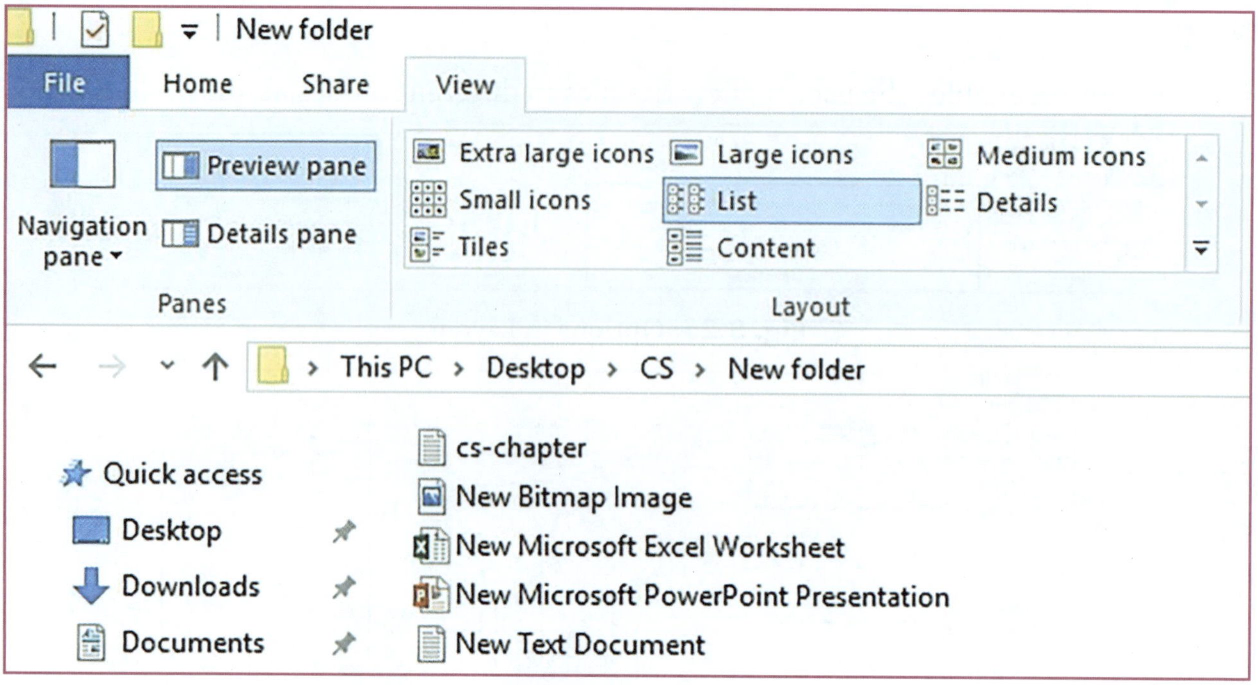

Fig. 3.25 (d)-1: List

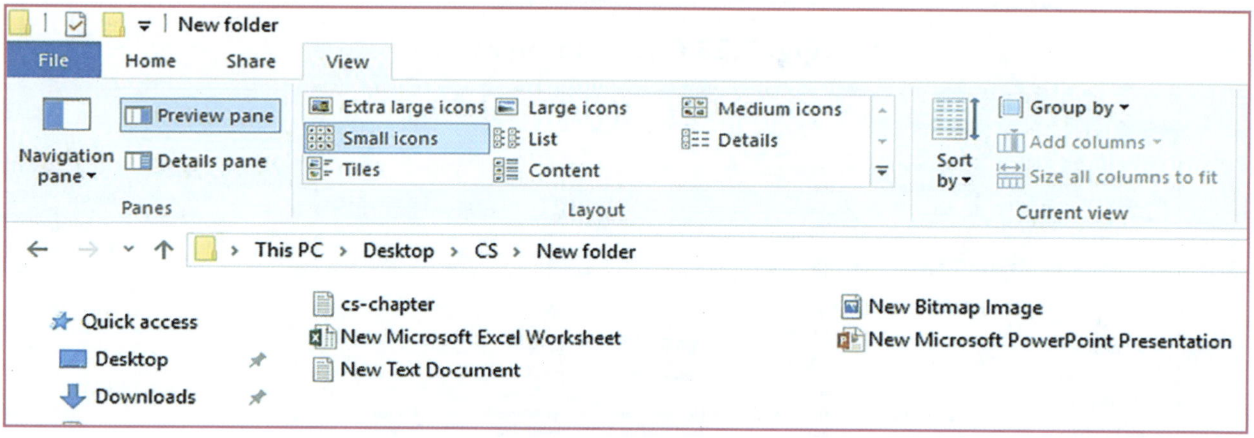

Fig. 3.25 (d)-2: Small icons

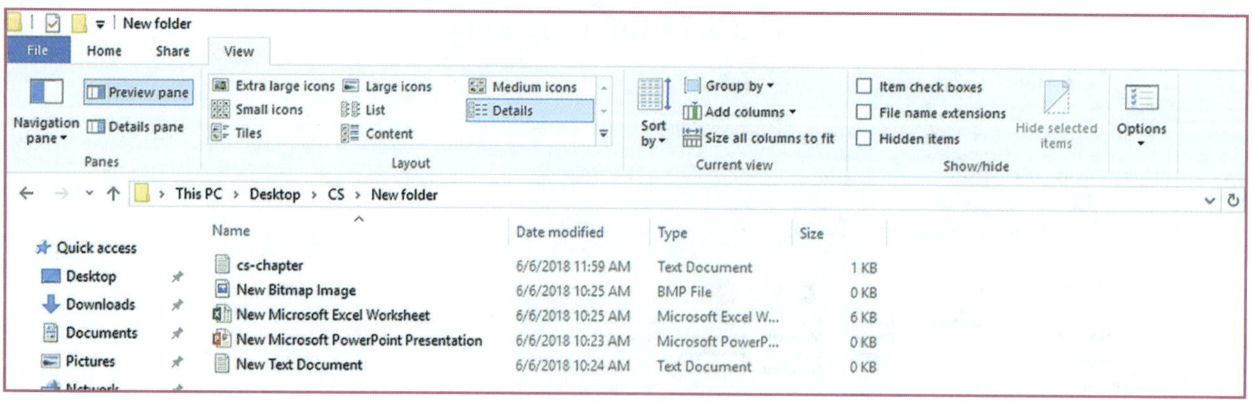

Fig. 3.25 (e): Details

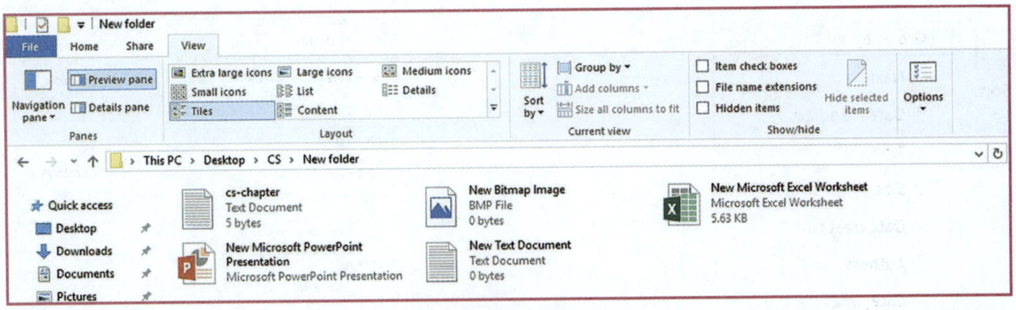

Fig. 3.25 (f): Tiles

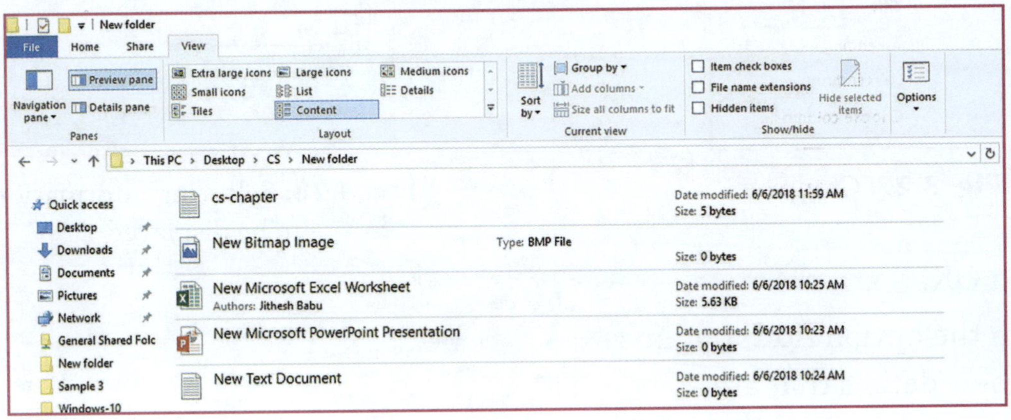

Fig. 3.25 (g): Content

Current view

The Current View option enables the user to organize the files and folders in different ways as discussed below.

Sort by and Group by

- To arrange the files and folders either in ascending or in descending order, select the relevant option from the drop-down menu in Sort by tab as in Fig 3.26.
- Sort by and Group by options help to arrange the files and folders as per the Name, Date modified, Type, Size, Date created, Authors, Tags and Title. Refer to Fig. 3.27.

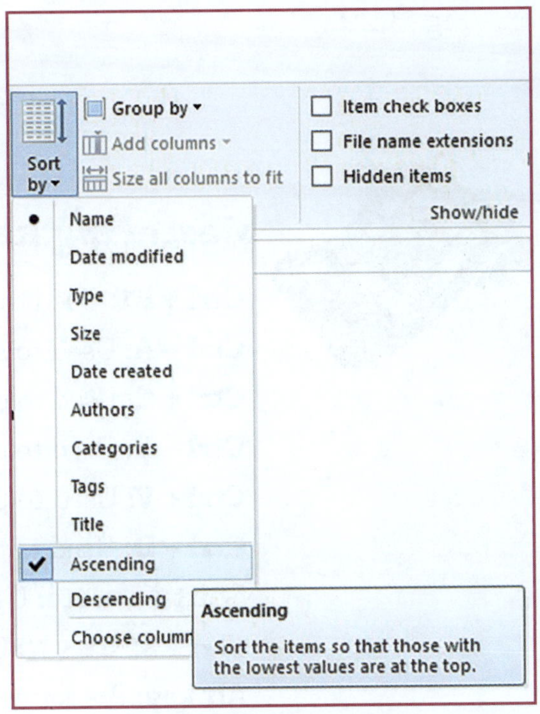

Fig. 3.26: Sort by tab

The information to be displayed in the Current view can be selected as given below:

- Select the option Choose columns as shown in Fig 3.28.
- Choose the appropriate detail that needs to be displayed from the drop-down menu.

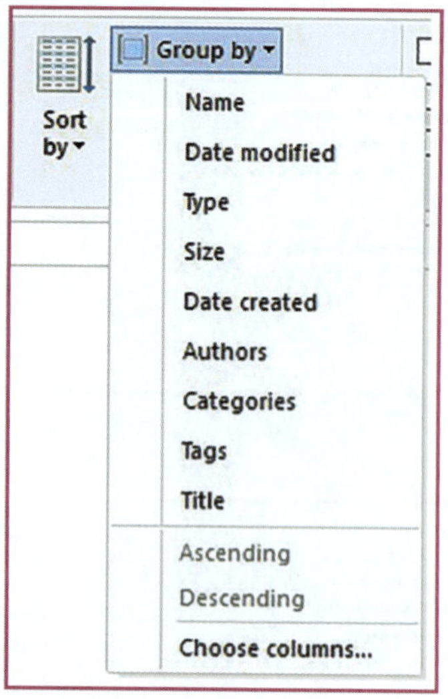

Fig. 3.27: Group by

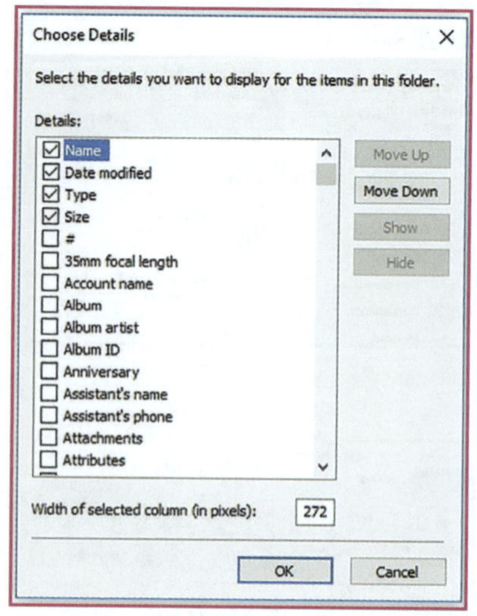

Fig. 3.28: Selecting information to be displayed

- Click on OK.
- Click on the option Add columns to add new details that are required to be displayed from the drop-down menu as shown in Fig. 3.29.

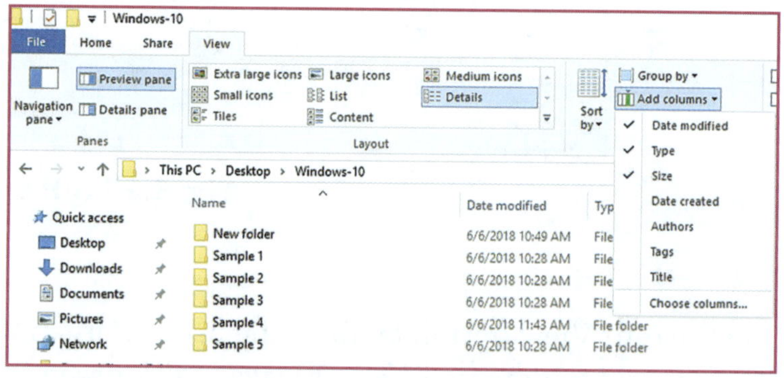

Fig. 3.29: Add columns

Mastering keyboard

Ctrl + F1: Used to minimize the ribbon button

Ctrl + A: Used to select all the files at a time in the folder

Ctrl + C: Used to copy the files

Ctrl + X: Used to cut the files

Ctrl + V: Used to paste the files

Ctrl + D: Used to move the files to recycle bin

Shift + Delete: Used to delete the files permanently

Ctrl + Shift + N: Used to create a new folder

Alt key: Pressing this key and by clicking and dragging the file creates a shortcut. (An arrow in the left corner of the file or folder icon indicates the shortcut.)

Digital geek

Zip Files

Zipped files are easier to transfer via Email and to store in a computer as they are smaller in size as compared to unzipped files. The size of the files can be compressed by following these steps given below:

- Select the files and folders that need to be zipped and right-click on them.
- Click on the option Send to and select the option Compressed (Zipped folder).

(Or)

- Select the files and folders that need to be zipped, click on the Share tab and then click on the Zip icon.
- A new zipped folder appears in the same location and this folder can be renamed, moved and shared.

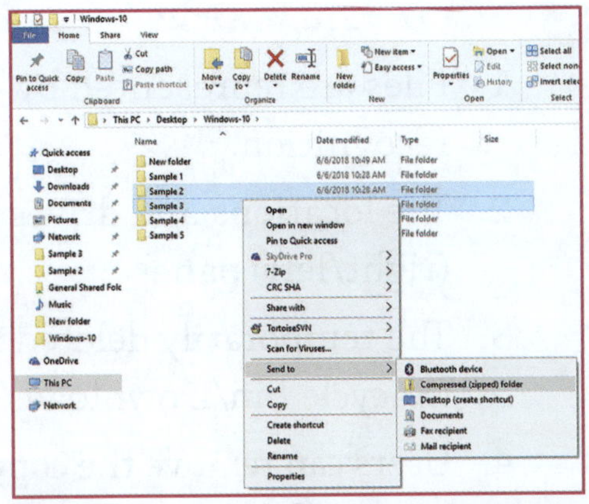

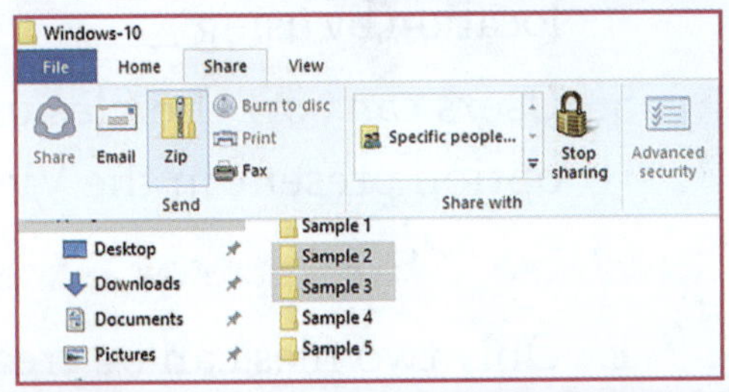

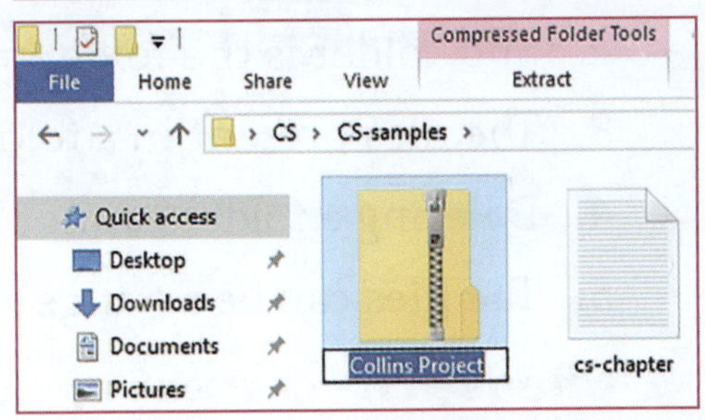

Concepts learnt

1. Organizing the files and folders in the system is essential to locate them easily.
2. All the information in the computer is saved in the form of files.
3. Files are saved in a folder. Sub-folder is the folder present within a folder.
4. File Explorer is used to create, view and organize the files and folders.
5. The Home tab of the File Explorer enables the users to create, rename, copy, select, move and delete files.
6. The View tab of the File Explorer enables the users to view and organize the files.

Exercise

A Fill in the blanks.

1. Files are represented by ________________ (icons/arrows) to make it easier for recognition.
2. The locations and drives of the system can be seen in the ________________ (right/left) pane.
3. The temporarily deleted files are stored in the system in ________________ (Recycle Bin/Downloads).
4. Users can remove the copy of files in the original location and move them to a new location by using ________________ (Cut/Move to) option in the Home tab.
5. Users can sort the files using the ________________ (Layout/Current view) option present in the View tab.

B Write T for True or F for False.

1. Only two files can be created within one folder. ☐
2. Sub-folder is the folder present within a folder. ☐
3. The files present in a folder cannot be moved to another folder. ☐
4. Deleting a folder cannot remove all the files present in it. ☐
5. The files can be arranged as per the date in which they were being created. ☐

C Choose the correct option.

1. We can create, view and organize the files in the system using one of the following options.
   (a) Settings (b) File Explorer
   (c) Apps (d) One drive
2. The location of the folder can be seen in one of the following.
   (a) Address bar (b) Quick Access Toolbar
   (c) Status bar (d) Ribbon Toolbar
3. Which of these options help to provide the desired name for the files?
   (a) Copy (b) Rename
   (c) Paste (d) Move to

4. Identify the tab used to select all the files at a time.
   (a) File
   (b) Home
   (c) Share
   (d) View
5. Which of these options is used to change the mode of the files from extra large icons to small icons?
   (a) Preview pane
   (b) Layout
   (c) Current view
   (d) Navigation pane

D Answer these questions briefly.

1. Explain the steps to create a new folder.
2. Distinguish between moving the files and copying the files.
3. How will you delete the contents of the folder permanently?
4. Write the various ways to select multiple files at a time.
5. How will you organize the files present in a folder in ascending order?

E Application-based question.

Manu selected the option of Recycle Bin under Delete tab whereas Madhav selected the option of Permanently delete under Delete tab to remove the files. What is the difference between these two options?

Computer is my mentor!

Create a folder named 'Importance of computers'. Create three sub- folders 'Science', 'Entertainment', and 'Education' in it. Place the folder in the desktop. Copy and move the entire content of the folder to one of the existing folders present in the system and rename the folder. Delete the sub-folder 'Science' temporarily from the system. Change the view of the folders to 'Details' from the existing view.

4 Editing and Formatting in MS Word 2013

Learning log

- Editing
- Formatting of text
- Saving a Word document

Introduction

Look at the two figures. Do you notice any difference between the two? List all the differences you notice in the figures.

COMPUTER

Computer is a device that can be instructed to carry out several operations. The computer can be connected to the Internet which further can connect millions of other computers.

COMPUTER

Computer is a device that can be instructed to carry out several operations. The computer can be connected to the Internet which further can connect millions of other computers.

In the above figure, although the content is the same, they look different in size, colour, clarity, etc. This is because both are created differently using various tools available in MS Word. In this chapter, you will be studying about the tools that will allow you to edit and format a document in MS Word.

Editing

Editing is the process of changing, correcting or modifying. Editing in Word involves modifying the content that has been typed. Editing tools are useful to make corrections in the document. Some of the commonly used editing tools are Cut, Copy and Paste. These options can be performed from the Clipboard group on the Ribbon as shown in Fig. 4.1.

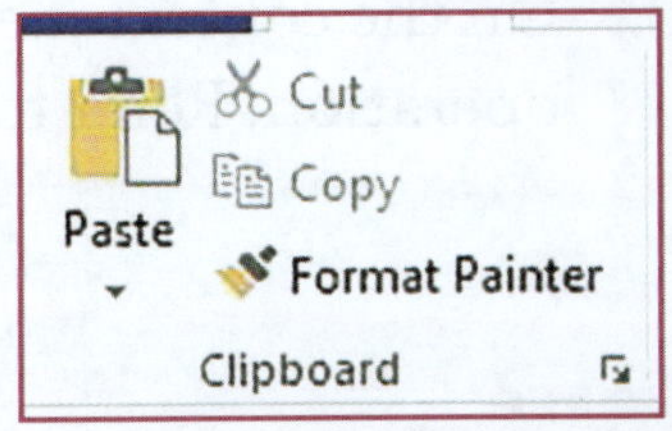

Fig. 4.1: Clipboard group containing Cut, Copy and Paste options

We shall study some of the important editing tools in detail along with alternate ways to execute the commands.

Cut

Cut is an editing tool that removes the selected item (like text, pictures, shapes, equations, etc.) from the document. Following are the steps to perform this operation:

1. Select the item and click the right-button of the mouse. Clicking the right-button of the mouse in MS Word opens the context menu.
2. Click on Cut in the context menu to execute the command as in Fig. 4.2.

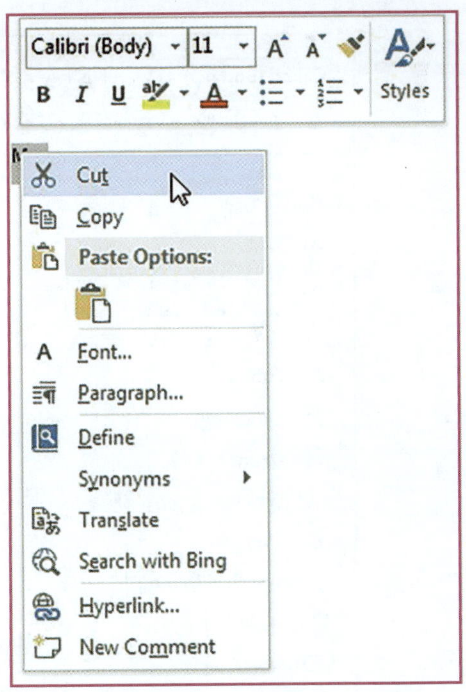

Fig. 4.2: The editing tool Cut

Word web

context menu: context menu is a list of tools/operations which appear when the right-button of the mouse is clicked. The operations in the list depend upon where the right-click is done.

Copy

Copy is a tool that duplicates the selected item. To carry out this command, follow the given steps:

1. Select the item to be copied.
2. Right-click on the mouse.
3. On the context menu, click on Copy to carry out the operation. Refer to Fig. 4.3.

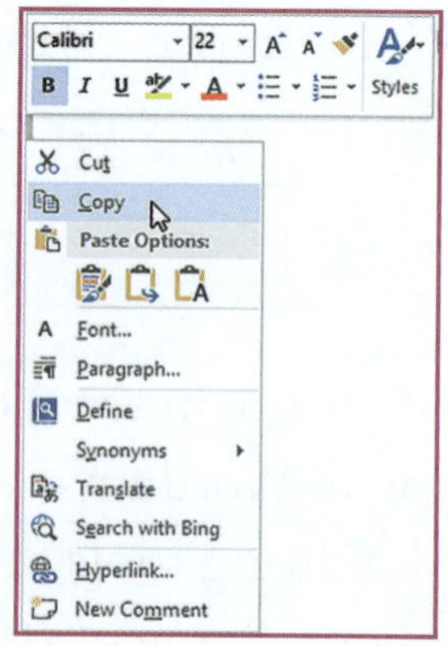

Fig. 4.3: The editing tool Copy

Paste

Pasting is the operation of inserting the item that was cut or copied. It is always performed after Cut or Copy operation. Once the item is cut or copied, it is ready to be pasted. Following is the procedure to perform this option:

1. Place the cursor where you want the item to be pasted and then click the right-button of the mouse.
2. Select the format in which you want to paste and the operation will be accordingly carried out. Refer to Fig. 4.4.

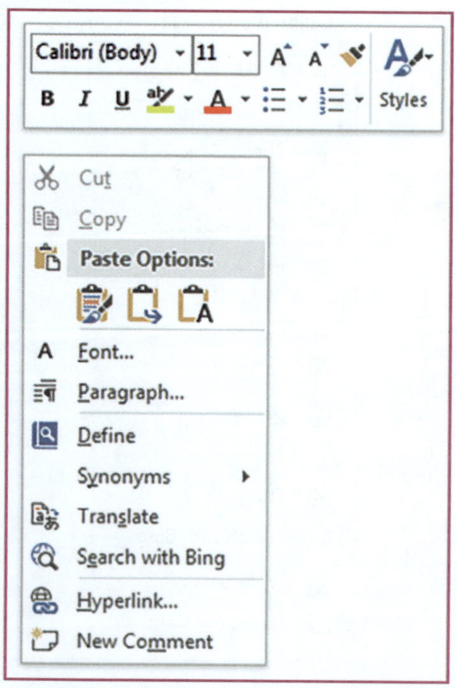

Fig. 4.4: The editing tool Paste

Digital geek

After an item is cut or copied, the computer stores the item in its memory which can be used by Paste operation when needed.

Paste Special operation gives different types of formats that can be used for pasting. This operation is useful when the item that is to be pasted differs in the format that you need.

Undo

Undo is a tool that reverses the previous action that was performed. For instance, you delete a few lines in a paragraph that you think are not needed. Later on, you feel those lines are needed. You can bring back those deleted lines by using Undo operation.

Redo

Redo operation reverses an undo operation that was performed. As explained in the example of Undo operation, performing the Undo operation brings back the deleted lines. Performing the Redo operation deletes those lines again.

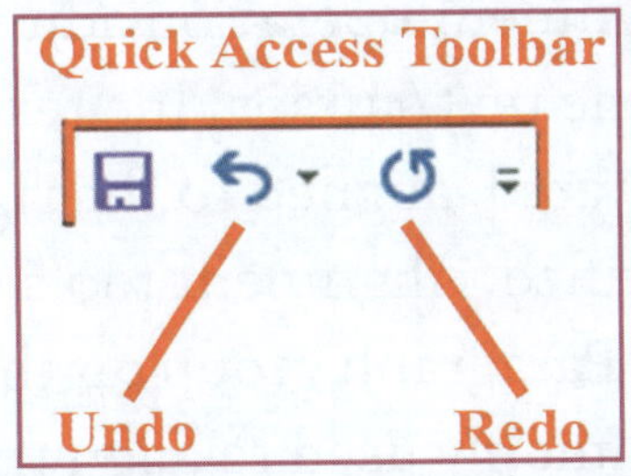

Fig. 4.5: Quick Access toolbar with Undo and Redo options

Undo and Redo operations are always on the Quick Access Toolbar by default.

Find and Replace

The Find operation searches and locates a specific word or phrase in the document. To perform the Find operation, click on the Find icon Find in the Editing group on the Ribbon. This opens a new pane (as shown in the Fig. 4.6) where the word or phrase to be located is entered.

The Replace operation substitutes words or phrases in the document with another. To perform this operation, click on Replace icon Replace in the Editing group and enter the word or phrase that you want to find in the **Find what** field and then enter the word or phrase that you want to replace it with in the **Replace with** field and click on Replace All as in Fig. 4.7.

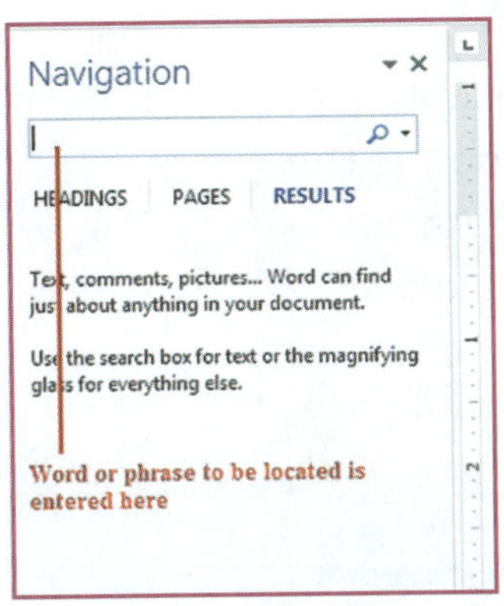

Fig. 4.6: The Find operation

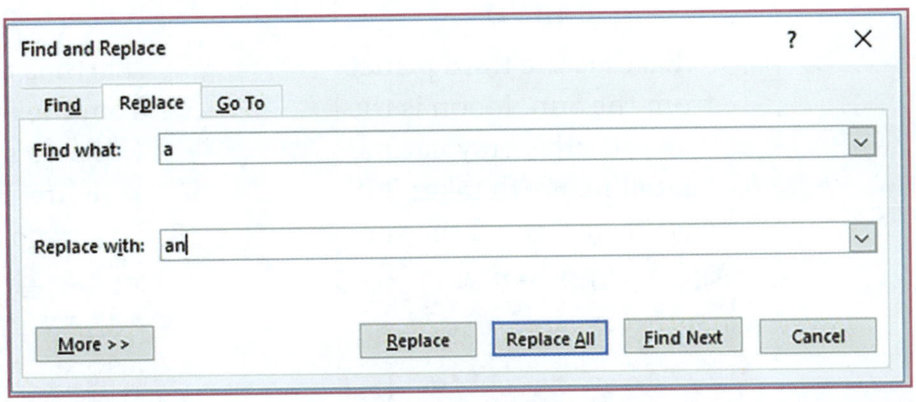

Fig. 4.7: Find and Replace

Formatting of Text

Formatting involves modifying the features of the item (like text, pictures, shapes, equations, etc.) that is entered or to be entered. Following are the formatting operations on MS Word 2013.

Alignment

Alignment operation adjusts the position of the text/cursor. The text/cursor can be centered, aligned to the right or left and justified. Alignment tools can be found in the Paragraph group on the Ribbon. It is commonly used to align the headings.

Fig 4.9 shows the different types of alignment that are possible.

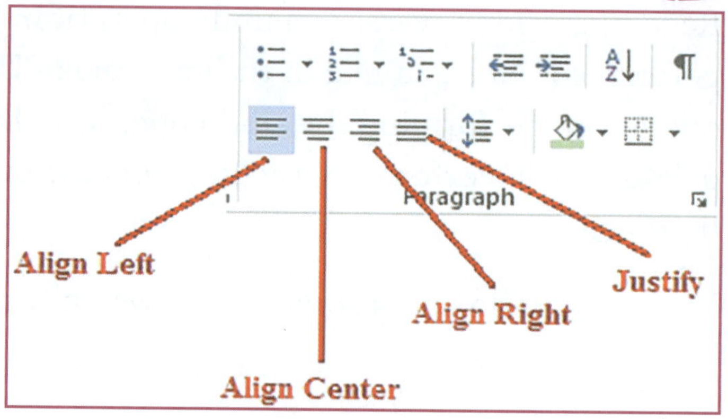

Fig. 4.8: Alignment tools

You should know

MS Word 2013 is available in many languages such as Arabic, Chinese, Dutch, English, French,

EARTH

Earth is the third planet from the Sun. Moon is the Earth's only natural satellite. Earth takes 365 days to go around the sun.

Left Alignment

The text is aligned along the left margin of the document area.

EARTH

Earth is the third planet from the Sun. Moon is the Earth's only natural satellite. Earth takes 365 days to go around the sun.

Right Alignment

The text is aligned along the right margin of the document area.

EARTH

Earth is the third planet from the Sun. Moon is the Earth's only natural satellite. Earth takes 365 days to go around the sun.

Center Alignment

The text is aligned around the midpoint of the document area.

Fig. 4.9: Different types of alignments

Justification is another alignment option where text is aligned to both left and right, and space is added wherever necessary. This gives a clean look to the text.

To perform this operation, select the entire text and click on the Justify icon ≡ in the Paragraph group. Fig. 4.10 shows the difference between justified and unjustified text.

JUSTIFIED TEXT	UNJUSTIFIED TEXT
Earth is the third planet from the Sun and the only planet where life exists. Moon is the Earth's only natural satellite. Earth revolves around the sun and takes 365 days to go around the sun. About 71% of Earth's surface is covered with water, mostly by oceans and the remaining 29% is land consisting of continents and islands.	Earth is the third planet from the Sun and the only planet where life exists. Moon is the Earth's only natural satellite. Earth revolves around the sun and takes 365 days to go around the sun. About 71% of Earth's surface is covered with water, mostly by oceans and the remaining 29% is land consisting of continents and islands.

Fig. 4.10: Justified and Unjustified text

Text modification

Text modification involves changing the features of text. Following are some of the text modification tools which are in the Font group:

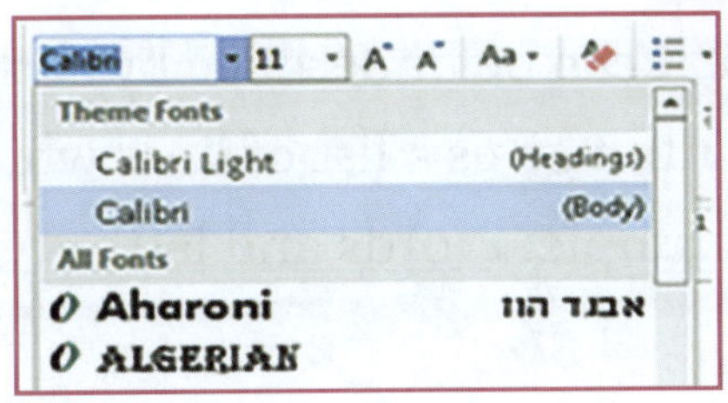

Fig. 4.11: Selecting a Font style

Font

Font is a set of characters of text like weight, style, width, etc. To choose the font style, click on the drop-down button next to the Font icon Calibri ▾. A list of font options drop. Choose the font which you need as in Fig 4.11.

Example: **Font style changes the style of the text.**

Font size

The size of the font can be either increased or decreased. To change the font size, click on the drop-down button next to 11 ▾ in the Font Size field and a drop-down menu of font sizes appears. Select a suitable font size from the drop-down menu as in Fig. 4.12.

Word web

drop-down button: it is the icon with a downward arrow ▾ next to the commands. Clicking on the drop-down button gives a list or menu of operations known as the drop-down menu.

Example: **Size of the letters can be changed.**

Bold

Bold is an operation that increases the thickness of the letters. To bold the text, select the text and click on the bold icon [B].

Example: **Letters can be bolded.**

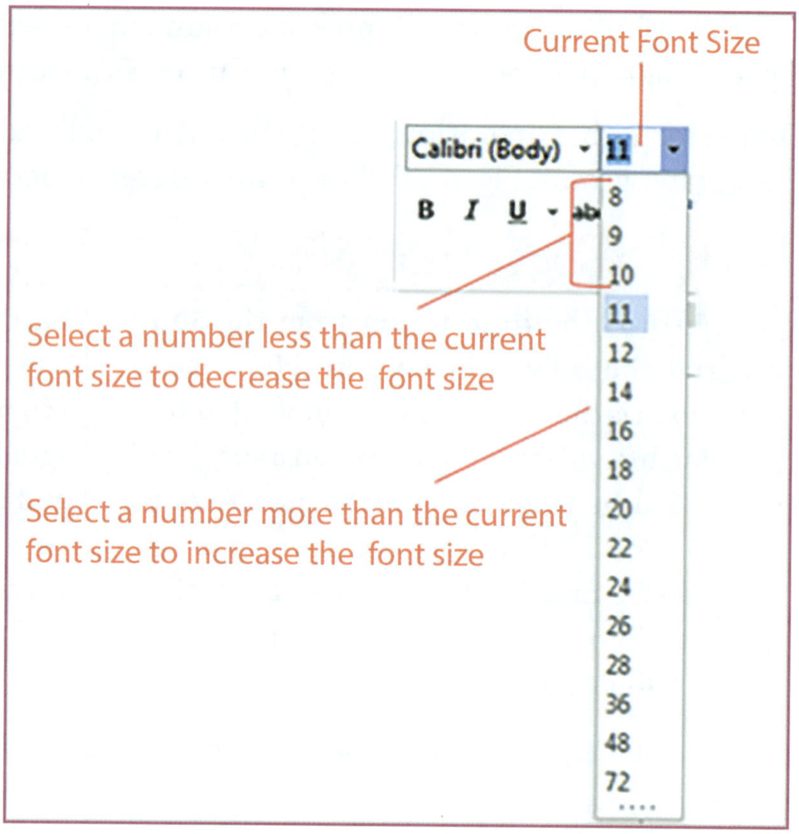

Fig. 4.12: Selecting the Font Size

Italics

Italic is a text tool which slants the letters to the right. To italicize the text, select the text and click on the Italic icon [*I*].

Example: *Words can be italicized.*

Underline

Text can be underlined by clicking the Underline icon [U ▾]. Clicking on the drop-down button gives a list of lines which can be used to change the type of line used for underlining. Example: Words and letters can be underlined.

Font color

Colour of the font can be changed by the following steps:

1. Select the text and then click the drop button on the Font Color icon [A ▾]
2. Click on the colour you need in the palette which will change the colour of the text.

Example: Color of the font can be changed.

Text highlight color

Fig. 4.13: Text Highlight Colour

We highlight important words, sentences or phrases in books with a highlighter pen. Similarly, highlighting can be done in an MS Word document, which applies colour over the text. To highlight, select the text and click on highlighter icon and select the highlighter colour as in Fig. 4.13.

Example: Text can be highlighted.

Text effects and typography

Extra features and effects to the font like shadows, reflections, changing styles, etc., can be added by using Text Effects and Typography tools.

To use these tools, select the text to which effects need to be added and click on Text Effects and Typography icon . Choose the style of the font that you need. Refer to Fig. 4.14.

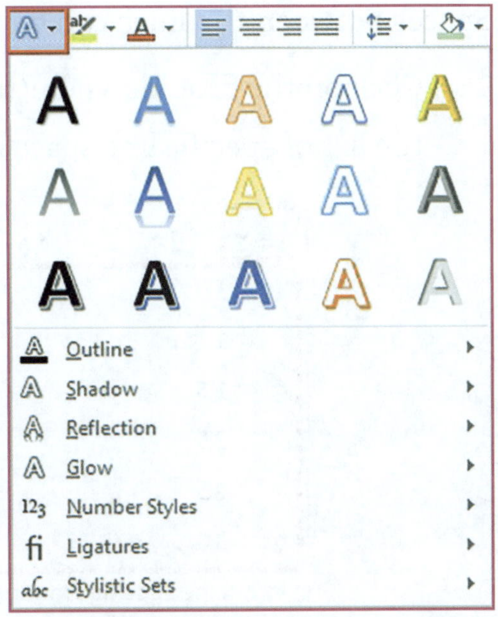

Fig. 4.14: Text Effects and Typography

Example: **Effects can be added**

Line spacing

Line spacing is the gap between consecutive lines. Fig. 4.15 compares different line spacing.

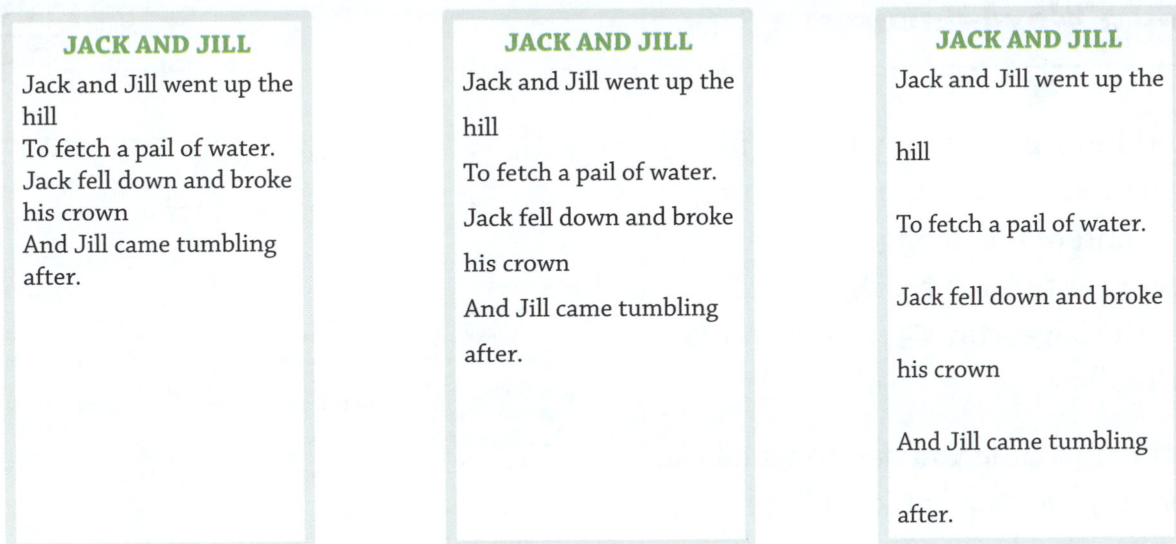

Fig. 4.15: Line Spacing

Spaces between the lines can be varied using the following operations:

1. Click on the drop-down button on line spacing icon in the Paragraph group. From the list of specific line space values, choose the line spacing needed as in Fig. 4.16.

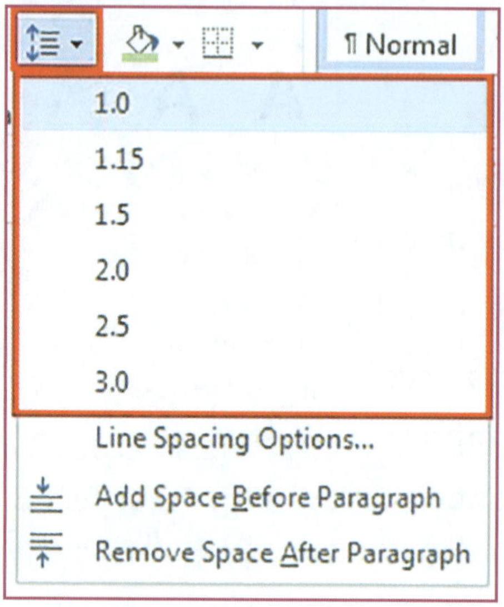

Fig. 4.16: Line Spacing Options

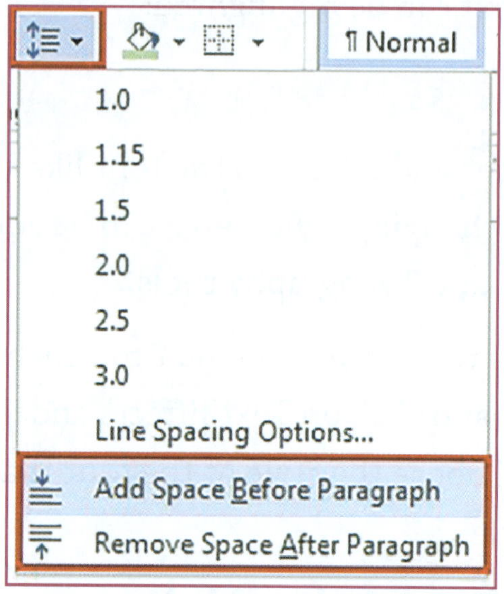

Fig. 4.17: Changing the space between paragraphs

2. Spaces between paragraphs can also be changed by using the options Add Space Before Paragraph and Remove Space After Paragraph in the Paragraph group as in Fig. 4.17.

Saving a Word document

After working on a document, the file needs to be saved to retain everything that was entered or changed in the document for future use. To save a file, click on the Save icon in the Quick Access Toolbar.

If it is the first time you have opened the document, provide a name and the location for the document as shown in Fig. 4.18.

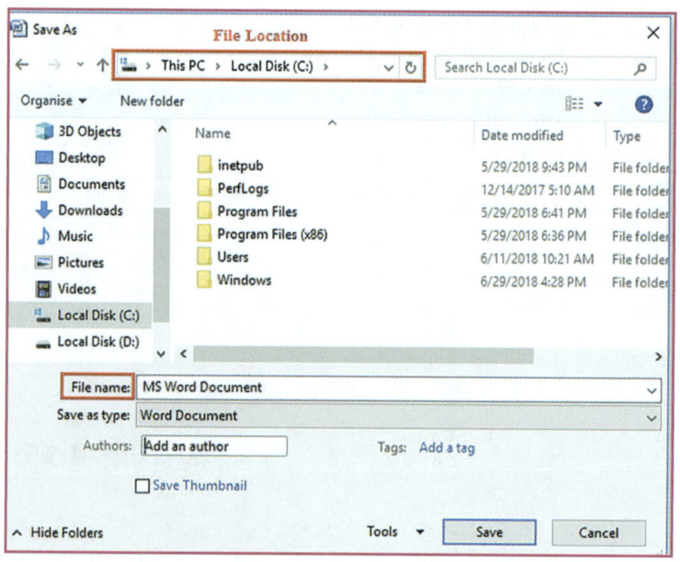

Fig. 4.18: File saving window

Mastering keyboard

Ctrl + U	Underline
Ctrl + E	Align Center
Ctrl + Shift + <	Decrease font
Ctrl + I	Italics
Ctrl + J	Justify

Concepts learnt

1. Editing is the process of changing, correcting or modifying.
2. Cut, Copy, Paste and Paste Special are some of the frequently used editing operations in MS Word.
3. Undo, Redo, Find and Replace are also some of the commonly used editing operations.
4. There are many tools for formatting in MS Word. Some of the operations that are often used for formatting are alignment, text modification, justification and line spacing.
5. Alignment operation adjusts the position of the text/cursor.
6. Line spacing is the gap between consecutive lines.
7. It is important to save a file before closing to retain all the information on the document.

Hands-on practice

Imagine yourself to be the school head boy/girl, prepare the list of events for your school's Sports Day. Save the document. Due to unavoidable circumstances, the Principal has asked you to change the date and flip the events planned for the afternoon with the ones planned for the morning. Use Find and Replace option to do that and fix the formatting again. Write the steps you followed in the space given below.

Exercise

A Fill in the blanks.

1. ________________ (Redo/Save) operation reverses an undo operation that was performed.
2. ________________ (Font/Table) is a set of characters of text like weight, style and width.
3. Italics is a text tool which slants the letters to the ________________ (left/right).
4. A Word document needs to be ________________ (saved/deleted) after working on it to retain the information in the document.
5. ________________ (Format/Color) painter copies all of the formatting from one item and applies it to another one.

B Write T for True or F for False.

1. Clicking the right mouse button in MS Word opens the context menu. ☐
2. Copy operation removes the item that was selected. ☐
3. Highlighter in MS Word is used to apply color over text. ☐
4. Text Effects and Typography tool is found in Styles group. ☐
5. Spacing between the lines cannot be changed in MS Word 2013. ☐

C Choose the correct option.

1. Which of the following operations does not change the features of the text?
   (a) Bold (b) Copy
   (c) Italics (d) Typography
2. Colour of the font can be changed by using the Font Color tool present in which one of the following groups?
   (a) Clipboard (b) Styles
   (c) Editing (d) Font
3. Which operation gives different types of formats that can be used for pasting?
   (a) Typography (b) Copy
   (c) Paste Special (d) Undo

4. Which of the following operations aligns the text to both left and right?
   (a) Justification
   (b) Copy
   (c) Paste Special
   (d) Text Effects and Typography
5. Which of the following operations inserts spaces between paragraphs?
   (a) Justification
   (b) Add Space Before Paragraphs
   (c) Remove Space Between Paragraphs
   (d) Line Spacing

D Answer these questions briefly.

1. Explain Undo, Redo and Paste operations in a sentence each.
2. Explain Find and Replace operations.
3. Explain the alignment of text.
4. What is the function of the Bold and Italic operations?
5. What are Text Effects and Typography tools?

E Application-based question.

1. A teacher in a school types an essay on an MS Word document and after typing, she wants to substitute the word 'common' by the word 'well-known' in all the paragraphs. What is the best way to do this that will save the teacher's time?
2. Vihaan types a paragraph on an MS Word document and closes it. When he comes back later to work on the computer, he does not find the document on the computer. What do you think Vihaan should have done before closing the document to have it on the computer?
3. There is a picture on the Word document which is aligned to center of the page, has borders and shadow effects. Another picture is copied from the Internet to the document which needs to have the same format as the other one. What tool can be used to copy the formats of one picture to the other?

Computer is my mentor!

Write a report of your Diwali celebrations. Use all the formatting tools mentioned in the lesson to prepare your report.

5 Inserting Tables in MS Word 2013

Learning log

- Inserting a table
- Modifying tables

Introduction

Look at the images given below. Can you recognize what are these? Yes, the first one is the calendar that is kept on a table in every house and office, and the second one is the school timetable that you and all the other school-going students have. Do you know how are they created?

DAY	PERIOD 1	2		3	4		5	6	7
Monday			SHORT BREAK			LUNCH BREAK			
Tuesday									
Wednesday									
Thursday									
Friday									
Saturday									

Calendars and timetables are created using a feature called **Tables**. A table is an arrangement of data in rows and columns. Each unit in a table is known as a **cell**. A simple example of a table is shown in Fig. 5.1.

Tables have a variety of uses like storing details of people in educational institutions and industries, performing mathematical calculations, etc. In this chapter, we will learn various operations that can be performed in a table.

A	B	C	D	E

Fig 5.1: Sample Table

Inserting a table

A table needs to be inserted in the document first. Following are the steps to insert a table:

Step 1: Click on the Insert tab in the Ribbon.

Step 2: Click on the drop-down button on the Table command in Tables group as in Fig. 5.2.

Clicking on the drop-down button opens a menu which is used to insert tables. Following are the methods to insert a table using the drop-down menu:

> **Word web**
>
> **grid:** a pattern or network of straight lines that cross each other to form squares or rectangles

1. The drop-down menu contains a grid of squares. Move the mouse over the grid to select the number of columns and rows in the table as in Fig. 5.3.

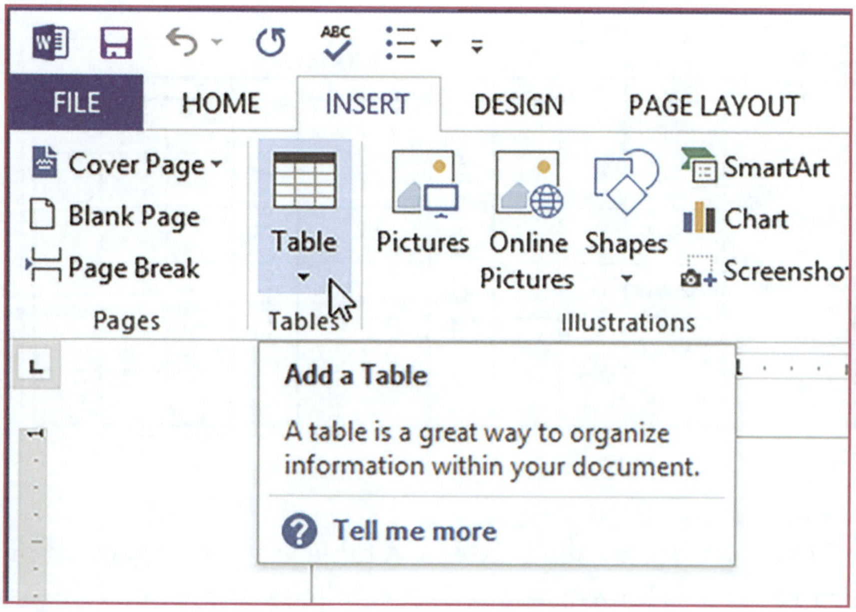

Fig. 5.2: Adding a table

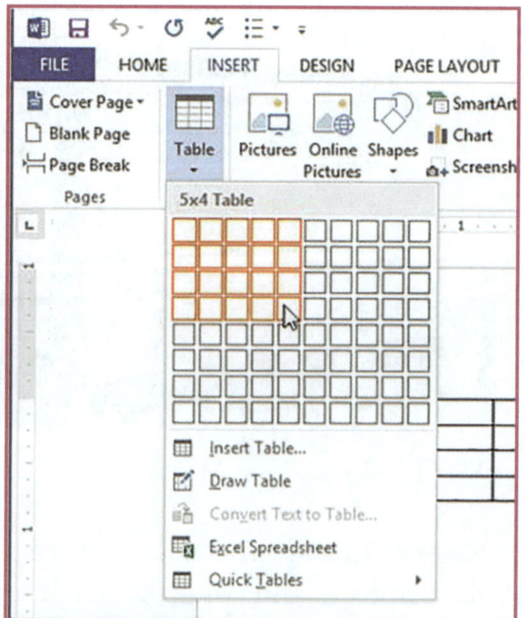

Fig. 5.3: Table Gridlines

2. Tables can be inserted using the Insert Table command from the drop-down menu. Fig. 5.4 shows the steps in which this command can be used.

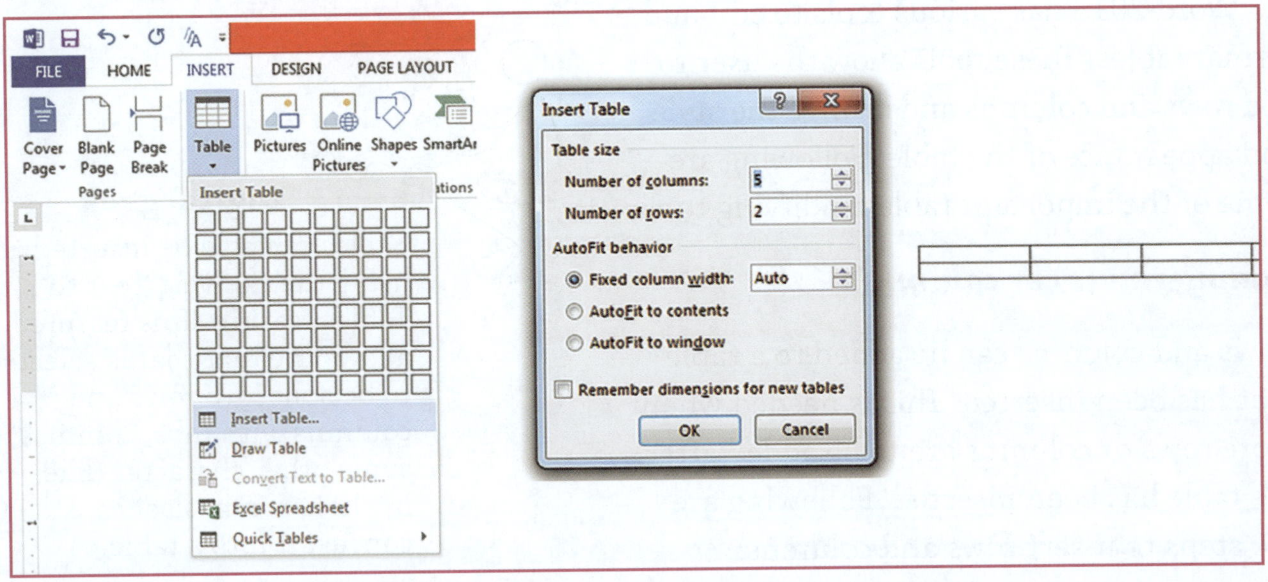

Fig. 5.4: Inserting table using Insert Table command

3. Quick Tables have a standard table format/template like calendars and tabular columns. They are used for preparing calendars while standard tables are used for official purposes. Fig. 5.5 shows some of the examples of Quick Tables.

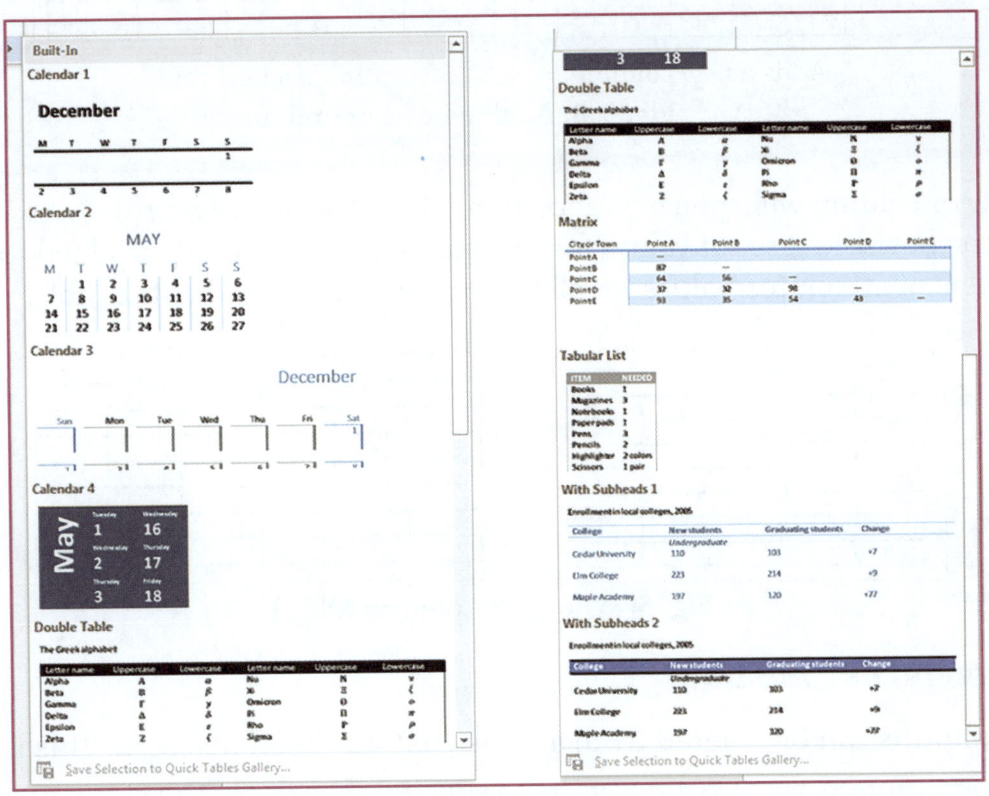

Fig. 5.5: Quick Tables

Modifying tables

MS Word 2013 has various tools to edit and format tables. These tools allow the user to add rows and columns and change the style and appearance of the table. Following are some of the important table modifying tools:

Digital geek

Tables can also be inserted using the Convert Text to Tables feature. This feature allows the text that is selected to be split into rows and columns with tabs, commas, or some other character (like hyphen, colon, slashes, etc.) to convert it into a table.

Adding row(s) or column(s)

Rows and columns can be added to a table that has been inserted. This is needed when more rows or columns are to be added after the table has been inserted. Following are the steps to insert rows and columns:

- Bring the cursor near the location where you want to add a row or column and then click the plus sign that appears as in Fig. 5.6.

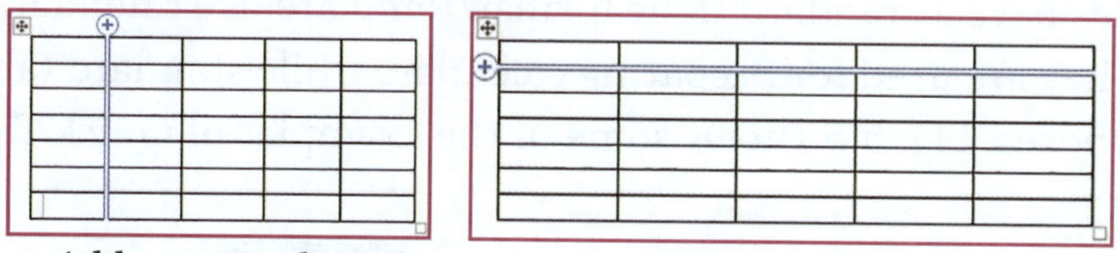

Adds a new column Adds a new row

Fig. 5.6: Adding Rows or Columns

- A new row or column will appear as shown in Fig. 5.7. Generally, a row is added to increase the horizontal set of values for one entity while a column is added to increase the numbers of attributes/values for all the entities mentioned in the table.

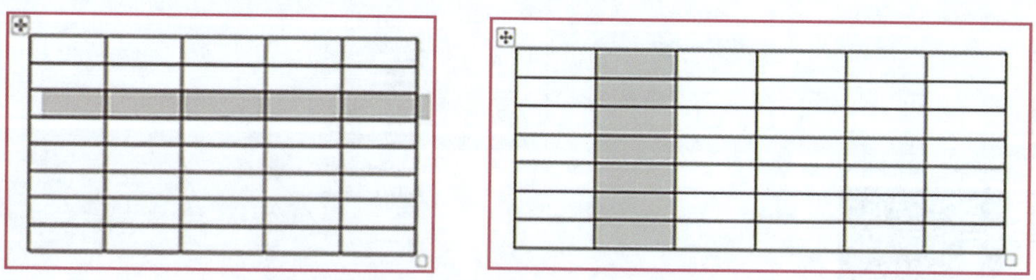

Fig. 5.7: Rows or Columns Added

Deleting row(s) or column(s)

Rows and columns can be deleted from a table that has been inserted. This is useful when there are more rows or columns than required. These are the steps to delete rows or columns:

1. Place the cursor in the row or column you want to delete. To delete multiple rows or columns, select the ones to be deleted.
2. Click the right button of the mouse and then select Delete Cells... from the drop-down menu as in Fig. 5.8.

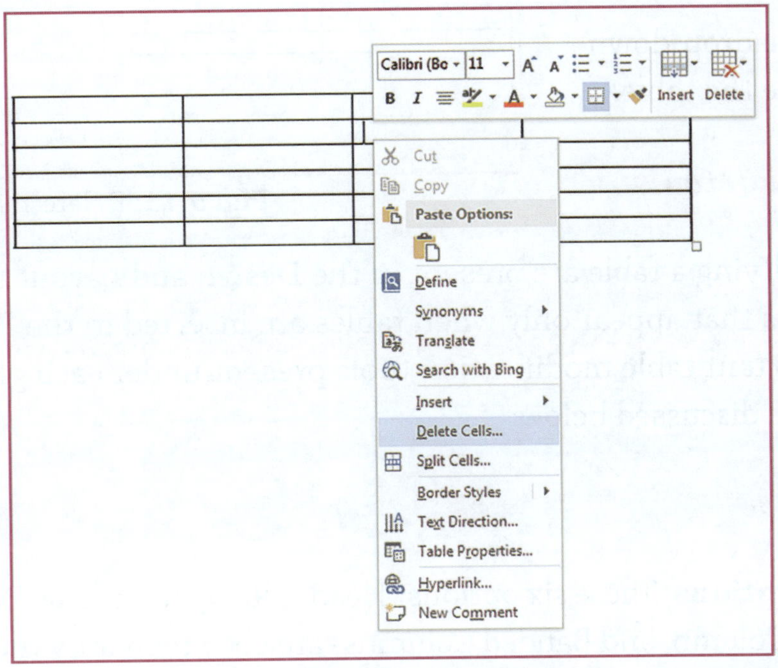

Fig. 5.8: Delete Cells

3. A dialog box will appear. Select the suitable option and then click OK as shown in Fig. 5.9. The column or row will be deleted.

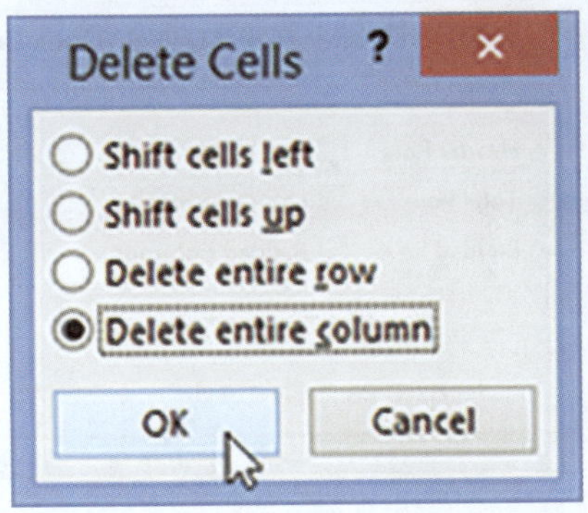

Fig. 5.9: Deleting Cells

Deleting a table

Deleting a table removes the table completely from the Word document. To delete a table, follow the steps given below:

1 Select the table by clicking on the crosshair sign on the left corner of the table. Crosshair sign appears as in Fig. 5.10.

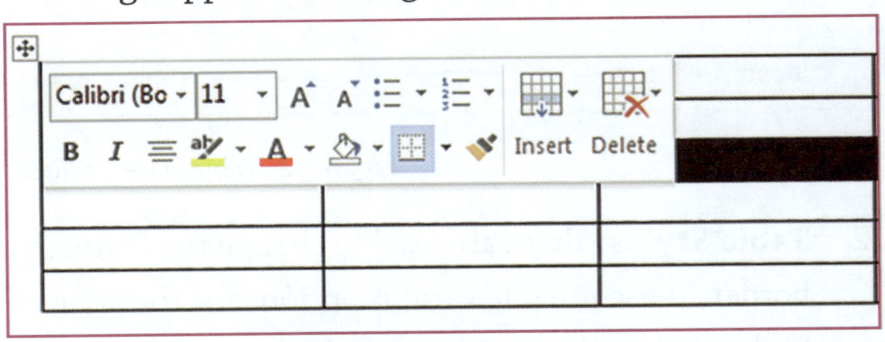

Fig. 5.10: Context menu

Word web

crosshair: two thin lines crossing at right angles, used as a marker.

2 On the context menu, as in Fig. 5.11 click on the Delete icon 

. Select Delete Table command in the drop-down menu to remove the table.

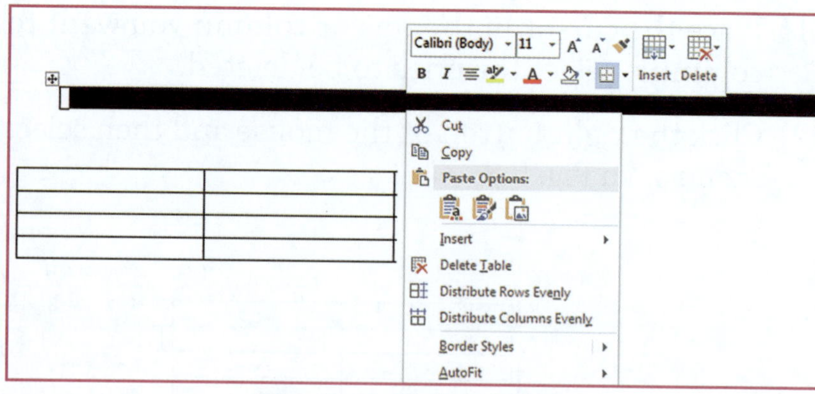

Fig. 5.11: Delete Table

Table modification tools

The tools for modifying a table are present in the Design and Layout tabs. These tabs are contextual tabs that appear only when tables are inserted in the Word document. Some of the important table modification tools present under each group in the Design and Layout tab are discussed below:

Groups in design tab

1. **Table Style Options**: These six options (Header Row, Total Row, Banded Rows, First Column, Last Column, and Banded Columns) are used to modify the way rows and columns of a table appear. Tools in this group provide different styles and combination of styles for rows and columns. Some of the examples are given in Fig. 5.12.

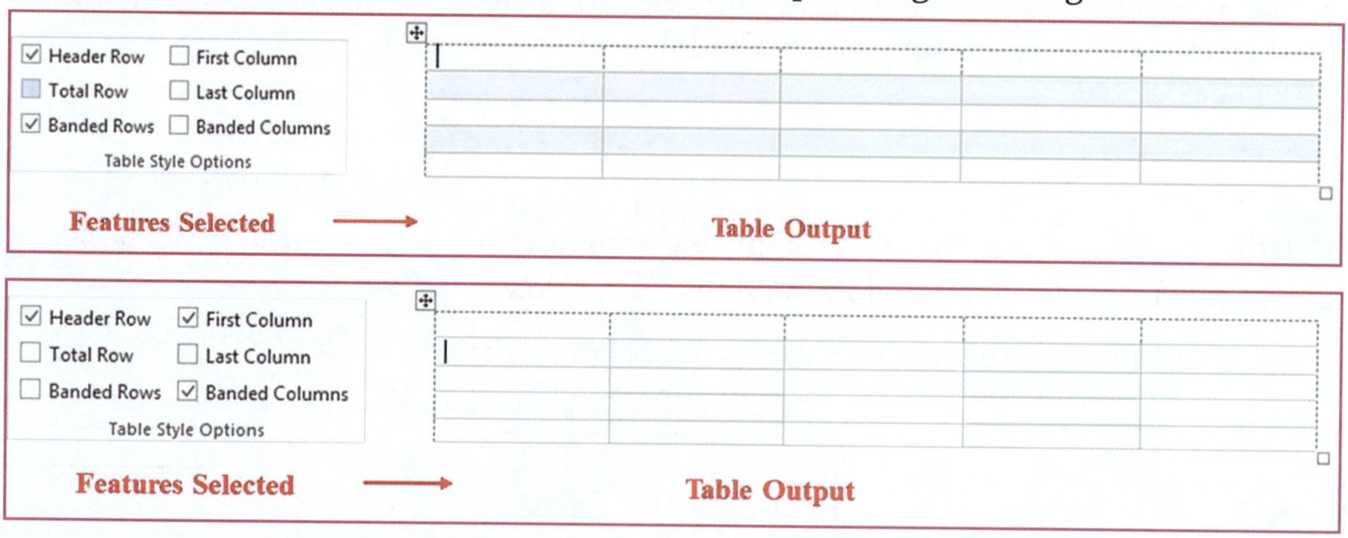

Fig. 5.12: Table style options

2. **Table Styles:** These are used to change the features of the table like colour and border. These provide various options for the style of the table. To apply Table Styles, follow the steps given below:

(a) On the Table Styles group, click on the More drop-down button to see all the available table styles as shown in Fig. 5.13.

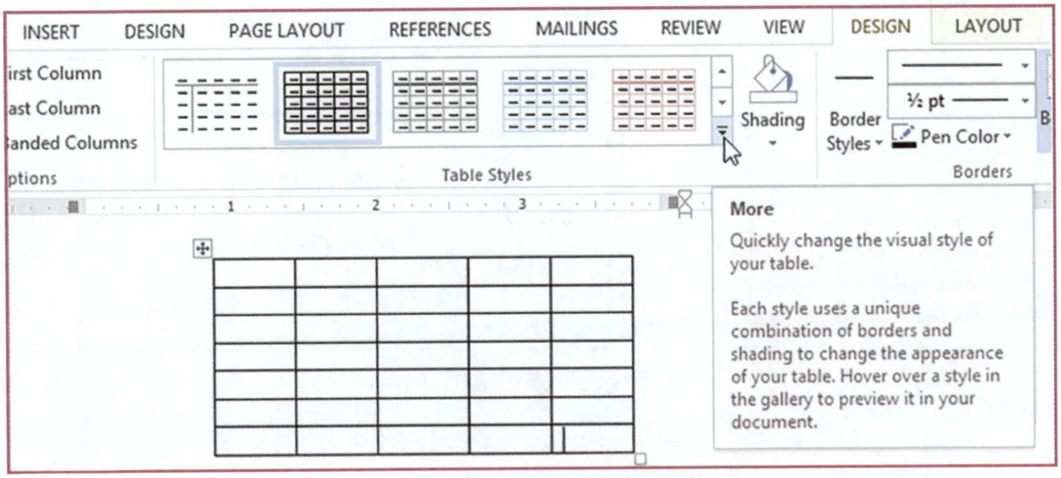

Fig. 5.13: Table Styles

(b) Click on the style that you need and the style will be reflected in the table as in Fig. 5.14. A table style (or Quick Style) is a combination of different formatting options, including colour combinations that are derived from the theme colours of the presentation.

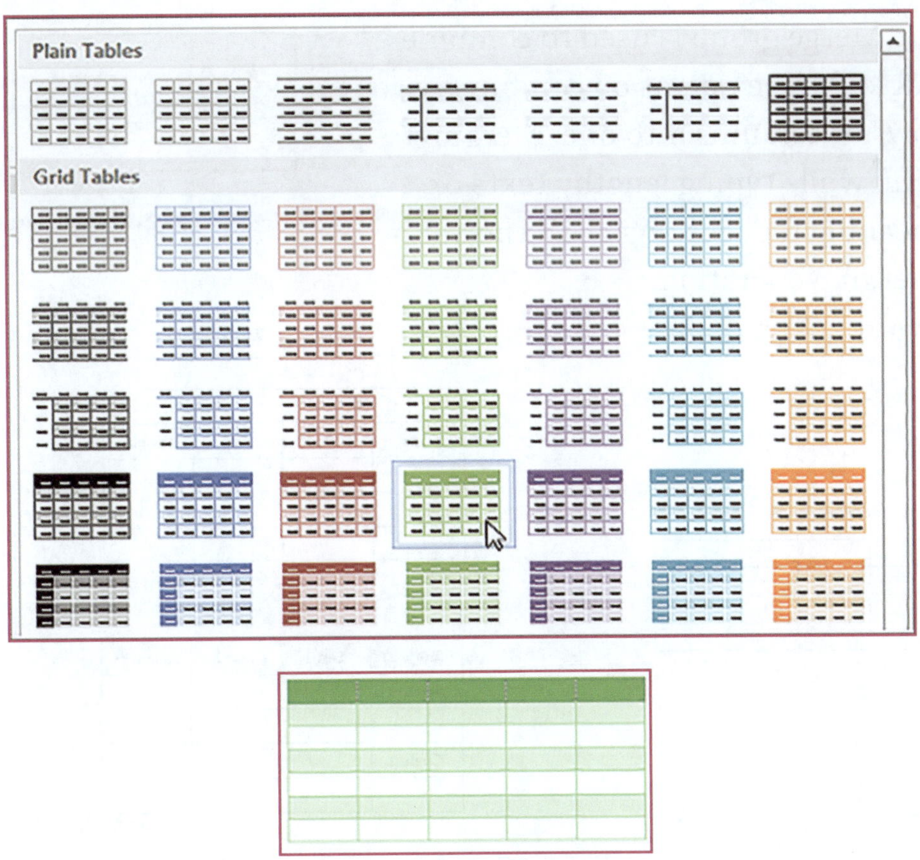

Fig. 5.14: Table Styles

3. **Borders:** Borders are lines/boundaries of a cell or the entire table. Tools in this group are useful in changing the features of the border like color, thickness and style. Fig. 5.15 shows the use of these tools.

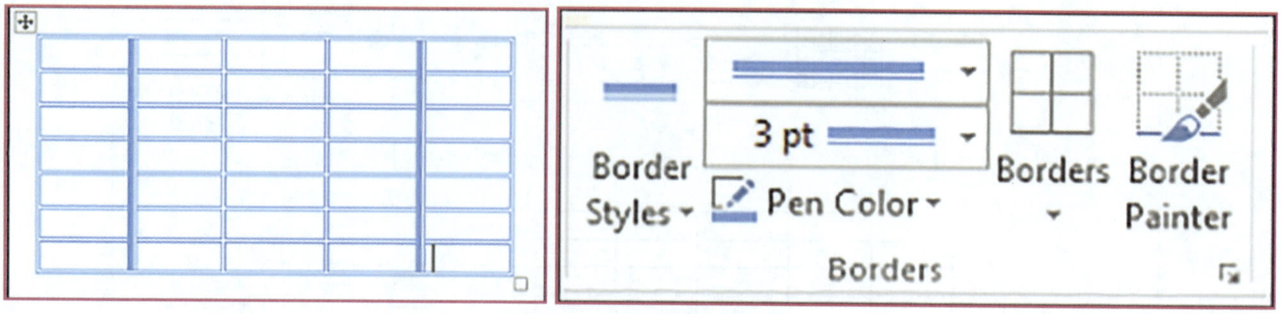

Fig. 5.15: Borders

Groups in layout tab

1. **Rows and Columns:** Tools in this group are used to add and delete cells (rows and columns) from the table. A table can also be deleted by using the Delete Table command present on the same group as shown in Fig. 5.16.

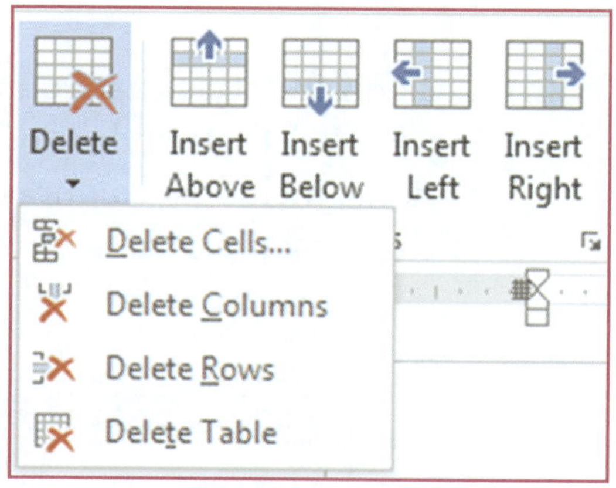

Fig. 5.16: Delete Cells

2. **Merge:** The Merge group is used to combine cells in a table. Merge operation combines two or more rows or columns into one. Merging cells is useful while typing lengthy texts or common heading for cells. Fig. 5.17 shows the usage of merging operation.

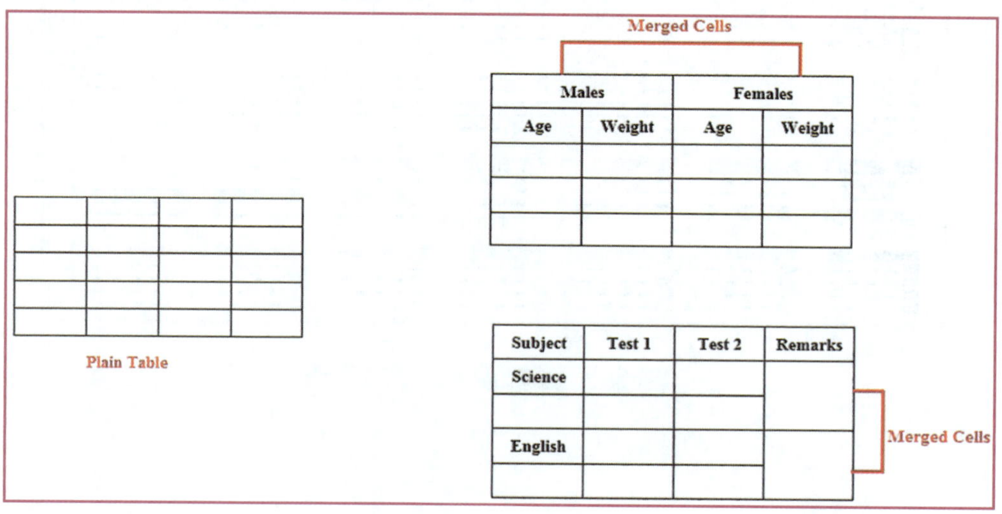

Fig. 5.17: Merging Cells

Following are the steps to merge cells in a table:

Step 1: Select the cells to be merged.

Step 2: Click on Merge Cells command on the Merge group. This will merge the cells (Fig. 5.18).

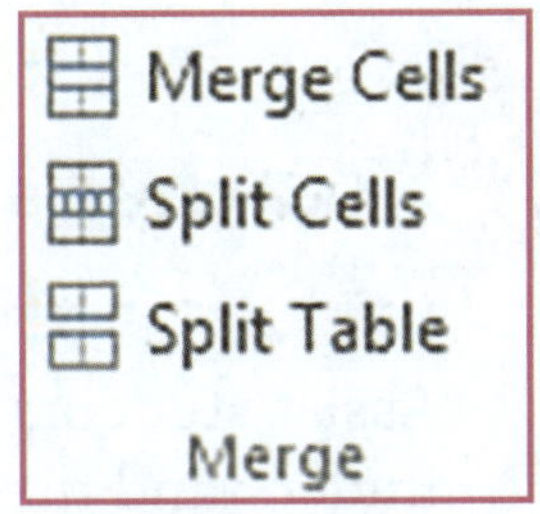

Fig. 5.18: Merge Cells command on the Merge group

3. **Cell Size**: Commands in the Cell Size group give options to vary the size of the cell. When a table is inserted, the cells will have a default size. Tools in the Cell Size group are useful when the cell size that we need is either smaller or bigger than the default size. The following image shows the functions of various commands in the group (Fig. 5.19):

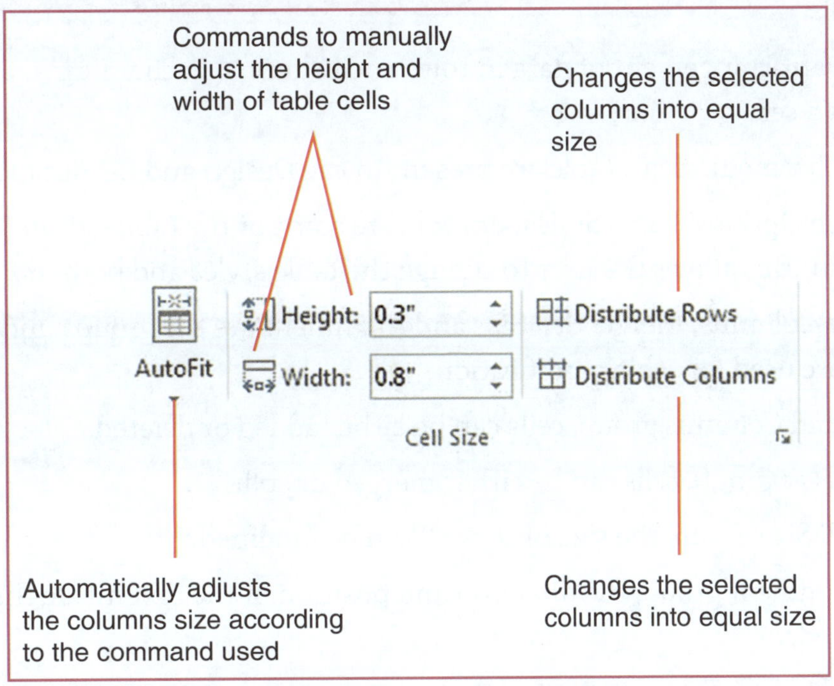

Fig. 5.19: Cell Size Commands

4. **Alignment:** Alignment in a cell is the direction and position of the text inside the cell. Tools in the Alignment group are used to change the direction and position of the text in the table. Fig. 5.20 shows some of the different alignments in a table.

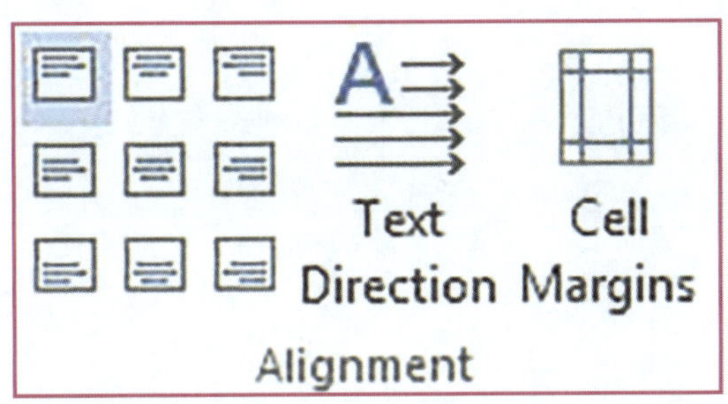

Fig. 5.20: Different alignments in a table

Teacher's note

Assist students to explore the commands mentioned above to completely understand their functions.

Concepts learnt

1. A table is an arrangement of data in rows and columns. Each unit in a table is known as a cell.
2. The tools for modifying a table are present in the Design and Layout tabs.
3. Table Style Options, Table Styles, Borders are some of the table-editing groups in Design tab. This allows the user to change the table styles and borders.
4. Rows and Columns, Merge, Cell Size and Alignment are the groups under Layout tab that are used for table modification.
5. In Rows and Columns group, cells can be either added or deleted.
6. Under Merge group, cells can be either merged or split.
7. In the Cell Size group, the size of the cell can be modified.
8. In the Alignment group, the direction and position of the text inside the cell can be modified.

Exercise

A Fill in the blanks.

1. Each unit in a table is known as a _______________ (Cell/Column).
2. Table is an arrangement of _______________ (Rows/Plates) and _______________ (Columns/Pillars).
3. Two cells can be combined to form a single cell using a command in the _______________ (Merge/Table Styles) group.
4. Two thin lines crossing at right angles, used as a marker is known as _______________ (Borders/Crosshairs).
5. The size of a cell can be varied using commands present in the _______________ (Cell Size/Alignment) group.

B Write T for True or F for False.

1. A table can also be deleted using a command in the Rows and Columns group. ☐
2. Merge operation combines only two or more columns. ☐
3. Layout tab is not a contextual tab. ☐
4. The size of the cells in a table is fixed and cannot be changed. ☐
5. Borders can be applied to both cell and table. ☐

C Choose the correct option.

1. Which of the following is a command to insert a table in a Word document?
   (a) Convert Text to Tables (b) Draw Table
   (c) Insert Table (d) All of these
2. Tables that have a standard format like calendars and tabular columns are known as
   (a) Quick Tables (b) Fast Tables
   (c) Swift Tables (d) Instant Tables
3. Using which of the following contextual tabs can rows and columns be added?
   (a) Design (b) Layout
   (c) Format (d) None of these

4. Which of following groups belongs to Layout tab?
   (a) Borders
   (b) Tables
   (c) Alignment
   (d) Symbols
5. Which of the following is a function of Cell Size group?
   (a) Apply different styles to the cell
   (b) Adjust the size of the cell
   (c) Add and delete rows and columns
   (d) Align text in different directions

D Answer these questions briefly.

1. Describe any two ways of inserting a table.
2. Differentiate between Table Style and Table Style Options groups.
3. What is the use of Alignment group?
4. Mention one use of the commands in Merge and Cell Size group.
5. What are the commands in Rows & Columns group useful for?

E Application-based question.

1. A class teacher while making the attendance sheet of her class wants a single heading across all the columns. How can the teacher do this?
2. A book publisher wants to gift his customers a calendar of the upcoming year. The publisher has MS Word 2013 to work on. How can calendars be prepared in MS Word 2013?

Computer is my mentor!

Make a timetable of your daily schedule from Monday to Friday using tables.

6 Introduction to MS PowerPoint 2013

Learning log

- How to start PowerPoint 2013?
- Components of PowerPoint Window
- Applications of PowerPoint 2013

Introduction

Microsoft PowerPoint (MS PowerPoint) is one of the many applications like MS Word, MS Excel, MS Access, MS Publisher, MS Outlook available in the MS Office package. With every version of MS PowerPoint, new features are brought in.

Microsoft PowerPoint 2013 is a program that helps to create and deliver effective presentations. It offers various themes, layouts and effects. MS PowerPoint lets you combine various media products available in the computer like text, graphics, videos, sounds, animations to create dynamic presentations and e-learning packages that grab the audience's attention.

MS PowerPoint is one of the most widely used presentation software. Other presentation software include Lotus Freelance, Apple Keynote and OpenOffice Impress.

The two terms that are commonly used in PowerPoint are slide and presentation. The individual page that is used in designing presentation is called **slide**, whereas **presentation** is a collection of individual slides that contains information on a specific topic. This can be in the form of text, images, audio clips and videos.

Starting PowerPoint 2013

You can start PowerPoint 2013 from the **Start** menu or by double-clicking an existing PowerPoint file. When you start the program without opening a specific file, the Start screen appears, prompting you to open an existing presentation or create a new presentation.

Method 1: Click the Start button, click Programs/Apps, click Microsoft Office 2013 and then click PowerPoint 2013 (Fig. 6.1).

Method 2: Search for the symbol with PowerPoint on the desktop and double-click on it (Fig. 6.2).

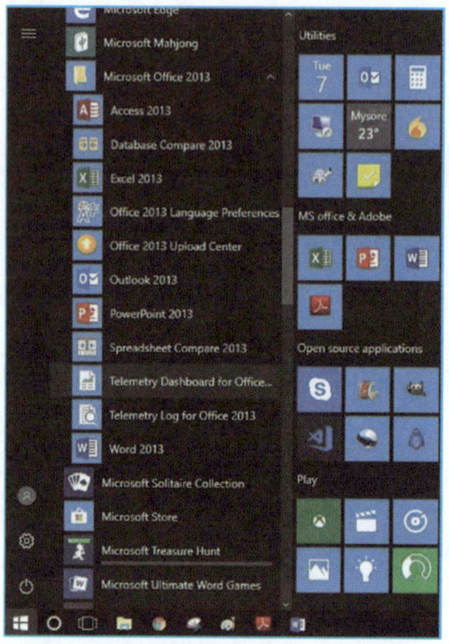

Fig. 6.1: Method 1- Starting Powerpoint 2013

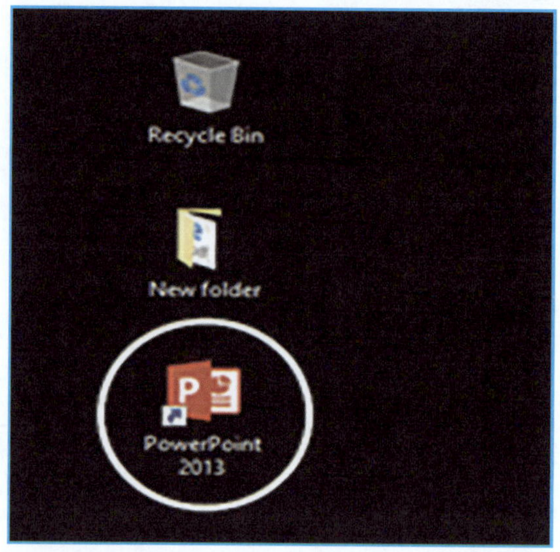

Fig. 6.2: Method 2- Starting Powerpoint 2013

Both the methods will take you to the Welcome Screen (Fig. 6.3).

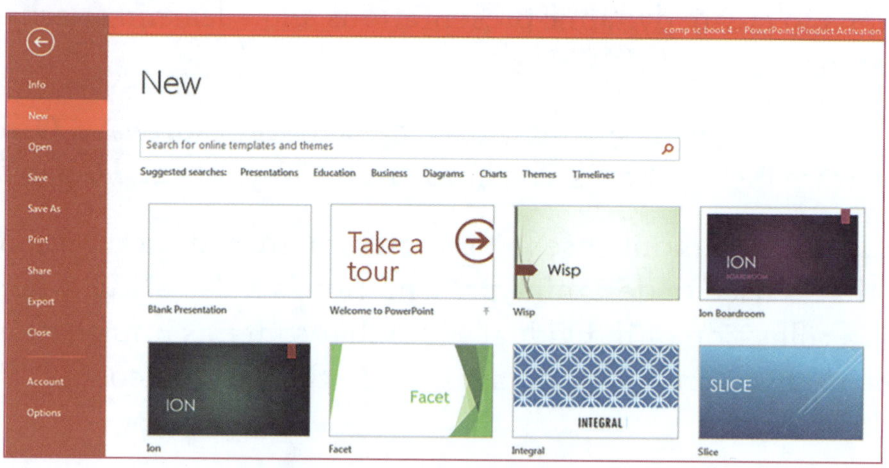

Fig. 6.3: Welcome Screen

Components of PowerPoint Window

All the Microsoft Office 2013 programs share a common user interface. The PowerPoint 2013 program window is easy to navigate and simple to use.

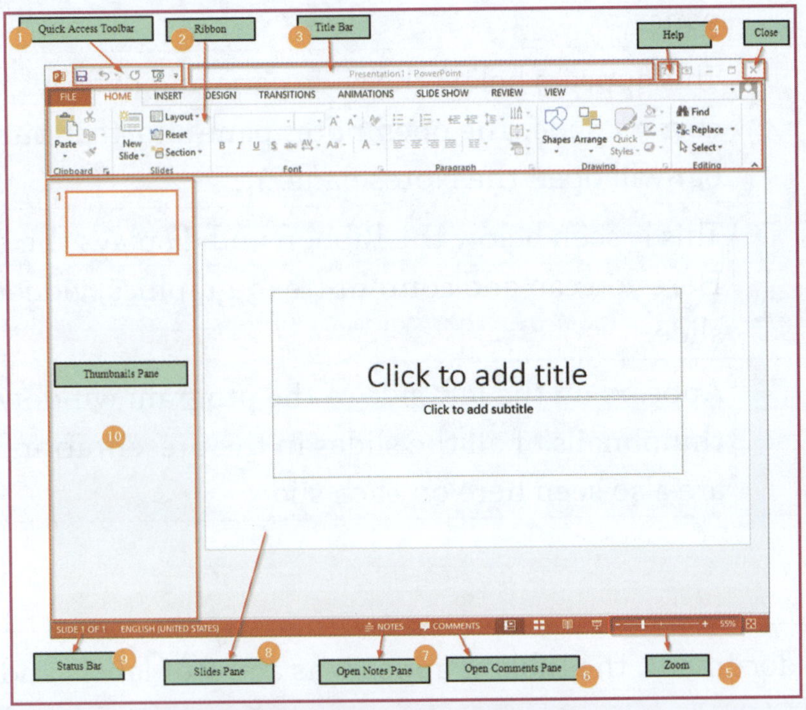

Fig. 6.4: Components of PowerPoint

The table below gives you brief information on the components of PowerPoint.

Name	Description
Quick Access toolbar **(1)**	This is seen on the left side of the Title bar. It provides one-click access to the frequently used commands.
Ribbon **(2)**	This extends across the top of the program window and is placed below the Title bar. It consists of a set of task-specific tabs.
Title bar **(3)**	This appears at the top of the program window and displays the name of the presentation and the program.
Help, Close **(4)**	These tabs are seen to the extreme right of the title bar. These buttons are used to get help; change the display of the Ribbon; Minimize, Restore, Maximize and Close the program window.
Status bar **(5) (9)**	This appears at the bottom of the program window and displays information about the presentation. Shortcuts for Comments pane, Notes pane and features like SLIDE SHOW, Zoom in and Zoom out are seen here.

Comments pane **(6)**	It appears on the right side of the program window and displays comments related to the current slide. This pane can be used to add, delete or reply to comments. The open Comment pane shortcut button on the Status bar will open up the Comment pane.
Notes pane **(7)**	This appears below the slide pane and displays notes about the current slide. The open notes pane shortcut button on the Status bar will open the Notes pane.
Slide pane **(8)**	This is seen below the Ribbon and displays the current slide. Here you can add content (text, graphics, videos, sounds) to each slide.
Thumbnails pane **(10)**	Appears on the left side of the program window and displays thumbnails of all the slides in the presentation. Slide numbers are also seen here on each slide.

Ribbon

In the PowerPoint document, the Ribbon appears as a row of labels and tabs.

The tools and functions that were formerly used in menus and toolbars in earlier versions of PowerPoint are now available under the Ribbon tab shown in Fig. 6.5.

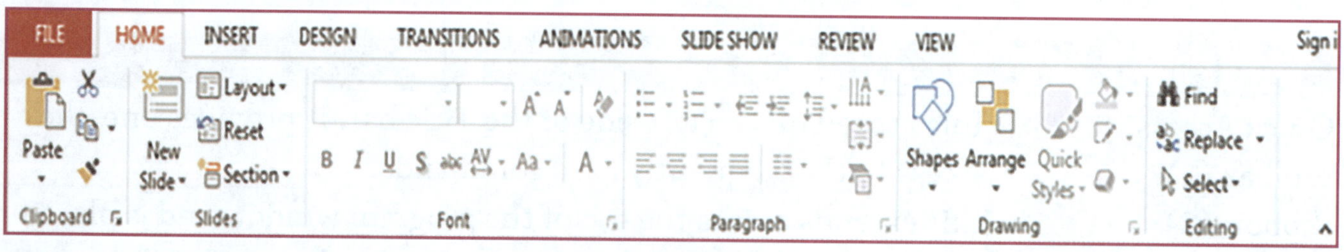

Fig. 6.5: Ribbon

The tabs are grouped based on their purpose. For example, to view a slide show you can use the SLIDE SHOW tab. The tools that you use to animate things on your slide would be on the Animations tab.

Let us have a look at the inclusions in the PowerPoint Ribbon tab.

Home

You find the Cut and Paste features, Font and Paragraph options, and all the other features that you need to add and organize slides, in the HOME tab as shown in Fig. 6.6.

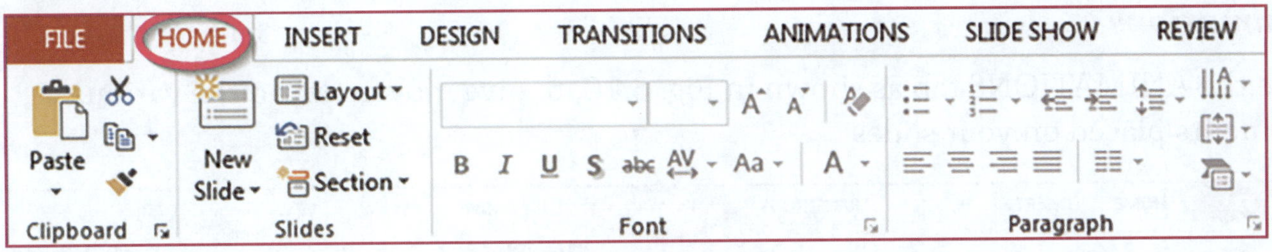

Fig. 6.6: HOME tab

Insert

Click INSERT to add something to a slide. This helps to insert pictures, shapes, charts, links, text boxes, video and more as shown in Fig. 6.7.

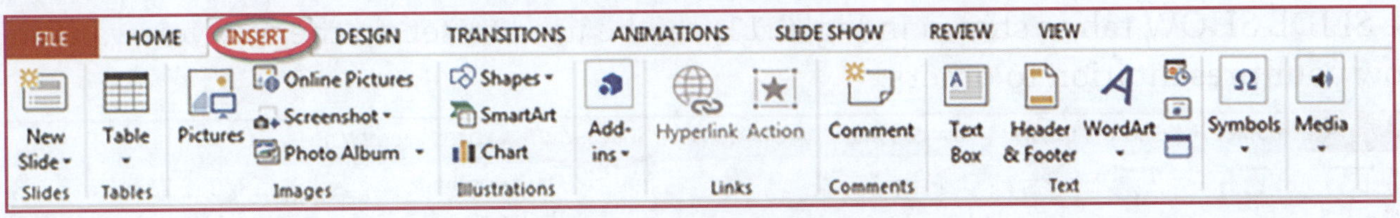

Fig. 6.7: INSERT tab

Design

On the DESIGN tab, you can add a theme or colour scheme, or format the slide background as shown in Fig. 6.8.

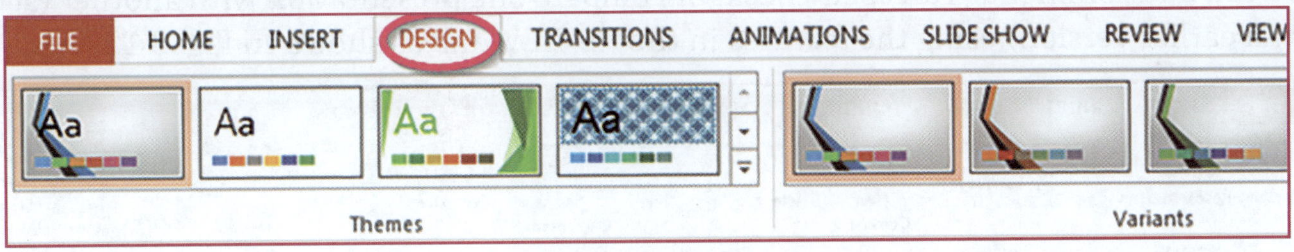

Fig. 6.8: DESIGN tab

Transitions

Using the features of TRANSITIONS tab, as shown in Fig. 6.9, you can set how the slides change from one to the next one.

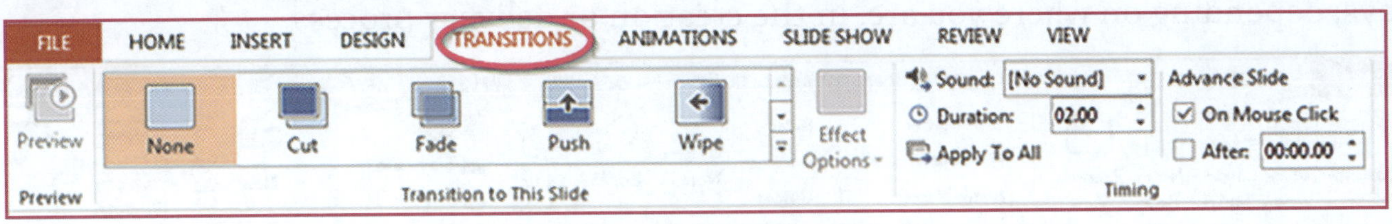

Fig. 6.9: TRANSITIONS tab

Animations

Use the ANIMATIONS tab as shown in Fig. 6.10, to give movement to the various elements placed on your slides.

Fig. 6.10: ANIMATIONS tab

SLIDE SHOW

The SLIDE SHOW tab as shown in Fig. 6.11, can be used to set up the way you want to show your presentation to others.

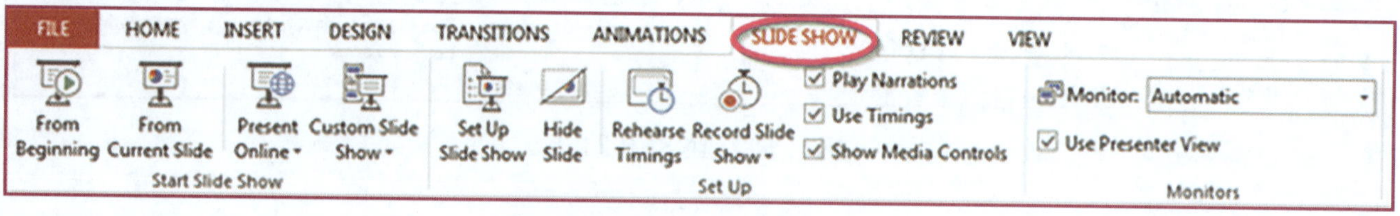

Fig. 6.11: SLIDE SHOW tab

Review

You can add comments, run spell-check, or compare one presentation with another (such as an earlier version) using the features in the REVIEW tab as shown in Fig. 6.12.

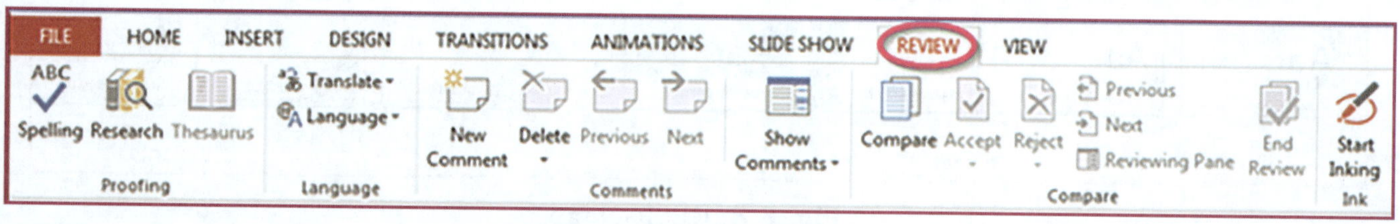

Fig. 6.12: REVIEW tab

View

The VIEW tab as shown in Fig. 6.13, allows you to look at your presentation in different ways, depending on where you are, in the creation or delivery process.

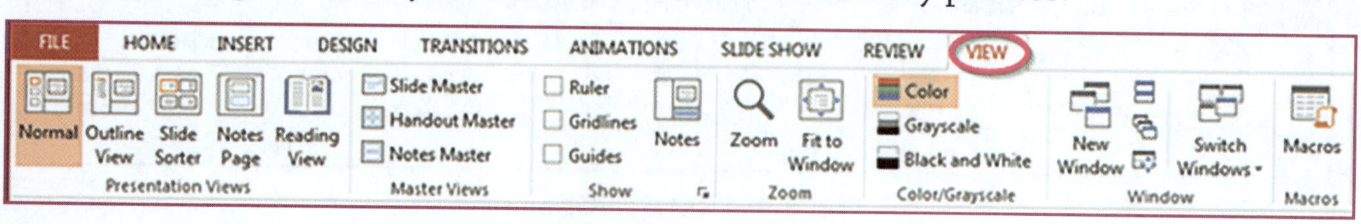

Fig. 6.13: VIEW tab

File

At one end of the Ribbon is the FILE tab, which you use for the operations, such as opening, saving, sharing, exporting, printing and managing your presentation.

Click the FILE tab to open a new view called the Backstage. This view is the place where you manage your files and the data about them — creating, saving, inspecting for hidden metadata or personal information and setting options.

Tool tabs

When you click some parts of your slides, such as pictures, shapes, SmartArt or text boxes, you might see a colourful new tab that appears at the end of the Ribbon.

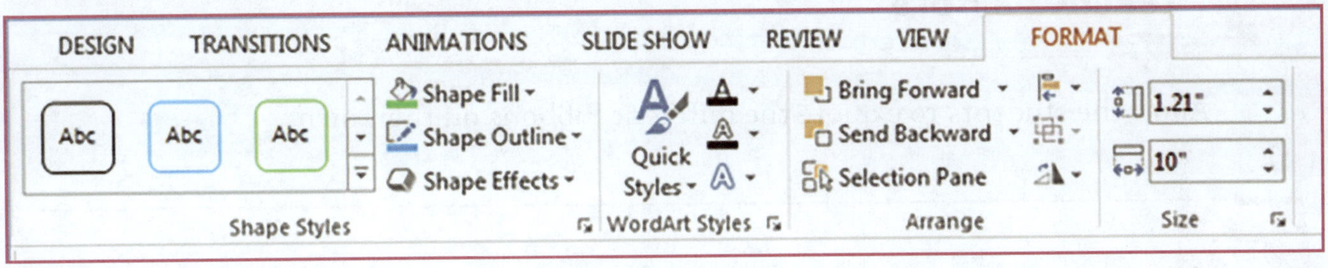

Fig. 6.14: Tool tab

The Drawing Tools tab appears when you click a shape or text box. When you click a picture, the Picture Tools tab appears. Other such tabs include SmartArt Tools, Chart Tools, Table Tools and Video Tools. These tabs disappear or change when you click something else in your presentation. These tabs are also called as contextual tabs.

Applications of PowerPoint 2013

PowerPoint is widely used across the world. It can be a powerful tool in creating clear, well-structured presentations that have a strong visual impact. Microsoft PowerPoint is widely used for making professional quality presentations in a variety of formats, including on-screen computer slide shows, black-and-white or colour overhead slides. You can also use it for making speaker's notes and audience hand-outs. In addition, PowerPoint can be used as a drawing package for preparing pictures, forms, posters and leaflets.

netsearch

The following are presentation software that can be used as alternative to MS PowerPoint and are freeware:

- LibreOffice - https://www.libreoffice.org/
- WPS Office - https://www.wps.com/
- SlideDog - https://slidedog.com/

Teacher's note

Allow the students to explore the different Ribbons on their own.

Concepts learnt

1. MS PowerPoint is one among the many available presentation software.
2. The feature SLIDE SHOW is used to run the slides sequentially in full screen mode.
3. The various components of PowerPoint are the Quick Access Toolbar, Title Bar, Ribbon, Thumbnails, Notes and Comments pane, Slide and Status Bar.
4. Many of the menus and toolbars are grouped in a tab called the Ribbon tab.
5. PowerPoint is a powerful tool in creating presentations with a powerful visual impact.

Exercise

A Fill in the blanks.

1. _______________ (MS PowerPoint/Apple Keynote) is a presentation program that is commonly used.
2. The latest version of MS Office is _______________ (MS Office 2013/MS Office 2016).
3. The bar that appears at the top of the program window is _______________ (Quick Access bar/Title bar).
4. A feature that you see on a Status bar is _______________ (Comments/Close).
5. The _______________ (Note/Slide) pane is used to add content to each slide.

B Write T for True or F for False.

1. Two presentation software are MS Publisher and Lotus Freelance. ☐
2. A slide consists of text, images, audio clips and videos. ☐
3. The Title bar gives you access to shortcuts like zoom in, zoom out, SLIDE SHOW and so on. ☐
4. To add themes or colour schemes, the TRANSITIONS tab is used. ☐
5. You can access Backstage through FILE tab. ☐

C Choose the correct option.

1. This pane appears on the right side of the program window and displays comments related to the current slide.
   (a) Thumbnails pane (b) Slide pane
   (c) Notes pane (d) Comments pane
2. The tab with access to cut, copy and paste is ___________.
   (a) VIEW (b) DESIGN
   (c) HOME (d) INSERT
3. Which of the features below is not an option available in Insert tab?
   (a) Table (b) Comment
   (c) Pictures (d) Layout

4. Which is the tab that contains the option to add themes to the slide?
   (a) INSERT (b) DESIGN
   (c) HOME (d) VIEW
5. Identify the false statement.
   (a) Tool tab can be accessed by clicking on certain parts of the slides.
   (b) Features like save, open, print are available in FILE tab.
   (c) The ANIMATIONS tab is used to change the design of the presentation.
   (d) Features to add comments, run spell-check are merged under REVIEW tab.

D Answer these questions briefly.

1. Give any two examples of presentation software.
2. Write a short note on Ribbon.
3. Write a note on the uses of MS PowerPoint.
4. Explain Tool tabs with an example.
5. What is Backstage view?

E Application-based question.

1. List out the places where presentation software is used.
2. List out the different features available in the Insert tab.

Computer is my mentor!

Create a PowerPoint presentation on a topic of your choice and explore the features of all the tabs in the Ribbon.

7 News and Computers Today

Learning log

- Importance of news
- Reading the news with the help of a computer
- Different ways of staying updated with the news

Introduction

The word news originates from Latin word *nova* that means new things. News comes to us through various media like newspaper, radio, television and even the computer today.

It helps us to stay informed about what is happening around the world. We should always keep in touch with the news and current affairs of our society to stay connected with the world outside our home. News helps us to know and understand the changing world. Our means of reaching out to news has changed with time. Can you list how people learnt about news around the world earlier?

1. ____________________.
2. ____________________.
3. ____________________.
4. ____________________.
5. ____________________.

Importance of News

We live in a world that is constantly evolving. Today in this competitive world, staying updated with news is important to have an idea of developments in different areas like politics, society, science, technology, language and arts.

Fig. 7.1: Newspapers–A Source of News

When we are updated with what is happening around us, we gain a better knowledge about the world around us. It helps us to reach out to more people by engaging in conversations on diverse topics. An updated person feels confident and can easily grasp day-to-day happenings in political, economical and social fields. News connects us to our history and our future. It enables us to identify our areas of interest and take important decisions. Knowledge is the most powerful weapon acquired during the course of time to prepare ourselves for the future.

Word web

evolving: developing

Reading the News with the help of a Computer

We use the computer for many purposes. One of these is to read news with the help of the Internet. To read news, type Today's news in the address bar of a Windows 10 computer browser – Windows Edge. News links of different websites will be displayed. Select any website

Word web

browser: a computer program to use the Internet

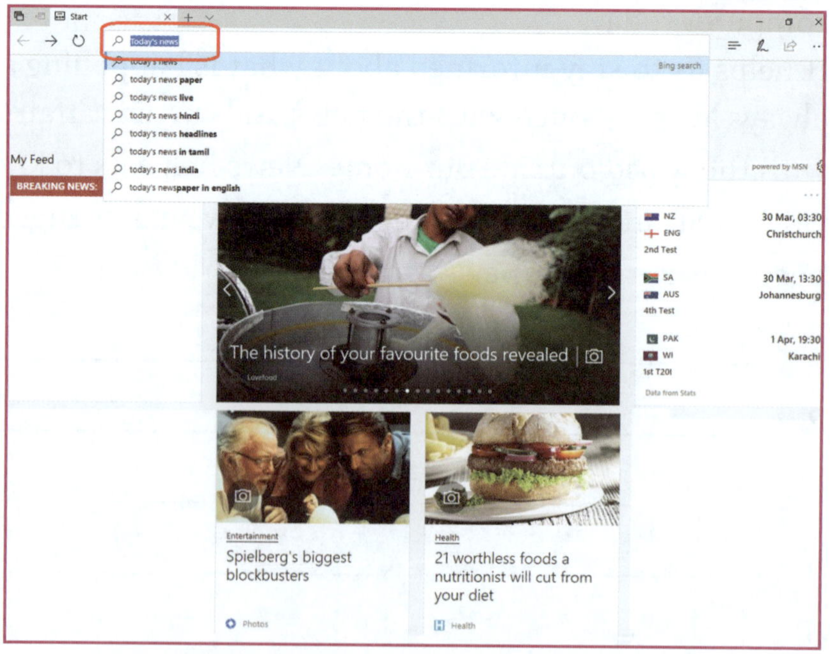

Fig. 7.2: Reading news from Windows Edge

to read the news. News will be displayed in categories like latest news, headlines, breaking news, health, lifestyle, sports, technology, entertainment, etc.

Different Ways of Staying Updated with the News

In this digital world, we have different ways to stay updated with the news around us. The computer and the Internet help us to stay connected and update our knowledge instantly. Let us discuss some popular ways of staying updated with the news around the world.

E-Newspaper

The newspaper is one of the most popular sources of getting information from all over the world. E-newspaper is an electronic newspaper that provides news in a digital format. We can read E-newspapers with the help of computers that have internet connectivity. E-newspapers are available in different languages. Almost all the newspaper companies publish E-newspapers. Examples of some of the popular E-newspapers in India are Times of India, The Hindu, Hindustan Times, Indian Express and Deccan Herald.

To read an E-newspaper on a computer, one has to type the name of the E-newspaper in the address bar. The respective newspaper will be displayed and then one can select the desired news from the paper and read it as shown in Fig. 7.3.

Fig. 7.3: An E-newspaper

Blogs

A blog is like a diary that is published online by an individual or a group in the form of web pages. Blog is the shortened name for weblogs. It provides information and invites discussion on various topics and it is updated regularly. Blogs are written on varied subjects as diverse as politics, cooking, travel, fashion and link to articles in other websites. Articles are listed chronologically in a blog, with the newest on top, as shown in Fig. 7.4. One who creates a blog is called a **blogger**. Using blogs to write and update information is called **blogging**.

> **Word web**
>
> **chronological:** described or shown in the order in which they happened

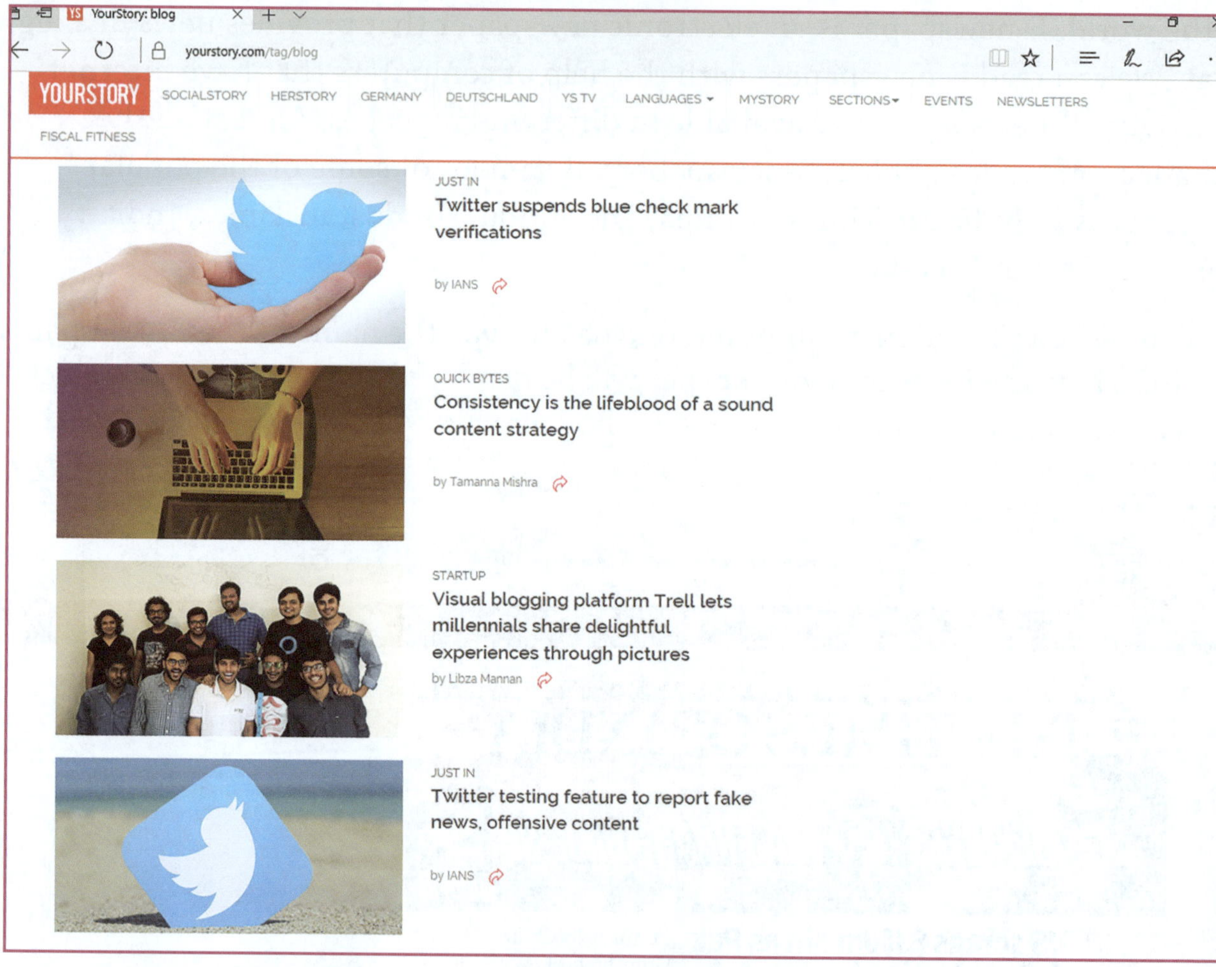

Fig. 7.4: A blog

One can read the blog by typing the names of the required blog in the address bar of the web browser.

Digital geek

Vlog is the short form of video blog or video log. It is similar to a web television where uploaded videos can be viewed by the users. Vlog helps to get updated information in the form of videos.

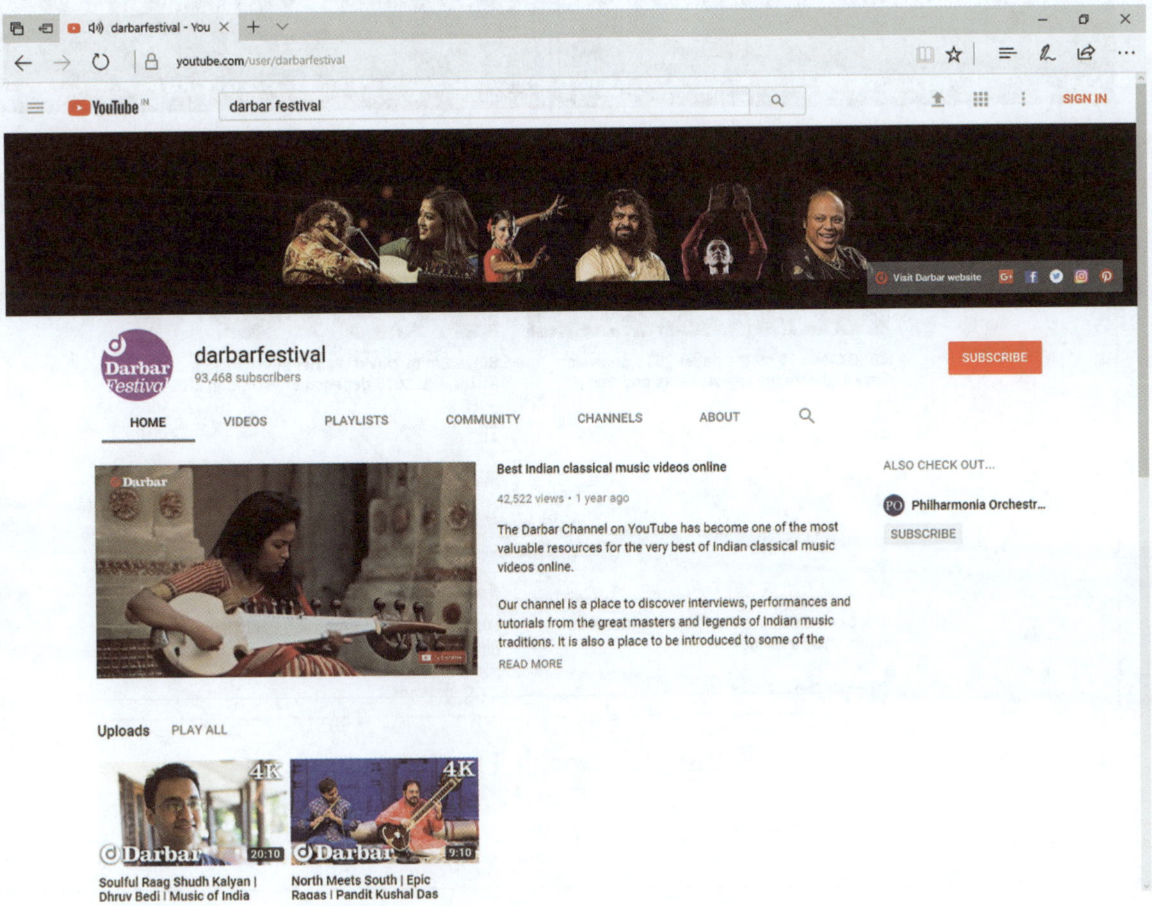

Darbar festival is a popular Vlog channel on YouTube on Indian classical music.

Google Play Newsstand

Newsstand is a place that sells newspapers and periodicals. Google Play Newsstand is a digital newsstand that provides ways to access and read the latest news from newspapers and magazines. It is a personalized newsreader which helps to read

Word web

periodicals: magazines or books published at regular intervals the news in one place. Google Play Newsstand is a news aggregator operated by Google. It automatically updates the news.

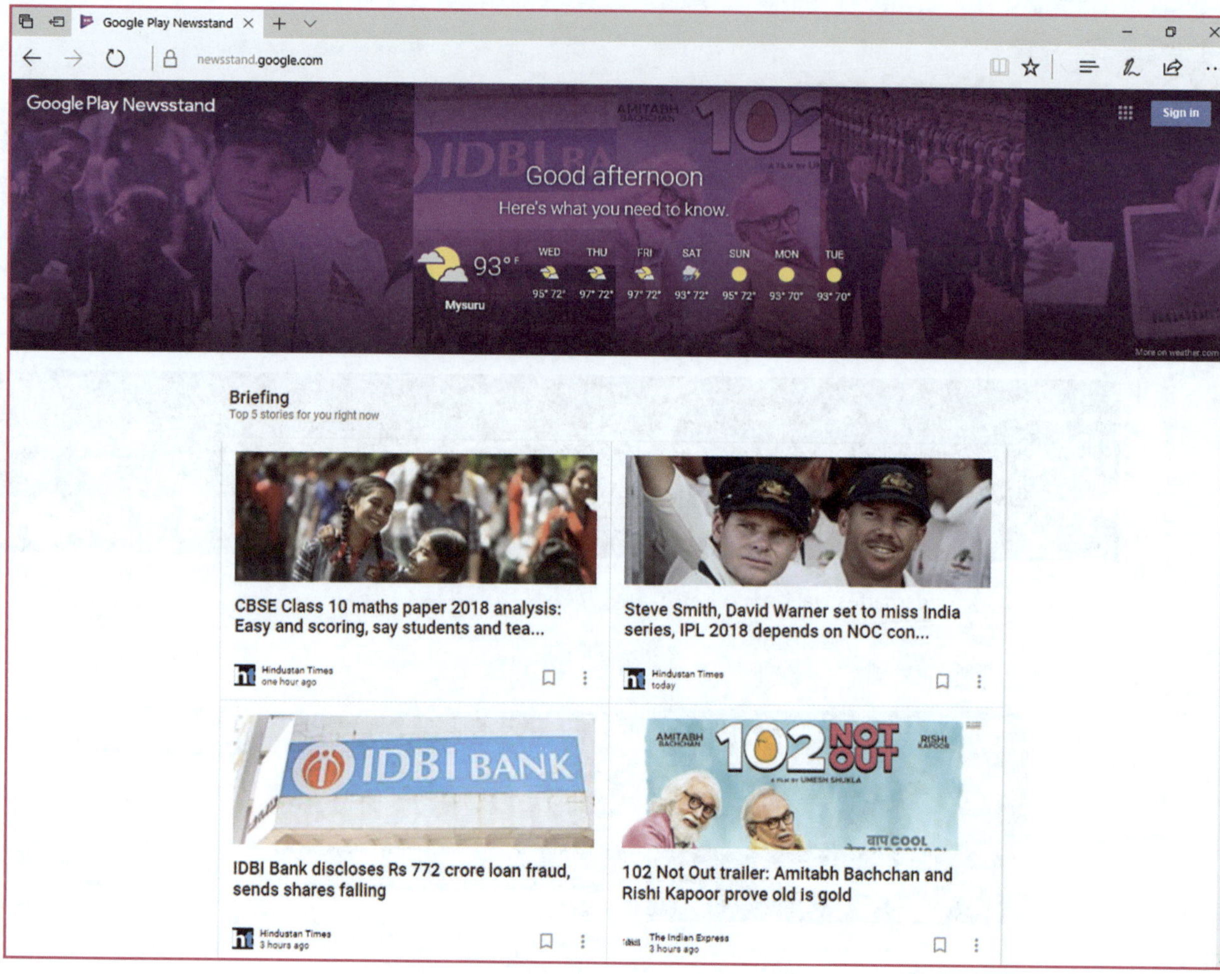

Fig. 7.5: Google Play Newsstand

Flipboard

Flipboard is a news aggregator which aggregates content from other websites in the form of text, images and videos. It shows the content in the form of a magazine. The content of Flipboard includes blog posts, stories, articles, etc. Flipboard can be accessed with the help of a web browser. It provides global news in different languages from various sources.

Word web

aggregator: a sum of many different things taken together

Using Flipboard, one can easily read the news from various fields from around the world one after the other like the way we read a magazine as shown in Fig. 7.6.

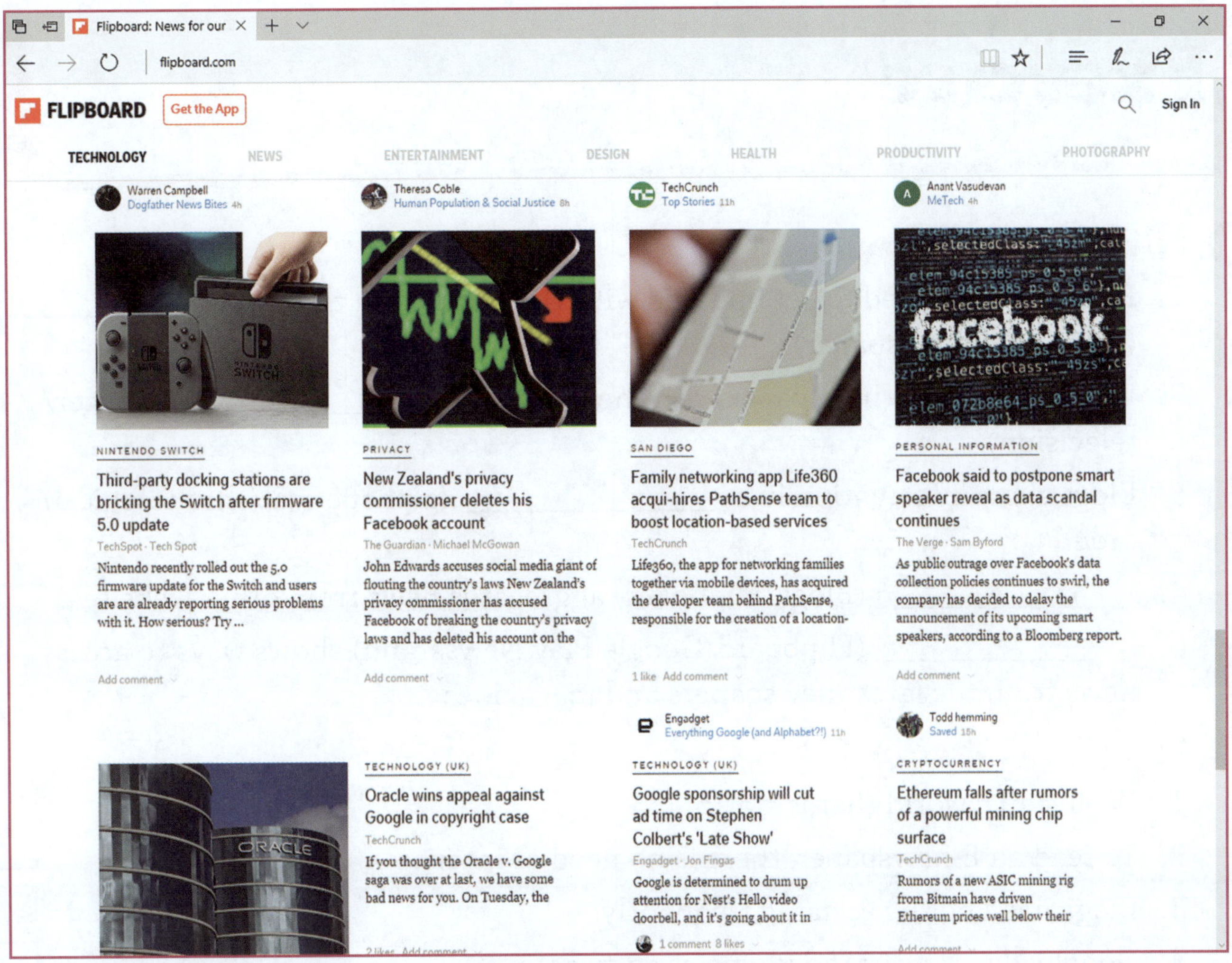

Fig. 7.6: Flipboard

Concepts Learnt

1. News helps us to stay updated with events.
2. Staying updated with news helps to increase our knowledge in variety of areas, connect with people and prepare ourselves for future.
3. We are living in a digital period where computer and the Internet serves as an easy medium to stay updated with news around us.
4. Some of the ways of updating news around us are E-newspaper, Blogs, Google Play Newsstand and Flipboard.

Exercise

A Fill in the blanks.

1. Earlier people used to get updated with the news from the ________________ (computers/newspaper).
2. We can read an E-newspaper with the help of ________________ (computer/television).
3. Blogs show information in a ________________ (alphabetical/chronological) order.
4. ________________ (Blogs/Flipboard) aggregates news from other websites.
5. ________________ (Flipboard/Google Play Newsstand) shows ways to access news from the latest newspapers and magazines.

B Write T for True or F for False.

1. We live in a world that is static. ☐
2. To read an E-newspaper, there is no need of internet. ☐
3. Blogs need not be updated frequently. ☐
4. Google Play Newsstand is a news aggregator. ☐
5. Flipboard only provides news on a particular topic. ☐

C Choose the correct option.

1. News helps us to
   (a) chat with friends. (b) stay updated.
   (c) have fun. (d) stay busy
2. What helps you to stay connected with the news around the world through an electronic means?
   (a) Books (b) Magazines
   (c) E-newspapers (d) Stories
3. Identify the E-newspaper from the following.
   (a) Indian Express (b) Blog
   (c) Flipboard (d) Google Play Newsstand

4. The purpose of a blog is to
   (a) play games.
   (b) chat with friends.
   (c) solve puzzles.
   (d) present an electronic diary.
5. Vlog is the short form of
   (a) video blog or video log.
   (b) weblog.
   (c) Virtual Log
   (d) Google Play Newsstand.

D Answer these questions briefly.

1. Explain the importance of staying updated with the latest news from around the world.
2. How can you read today's news using a computer?
3. How are blogs helpful to stay updated with diverse things in the world?
4. Explain how Google Play Newsstand helps to stay updated with the news.
5. Why is a Flipboard is called a news aggregator?

E Application-based question.

1. How can we get the recent update of a cricket match played in a country?
2. How can you prepare a live report of the Indian Prime Minister's visit to the USA?
3. A computer company has announced the launch of a new technology today. How will you collect information for a discussion with your colleagues on the new technology on the day of its launch?
4. You have to prepare an assignment on the updated status of ten events happening in different parts of the world. What will you do to prepare the assignment?

Computer is my mentor!

Explore E-newspapers, collect useful information and share it.
Visit various blogs and summarize the information.
Use Google Play Newsstand to collect updated news on any interesting topic.

8 Email

Learning log

- What is an Email?
- Creation of an Email account
- Features of Email account
- Advantages of Email
- Safety measures to be taken while using Email

Introduction

List some of the methods by which people exchanged messages in the past.

___

___

___

Observe the image shown here. There is a huge mailbox placed on a computer. Does this mean we can send mails using our computer?

Yes. We can send and receive mails using our computers. It is called Email.

What is an Email?

Electronic mail is popularly known as **Email**. It is similar to a letter; is used to send or receive letters using computers through the Internet. Email is one of the fastest means of communication. It is also a comfortable way of exchanging messages, documents, photos and videos between computers. We need an Email account and address to use the Email service.

Email account and address

Email account gives access to send and receive messages. Email address is the unique identity to access an Email account. This can be created with any of the Email service providers. The name of the service provider, also called the domain name, can be seen as a part of the Email address.

Email address is the combination of username and domain name. This username and domain name is separated by the symbol '@'. The username, as the word suggests, can be the name of the user or any combination of letters, numbers or special characters (like underscore (_), dot (.), etc.). The Email address of an individual is protected with a password. The user should not share his/her password with anyone.

Popular Email account providers

There are many Email service providers. Some of the popular service providers are:

- www.gmail.com
- www.yahoo.com
- www.rediffmail.com
- www.hotmail.com
- www.outlook.com
- www.icloud.com

Word web

Email: electronic mail

domain: the words used to identify a website

username: unique identity to access a computer/internet or network

password: a set of characters used to verify the username

Creation of an email account

Email account can be created by registering with the website of the Email account provider. The following are the steps to create an Email account.

1. Open the Website
2. Fill up the registration form
3. Verify the account

(The example for creating and operating an Email account discussed here is with the most popular Email account provider - Gmail.)

Open the website

- Type the name of any popular Email account provider on the browser.
- The URL opens as shown in Fig. 8.1.

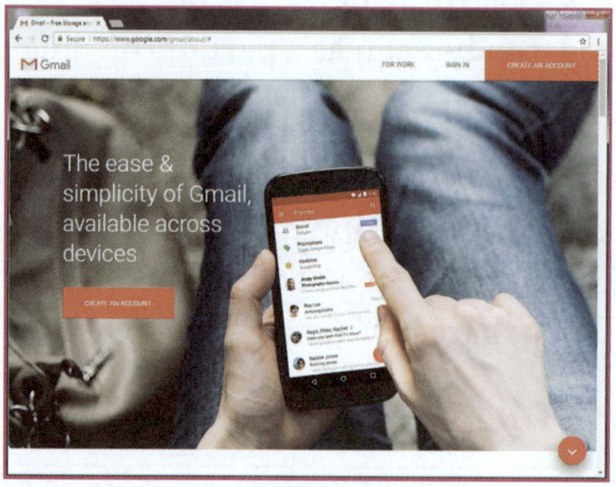

Fig. 8.1: Home page of an Email account provider website

- Click on **Create Account**. A new window will appear as shown in Fig. 8.2.

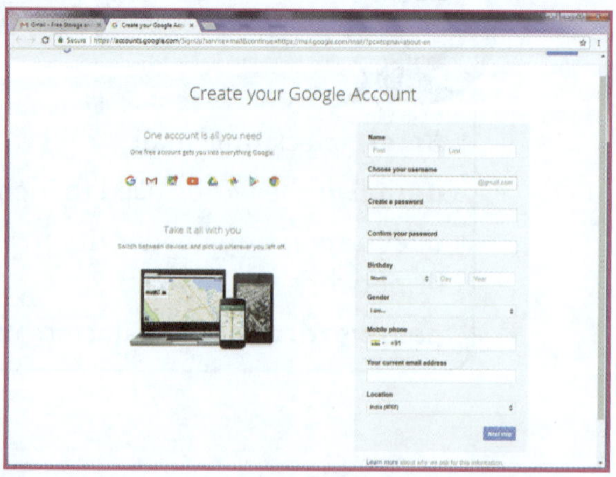

Fig. 8.2: New Email account creation form

Fill up the registration form

- In this form the First name, Last name, Username, Password, Date of Birth, Gender and Address have to be filled. While filling or choosing the username, it is suggested to check the availability of the username. Refer to Fig. 8.3.

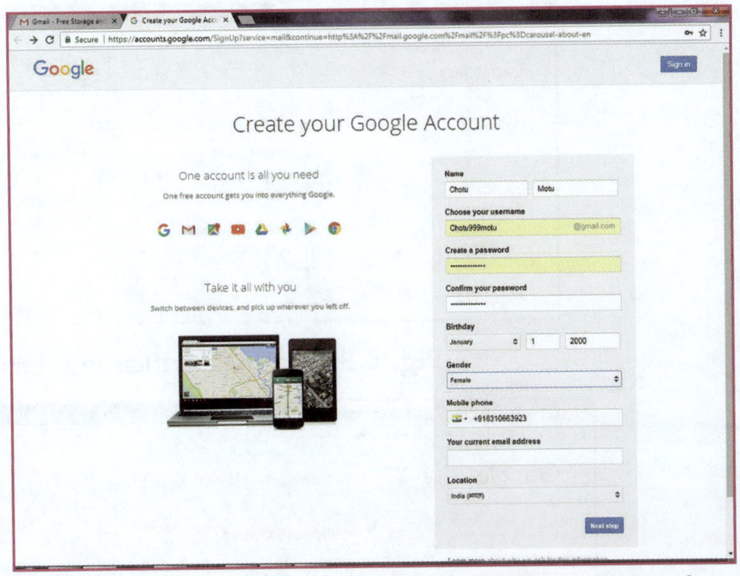

Fig. 8.3: Details filled in the Email creation request form

- Option 'Check the availability' is made available right below the username filling area. Letters used in the username are always to be in lower case, example: Chotu999motu.
- The password should have at least eight characters. These eight characters should include letters from capital case, small case, numbers and special characters, example: Ch!ntu123.

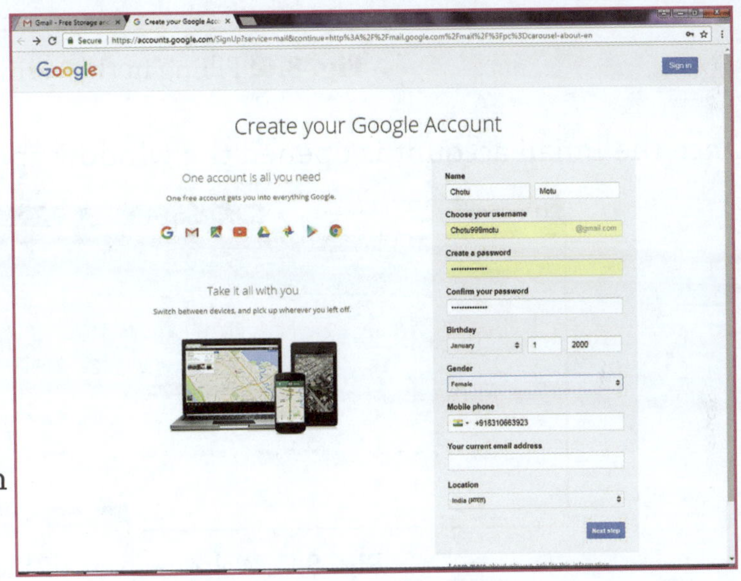

Fig. 8.4: Privacy and Terms form

- Accept the Privacy and Terms form that appears once the next step option is clicked after filling in the details as shown in Fig. 8.4. A new Email account is created.
- Email address will be the username you have selected followed by @ and the domain name.

Verify the account

A verification code will be sent to the registered mobile number or alternate Email address you have provided as in Fig. 8.5. Enter the verification code from either of the above to verify and get a confirmed registration as shown in Fig. 8.6.

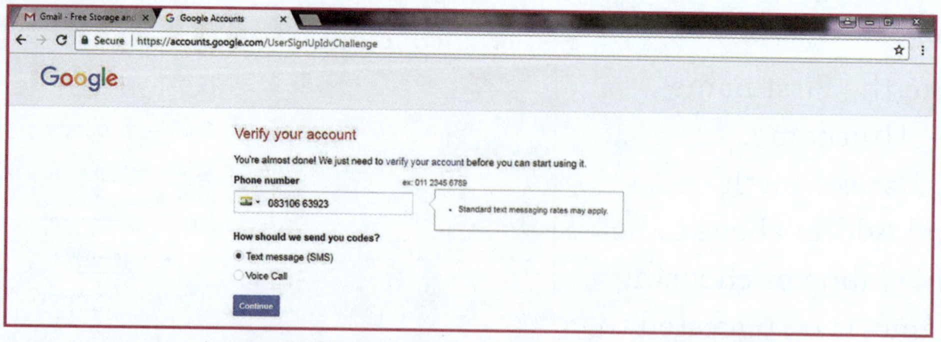

Fig. 8.5: Account verification through mobile number

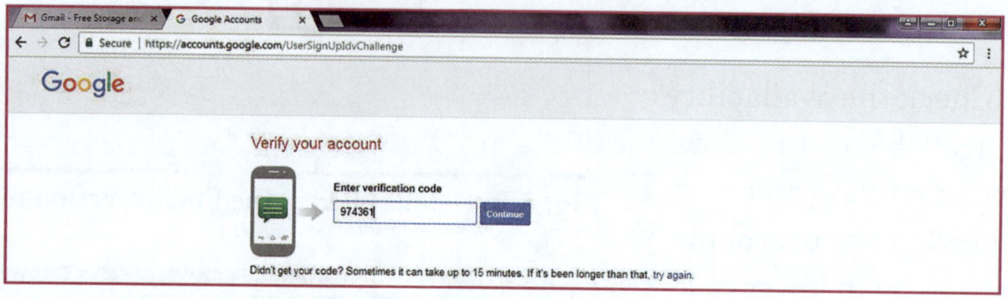

Fig. 8.6: Filling in the verification code

Once the Email account is opened the window appears as shown in Fig. 8.7.

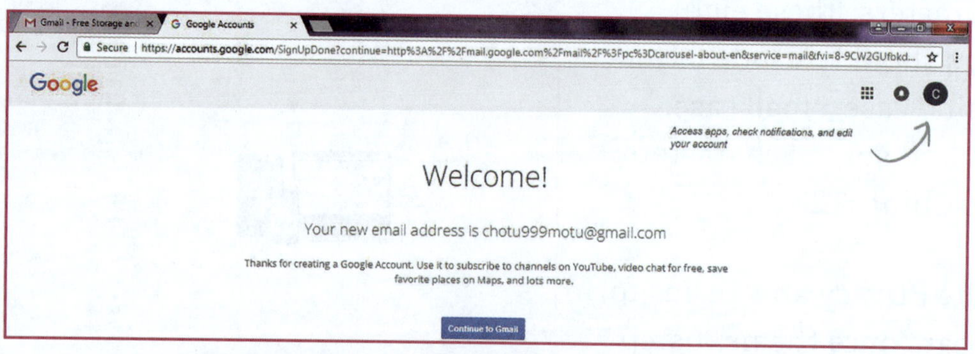

Fig. 8.7: Welcome page of the Email account

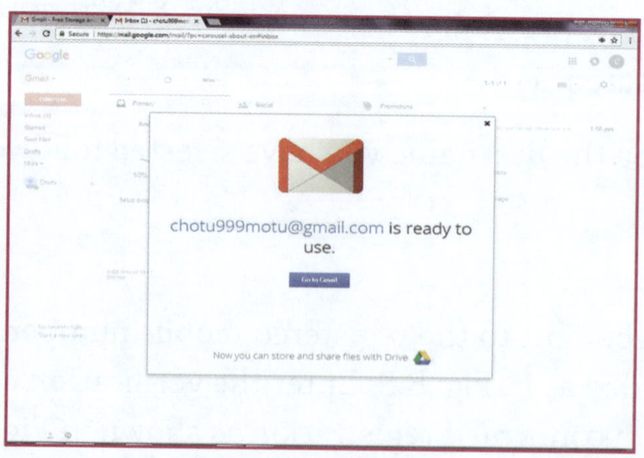

Fig. 8.8: Account displaying the confirmed Email address

Features of an email account

The layout of the Email account of each domain is unique and different from each other. Some features are common in all domains. Let us have a look at some of the features of a Gmail account.

Word web

layout of Email account: layout of the Email account is the structure or order in which the elements are arranged

Inbox

The Inbox is the storage space/folder in the Email account where all the mails received from different Email addresses from different domains are collected and stored. Unread mails in this folder are indicated in bold. By clicking on Inbox, details of the received message such as sender's name, subject, date and time can be seen as shown in Fig 8.9.

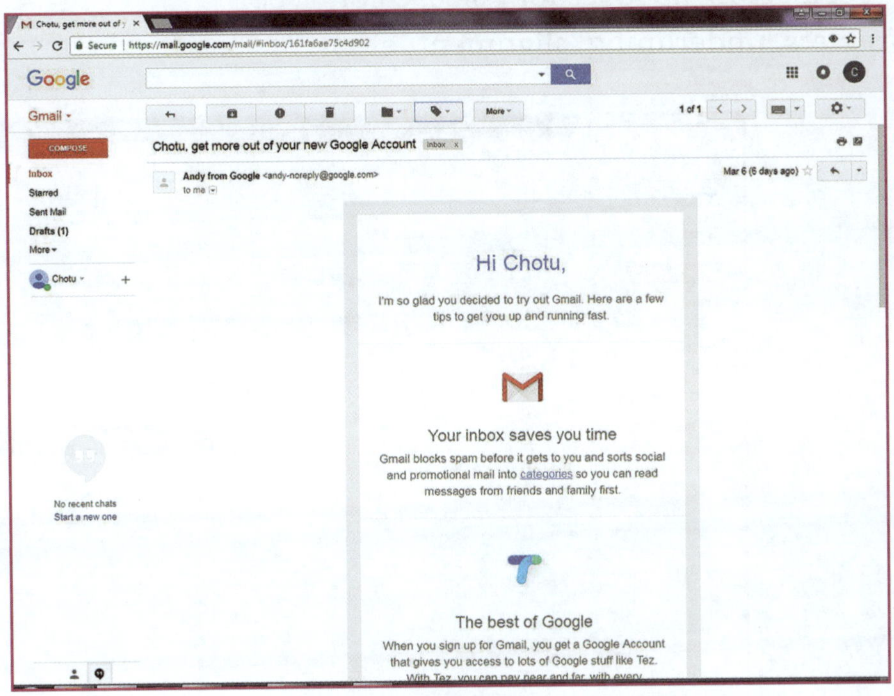

Fig. 8.9: Inbox

Compose mail

A new message can be written by using Compose Mail. Click on **Compose** and a new window will pop out. The following are the fields that are to be filled up before sending the composed mail.

To: Here the recipient's (the person to whom the Email is being sent) Email address has to be filled in.

Cc: Cc means **Carbon copy.** Type the address of the people to whom a copy of the composed mail has to be sent. The Email address in this is visible to other recipients as well. Cc mails are sent to people who have to be informed about the message in it.

Bcc: Bcc means **Blind carbon copy.** Type the address of the people to whom a copy of the composed mail has to be sent. The Email address in this is not visible to other recipients. It is used when you don't want people in To/Cc to know that the people in Bcc are getting the Email too.

Subject: A short title on which the mail composed is to be given.

Message: The text or the message can be typed in this blank space. Text message can be expressed using emoji as well.

A: The typed text message can be formatted using this tool as shown in Fig. 8.10. (Formatting includes font size, color, type, bullets, underlining, alignment, etc.)

Word web

Cc: carbon copy of mail
Bcc: blind carbon copy of mail
emoji: a small digital image or icon used to express an idea or emotion in electronic communication

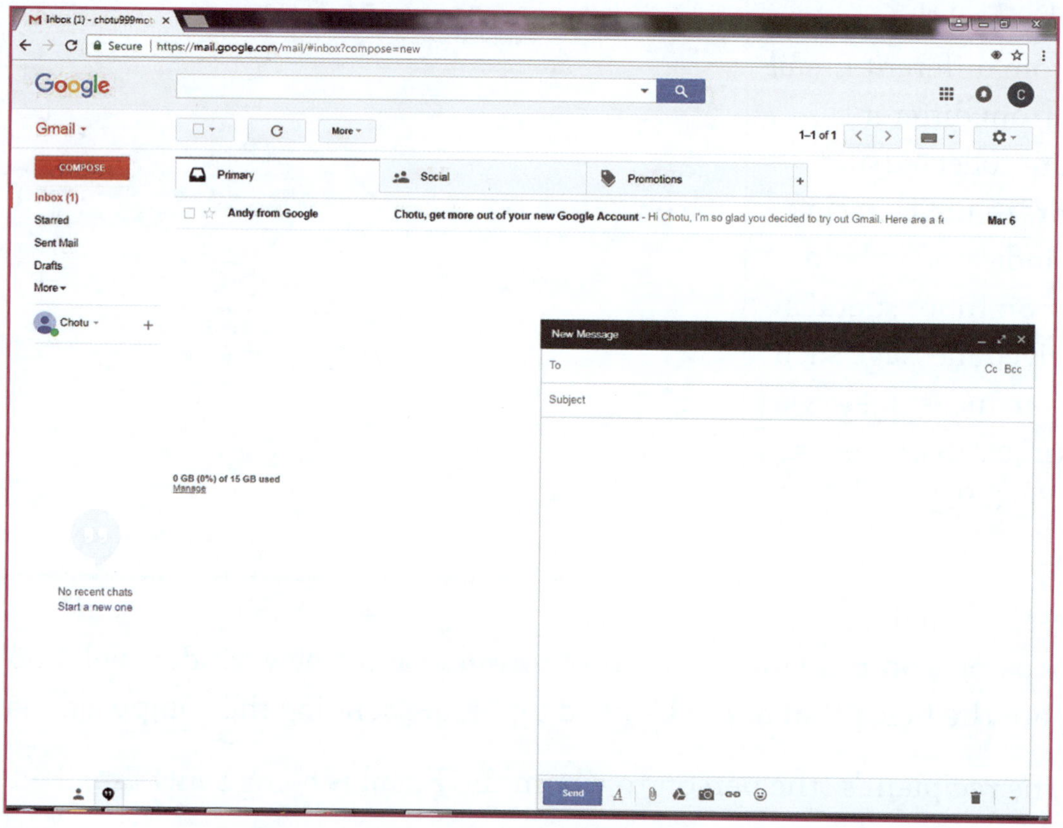

Fig. 8.10: Compose new mail layout and its components

Attachments: Pictures, files and documents can be attached along with the mail and sent through Email. Following are the steps to attach any document and send it to the recipient:

Step 1. Click on  (attachment). A new window will pop out. See Fig. 8.11.

Step 2. Browse and choose the document to be sent to the recipient and click Open.

After filling all the required fields and attachments click on **Send** to send the mail.

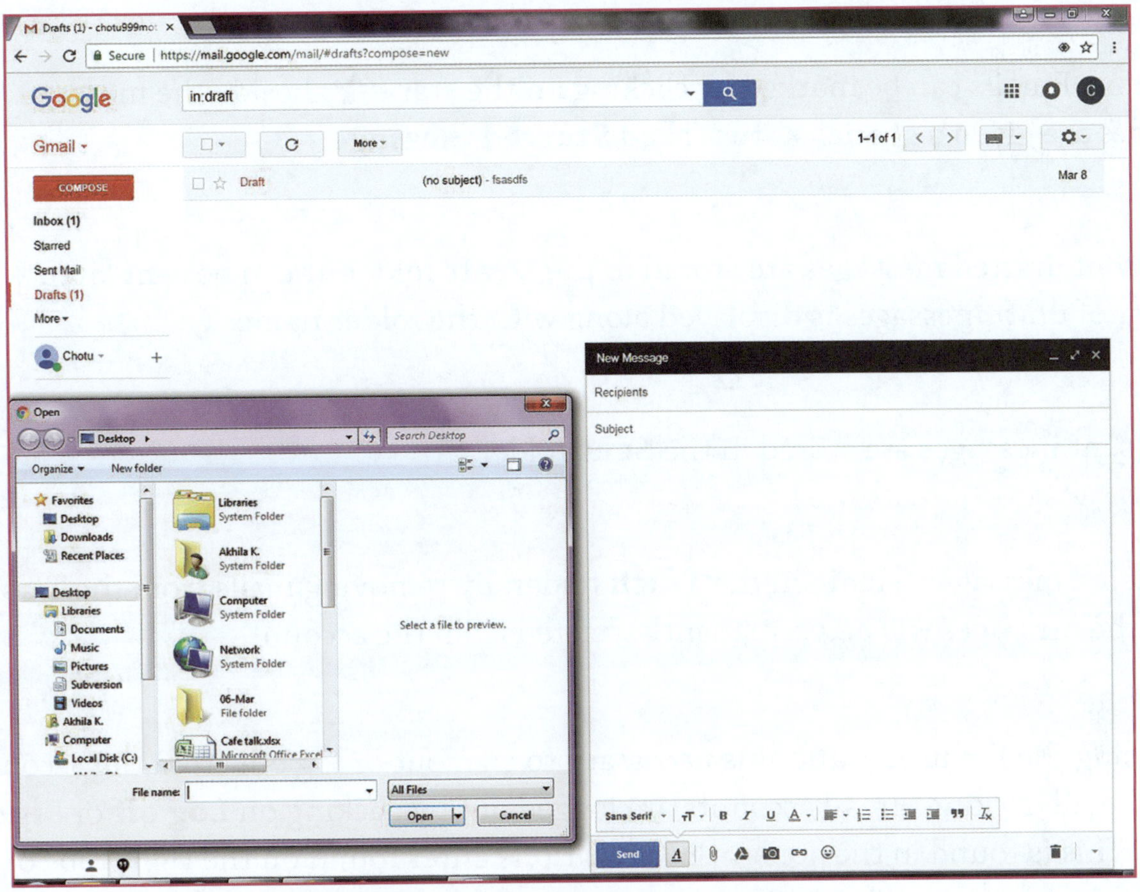

Fig. 8.11: Attaching a document to the mail

Replying to an Email

Once the Inbox message is read, one can reply to the same mail by clicking on **Reply** button. Mails can be replied to one particular recipient or to all recipients who are under Cc.

Forwarding an Email

The Inbox mails can be forwarded to other recipients by clicking on **Forward** button. The mail along with the attachments if any will be forwarded to recipients.

Deleting an Email

The mail in the Inbox can be deleted (if not required for future use) by clicking on **Delete** button. This will reduce the storage space in the domain.

Spam

Unwanted advertising mails from unknown recipients will be placed in the **Spam** folder. Sometimes these advertising mails may have viruses which may affect the software. Number of Spam messages is displayed along with the folder name.

Starred

Important Emails can be marked by clicking on the star (☆) beside the message. These messages are given a special status called **Starred message**.

Draft

The unsent drafted messages are stored in the **Draft** folder. It can be sent later. Number of draft messages is displayed along with the folder name.

Sent

All the sent messages are stored in the **Sent** folder.

Trash

The deleted messages remain in the **Trash** folder. By removing mails from the Trash folder, the messages will be permanently deleted from the account.

Sign out

After using the Email account, it is necessary to sign out or log out from the account to prevent mail hacking. Email accounts are logged out by clicking on **Log off** or **Sign out** button. This is found in the account information center found on the right top corner of the screen as shown in Fig. 8.12.

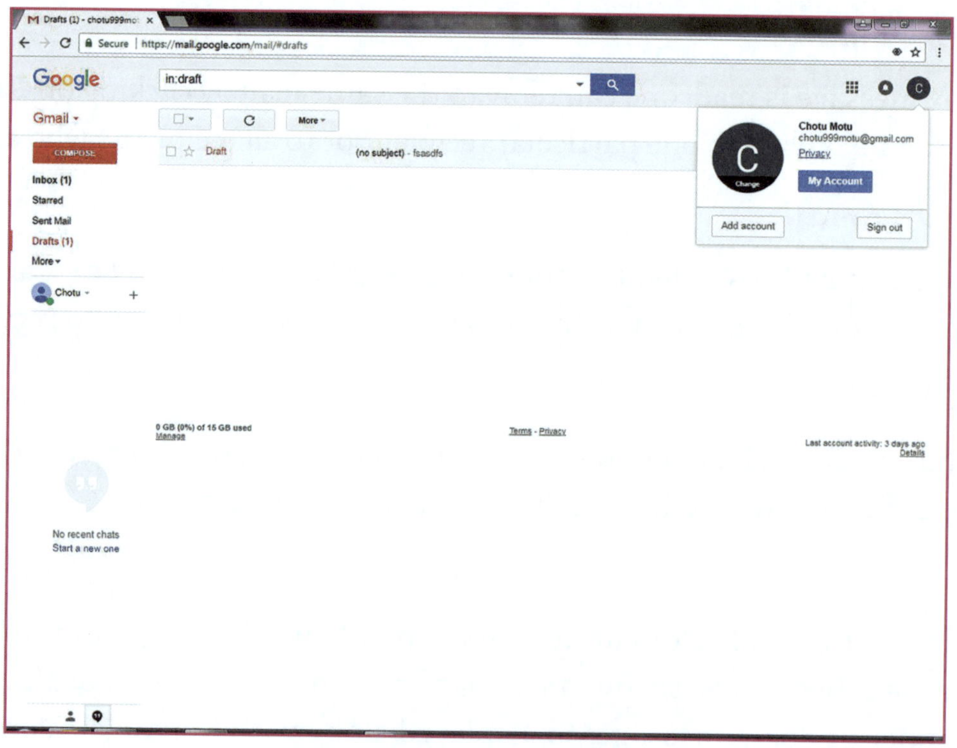

Fig. 8.12: Sign out screen

Advantages of Email

- Email is one of the fastest means of communication. The recipient receives the Email as soon as they go online and check their mail.
- It is cheaper than post or courier services.
- Photos, documents and other files can be attached to an Email so that more information can be shared.
- One Email can be sent to more than one recipient at a time.

Safety measures to be taken while using Email

- The password should be changed regularly.
- The password should not be shared with anyone.
- Do not open attached documents sent by unknown people.
- After the use of the Email account, remember to log off/sign out from the account.
- Do not reply to Spam Emails.
- Keep your personal information to yourself—do not share bank or credit card information through Email.
- Make sure that you have an antivirus software installed and keep it up-to-date.

Concepts learnt

1. Electronic mail is popularly known as Email and it can be accessed through an Email account.
2. Email address is a unique identity that is used to access an Email account and it is protected with a password.
3. Email account can be created by registering with an Email service provider.
4. Email account is used to compose messages, send messages, forward messages and reply to messages.
5. Inbox, Sent, Compose, Starred, Spam, Trash, etc., are some of the features of Email account.

Hands-on practice

With the permission from your teacher, create your new Email account. Send an Email to your friend, describing your experience. Write the steps you followed in the space given below.

Exercise

A Fill in the blanks.

1. Username is protected by the ______________________ (Email/password).
2. ______________________ (Inbox/Outbox) shows the number of unread mails in the Email account.
3. _________ (Inbox/Subject) gives the description of the mail.
4. Pictures, files and documents can be sent through _______________ (Spam/ Attachments).
5. The unsent composed messages are stored in ____________ (Draft/Spam).

B Write T for True or F for False.

1. Email address is the combination of both user name and domain name. ☐
2. Password should have at least six characters. ☐
3. Bcc recipients are visible to other recipients. ☐
4. By clicking on 'Forward', the received mail can be sent along with the attachment/s received. ☐
5. Email account need not be logged off or signed off after usage. ☐

C Choose the correct option.

1. Which of the following websites do not provide Email service?
   (a) www.gmail.com
   (b) www.yahoo.com
   (c) www.outlook.com
   (d) www.sendemail.com
2. Which of the following information is not given while filling an Email account registration form?
   (a) Class and school name
   (b) First name
   (c) Date of birth
   (d) Gender
3. Which of the following folders will have the deleted mails?
   (a) Spam
   (b) Inbox
   (c) Trash
   (d) Starred

4. Which of the following icons is clicked to attach a file in the mail?

   (a)  (b) 

   (c)  (d) 

5. Which of the following is used to format the text?

   (a) A (b) Bcc

   (c) Cc (d) To

D Answer these questions briefly.

1. What is an Email and why is it needed?
2. List four advantages of Email.
3. What are the precautions to be taken while choosing a password?
4. List the precautions to be taken while using an Email account.
5. What is the difference between a Spam and Starred mail?

E Application-based questions.

1. List four possible usernames to create an Email account in www.yahoo.com.
2. Sujan has received an Email from Jagan. Sujan wants to send the same Email to Sudhir. Which option in the Email account should Sujan use?
3. Naveen and four of his friends have received a mail about their working project. Naveen wants to reply only to his manager and not to his friends. Which option in Email should Naveen use to reply to his manager?
4. Kiran wants to remove all the unwanted mail from her Inbox. Which option will help Kiran?
5. Seema has received an Email along with some attachment from an unknown person. Should she open the attachment and reply? If not why?

Computer is my mentor!

Open an Email account. Compose a mail and send it to your computer teacher.

Note: The teacher should share his/her Email id with the students.

9 Introduction to Scratch Programming

Learning log

- What is Scratch?
- How to get started with Scratch?
- Features of Scratch

Introduction

The butterfly in the picture wants to reach the flower. Can you make it reach the destination?

Yes, it is possible for you to make the butterfly move towards the flower. You can do such interesting movements on screen called **animations** using a simple programming language called **Scratch**.

What is Scratch?

Scratch is a free online application that can be downloaded over the Internet. It helps us create interesting games and animations using pre-set programming codes.

The output of a Scratch program can be shared over the Internet. This application helps us learn programming in a simple way. Familiarity with Scratch will help you express yourself more creatively and make connections with more powerful ideas. Scratch will also help you learn strategies that are important in today's world for solving problems and designing projects.

Word web

programming codes: these are a set of instructions that specify the actions to be performed by a computer

Getting started with Scratch

To start working on Scratch one must double click on the icon (↗) present on the monitor. The shortcut icon for Scratch on desktop appears as below. (Fig.9.1).

Fig. 9.1: Scratch program shortcut on a monitor screen

You should know

Scratch is developed by the 'MIT Media Lab Lifelong Kindergarten Group'. This simple programming language was designed by Mitchel Resnick in the year 2002.

Mitchel Resnick

On opening Scratch, a default screen (Fig.9.2) is displayed.

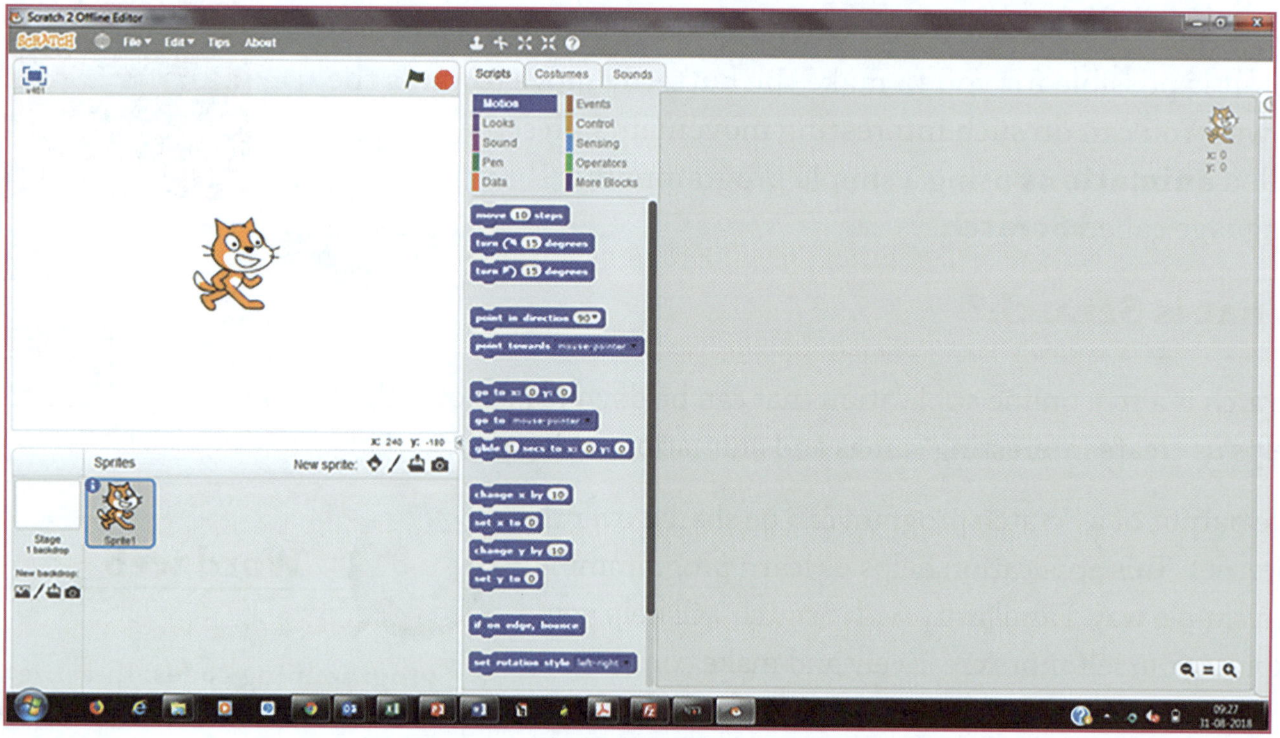

Fig. 9.2: Default screen that appears on opening Scratch

The top left space (Fig. 9.3) is the area where the output appears.

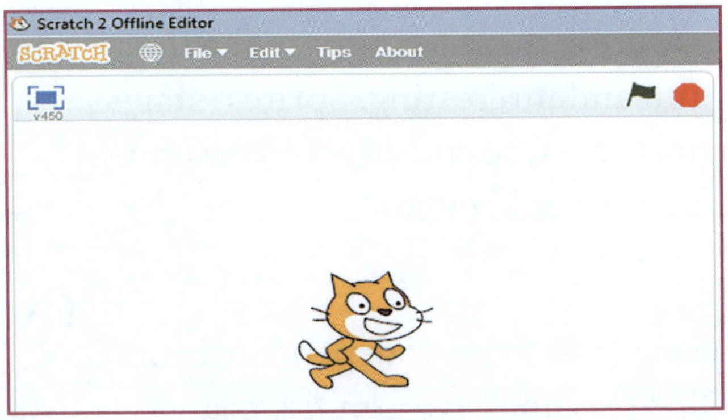

Fig. 9.3: Output screen

The bottom left space (Fig. 9.4) is the area where the objects and images selected for animation appear.

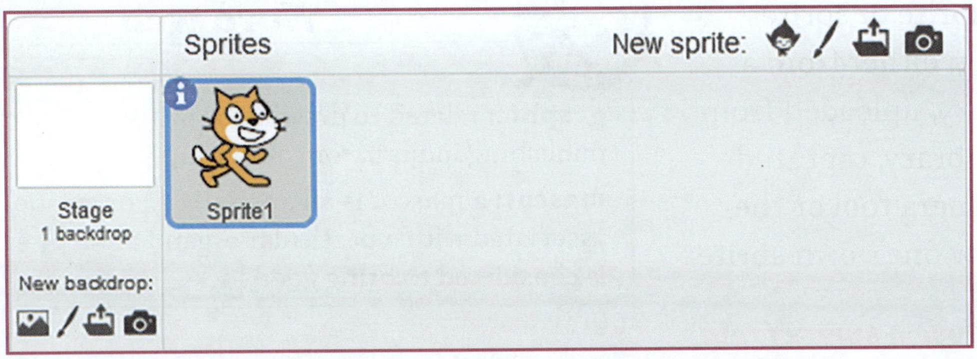

Fig. 9.4: Area for animation objects and images

The right side of the screen (Fig. 9.5) is the area used for programming the animation.

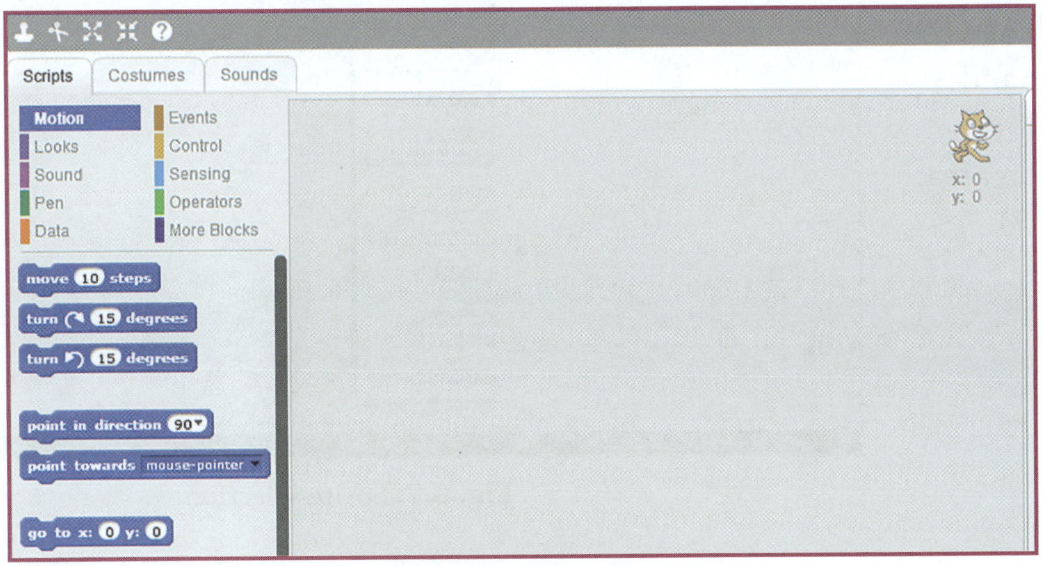

Fig. 9.5: Programming area

Features of Scratch

Scratch comes with a kit of features. These features make the experience of programming fun and interesting. Sprites, stage backdrop, control tools, support tools, sound effects, costumes and scripts are some of the features of Scratch.

Fig. 9.6: Default sprite

Sprites

A small graphic which can be made to move independently on the screen is called a sprite. Sprites can move around, change appearances, talk and play sounds and music. The default sprite in Scratch is an orange cat called **'Scratch Cat'**. It is the mascot for Scratch.

A different sprite or sprites can be chosen either from a Scratch library, uploaded from the system library, captured using the camera tool or the user can draw one's own sprite.

Word web

graphic: related to drawing or pictures, especially in publishing industry or computing

mascot: a mascot is an animal, toy, or symbol which is associated with a particular organization or event, and is considered to bring good luck

Steps to choose a sprite from a Scratch library

1) Click on the sprite icon available in the objects and images selection area (Fig. 9.7).

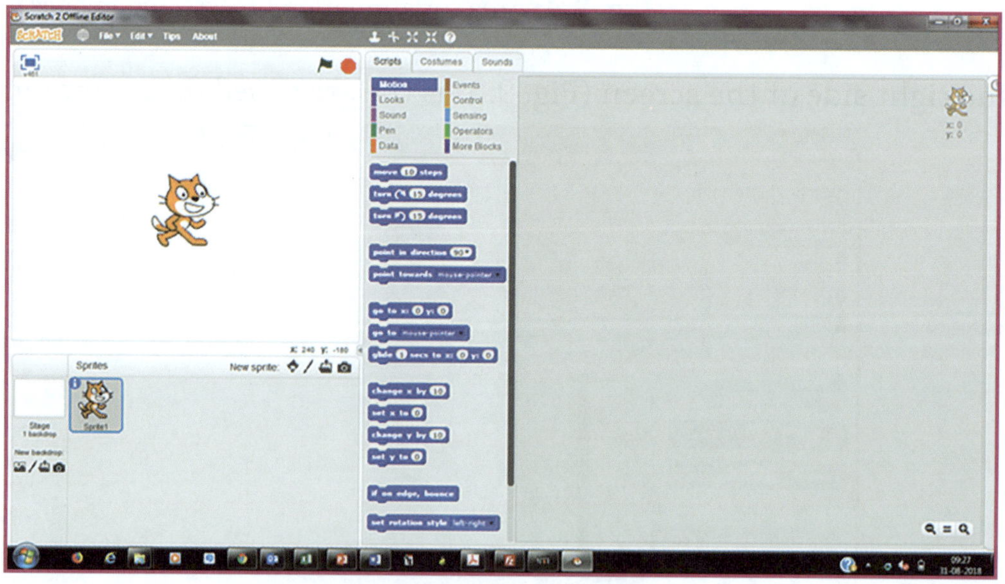

Fig. 9.7: Sprite selection

2) A library of objects categorized for filtering is available to view and choose. Select the required sprite and click OK (Fig. 9.8).

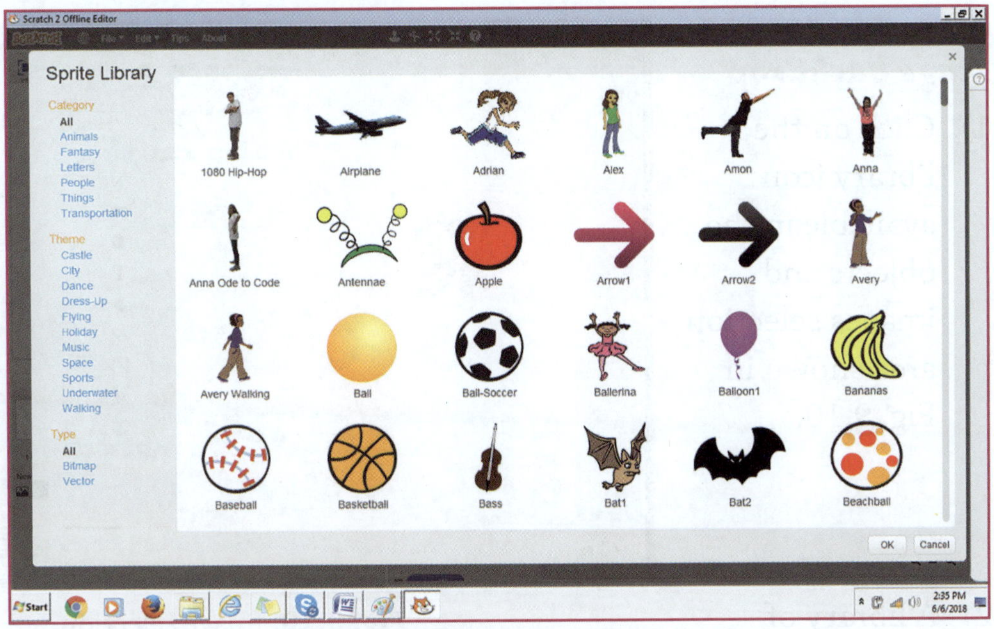

Fig. 9.8: Select sprite

Stage backdrop

The background in which we want our sprite to move is called stage backdrop. The default stage backdrop is always a white screen as shown in Fig. 9.9.

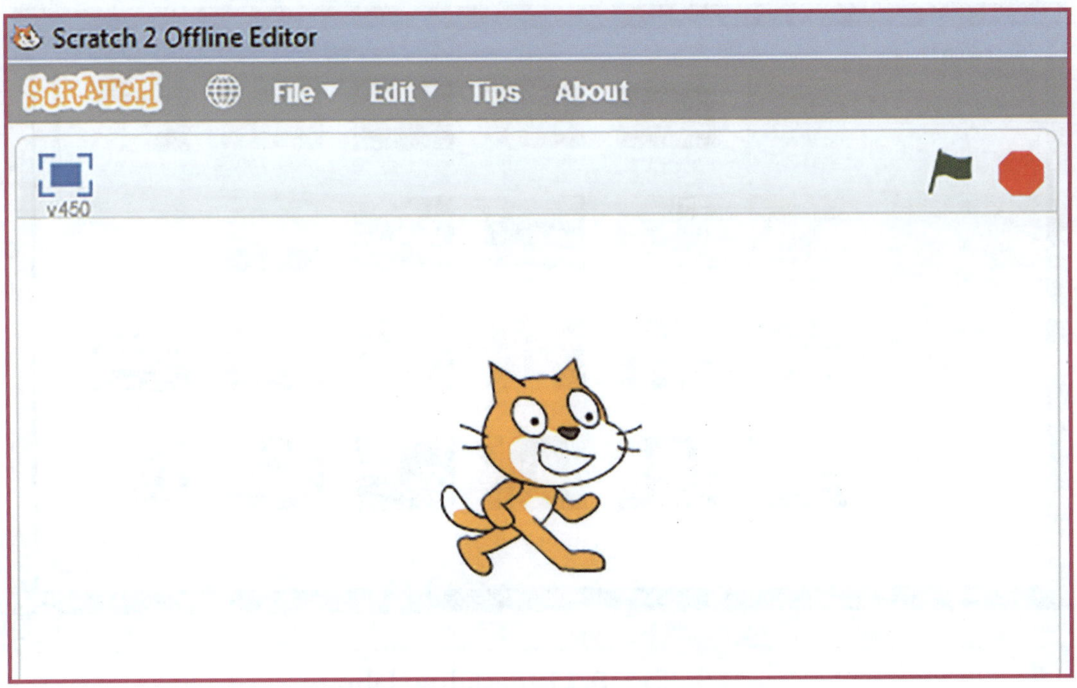

Fig. 9.9: Default stage backdrop

A different stage backdrop can be chosen from a library in Scratch, uploaded from the system library, captured using the camera tool or the user can draw one's own stage backdrop.

Steps to choose a stage backdrop

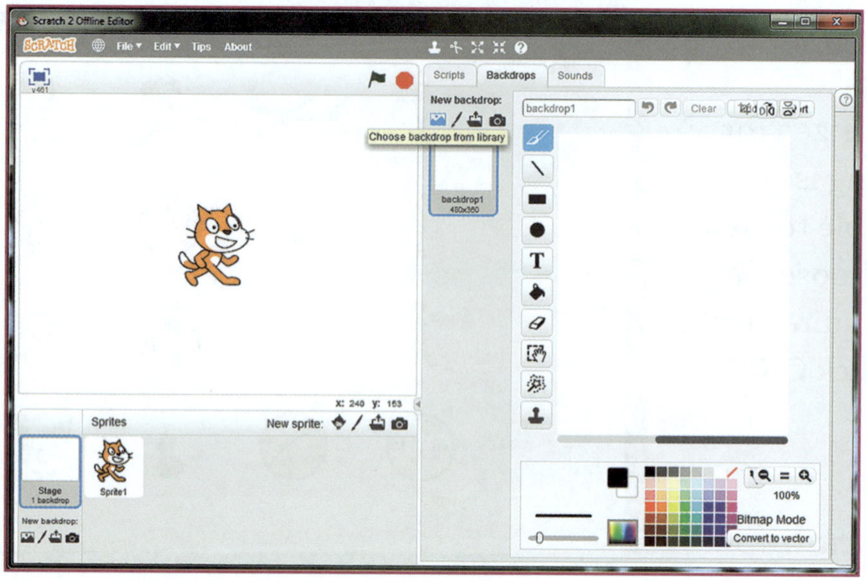

1) Click on the library icon available in the objects and images selection area shown in Fig. 9.10.

Fig. 9.10: Image selection

2) A library of backdrops categorized for filtering is available to view and choose. Select the required backdrop and click OK. Refer to Fig. 9.11.

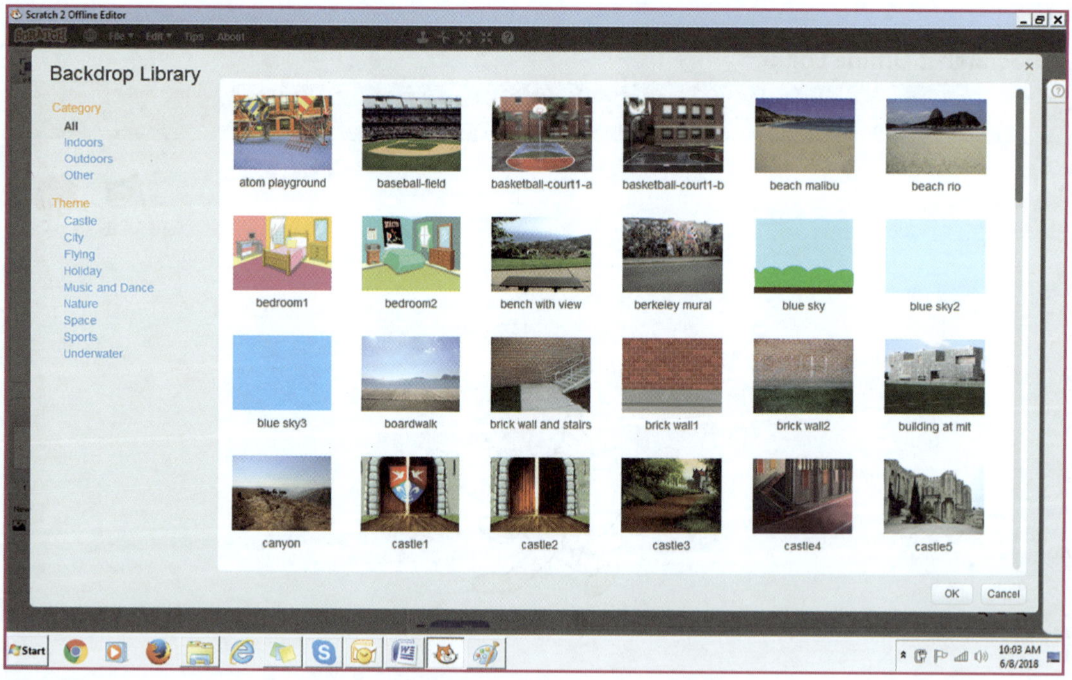

Fig. 9.11: Backdrop Library

Control tools

In Scratch, one can switch between normal view to full screen view and back. The animations can be started and stopped with the help of the control tools provided.

Stop, start and full screen are the control tools that are available in the output screen as shown in Fig. 9.12.

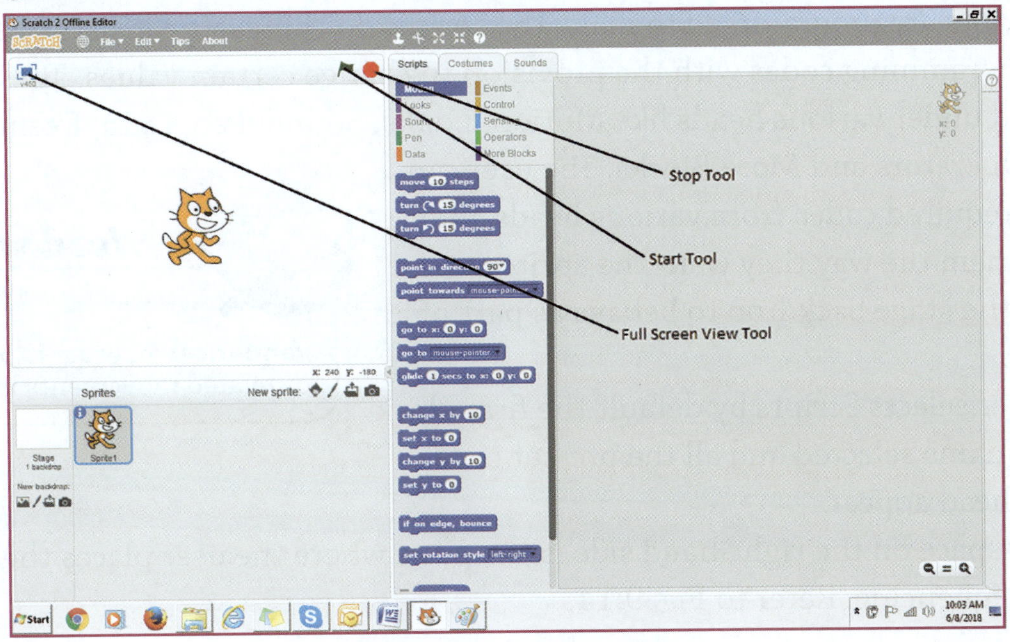

Fig. 9.12: Control tools

Support tools

Scratch comes with support tools like Duplicate, Delete, Grow and Shrink. The Duplicate tool helps us replicate an existing sprite; Delete tool can be used to delete a sprite or a backdrop; Grow tool helps us in increasing the size of a sprite and Shrink tool helps in reducing the size of a sprite. See Fig. 9.13 below.

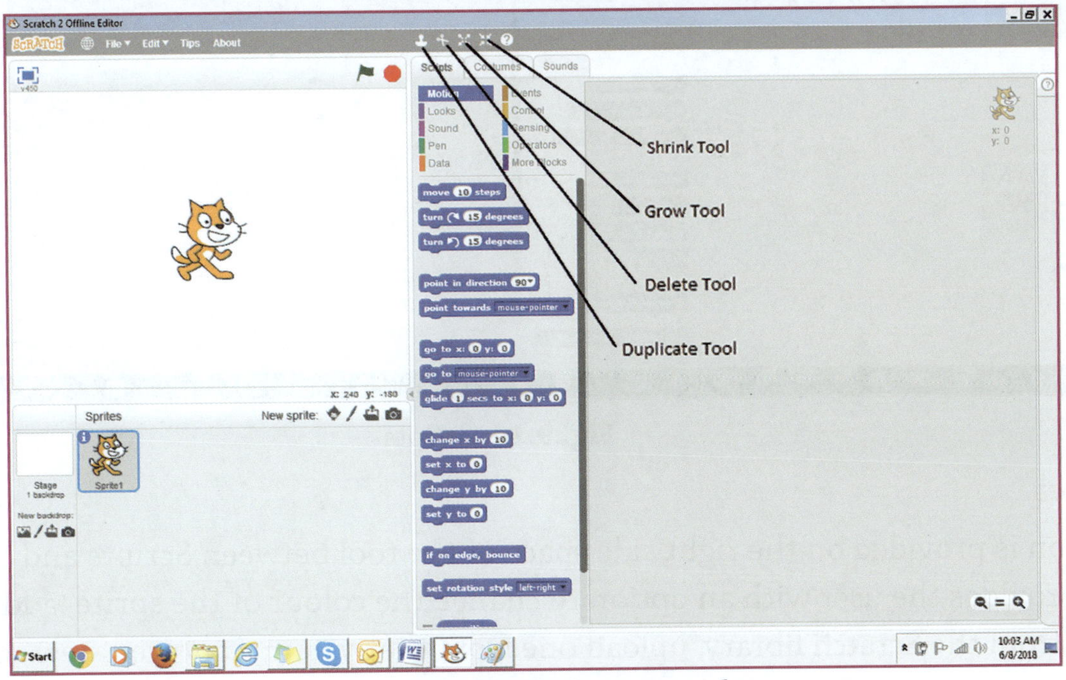

Fig. 9.13: Support tools

Scripts

This option is provided on the right side space of the tool alongside Costumes and Sound. Scripts are programmed to make the sprites do things. It consists of several pre-set programming codes with the provision to change certain values. These are categorized under various heads like Motion, Looks, Sound, Pen, Data, Events, Control, Sensing, Operators and More Blocks. The user can select the required codes from various heads and sequence them the way they want the sprite to behave or the stage backdrop to behave as part of an animation.

Word web

sequence: an order in which a set of related movements is seen

When a user selects Scripts by default the first block Motion remains selected and all the pre-set codes under the head appear.

The empty space on the right-hand side is the place where the user places the selected codes for sequencing. Refer to Fig. 9.14.

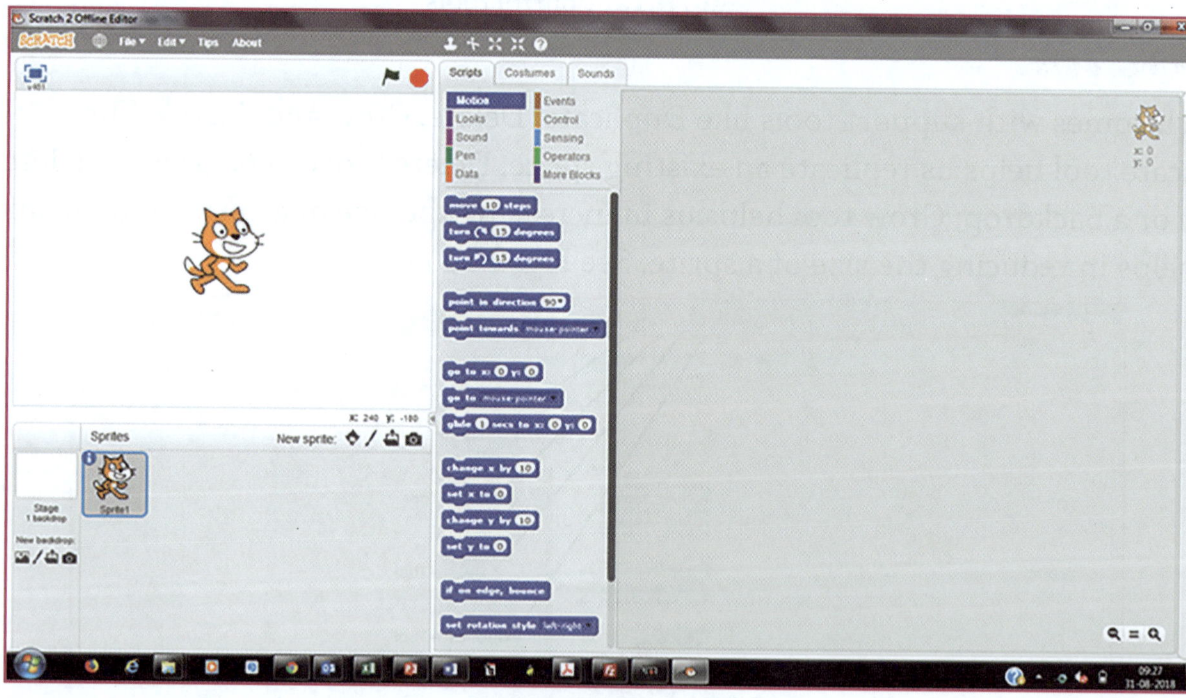

Fig. 9.14: Scripts

Costumes

This option is provided on the right side space of the tool between Scripts and Sound. Scratch provides the user with an option to change the colour of the sprite, add a new costume from the Scratch library, upload one from the system, capture a new costume using the camera tool or draw an additional layer to the sprite. This feature helps enhance the creativity of the user. Refer to Fig. 9.15.

Word web

layer: a transparent sheet used to edit different elements in an image

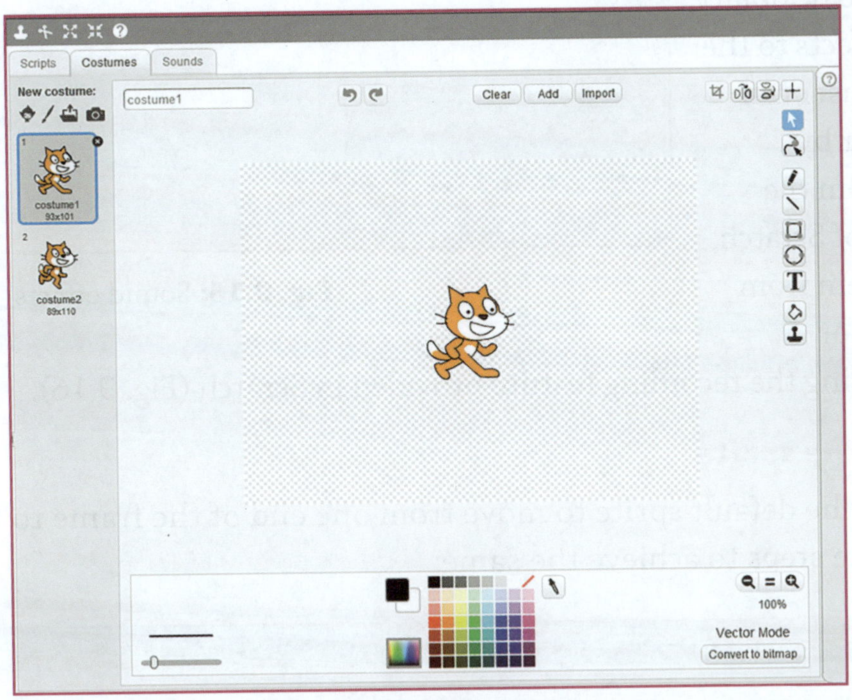

Fig. 9.15(a): Select costumes

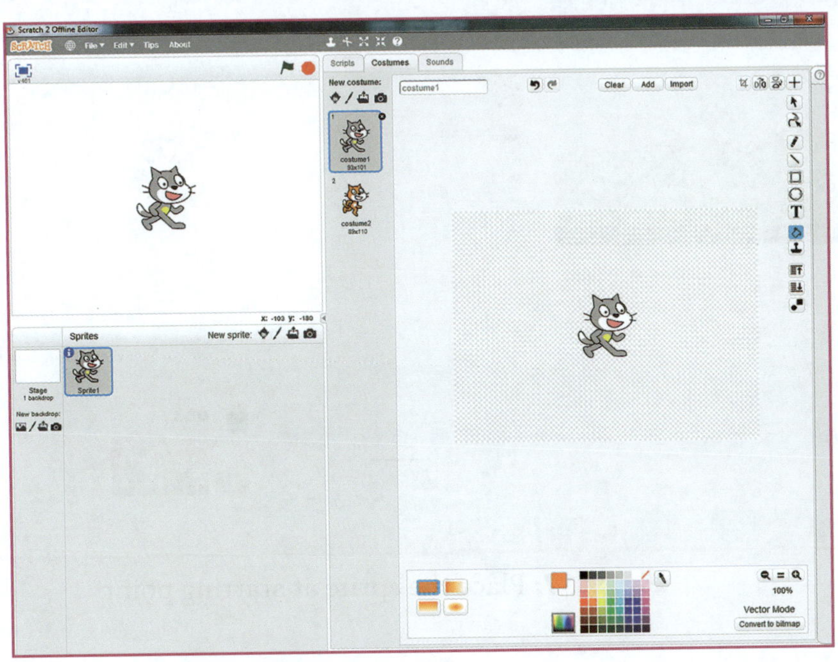

Fig. 9.15(b): Effect of selected costume

Sound effect

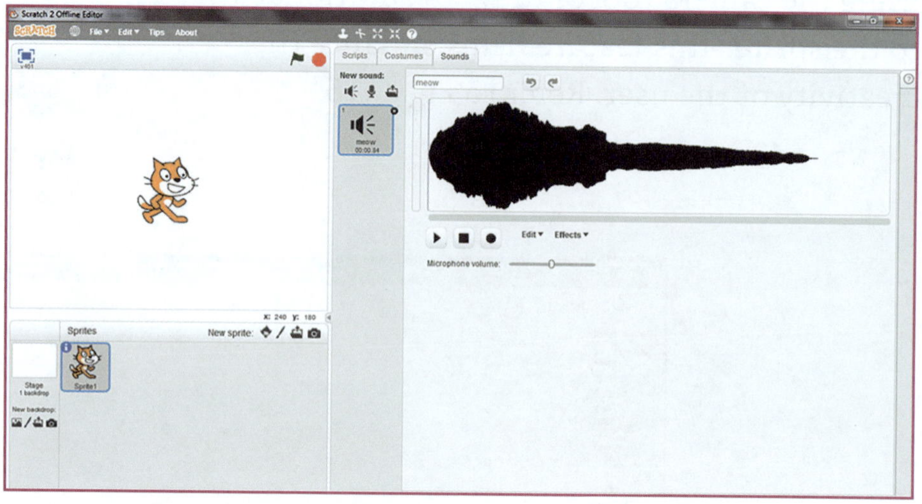

Fig. 9.16: Sound effects

This option is provided on the right side space of the tool alongside Scripts and Costumes. Scratch provides the user with the flexibility to add sound effects to the animation. The user can add Sound either by picking them from the existing library of Scratch, by uploading them from the local system or recording one using the recording feature provided in Scratch (Fig. 9.16).

Movement of the sprite

Let us program the default sprite to move from one end of the frame to the other. Following are the steps to achieve the same:

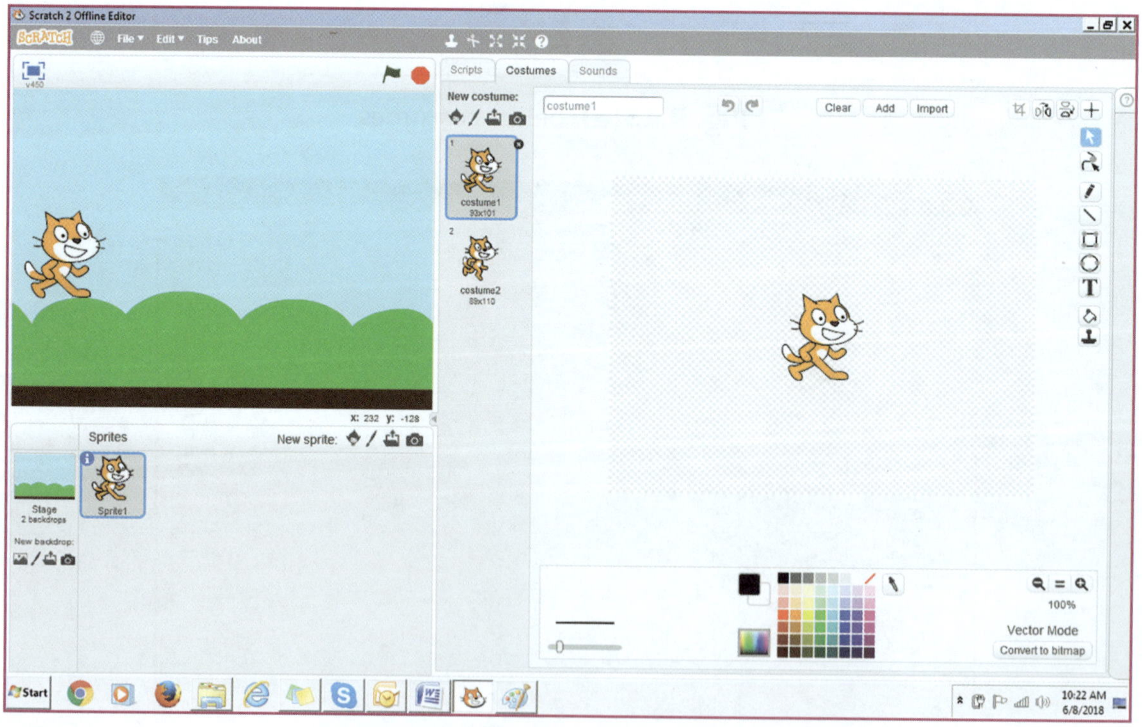

Fig. 9.17: Place the sprite at starting point

1. Let the sprite be the default Scratch Cat.
2. Select 'blue sky' backdrop from the library.
3. Select the sprite and place it at the starting of the screen (Fig. 9.17).
4. Go to Scripts and select Motion. Select the 'move 10 steps' code and place it on right hand side of the screen. Change 10 steps to 100 steps. This code is required to move the sprite. Refer to Fig. 9.18.

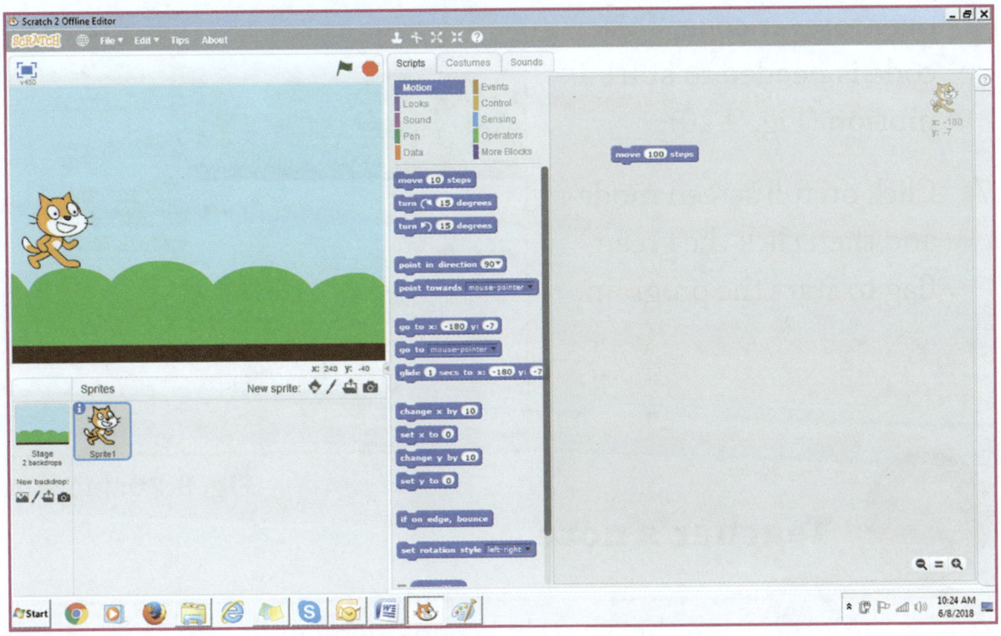

Fig. 9.18: Moving the sprite

5. Go to controls and select forever code and move it to the right side of the screen such that 'move 100 steps' code gets wrapped within forever code. This code will make the sprite move 100 steps whenever we start the script (Fig. 9.19).

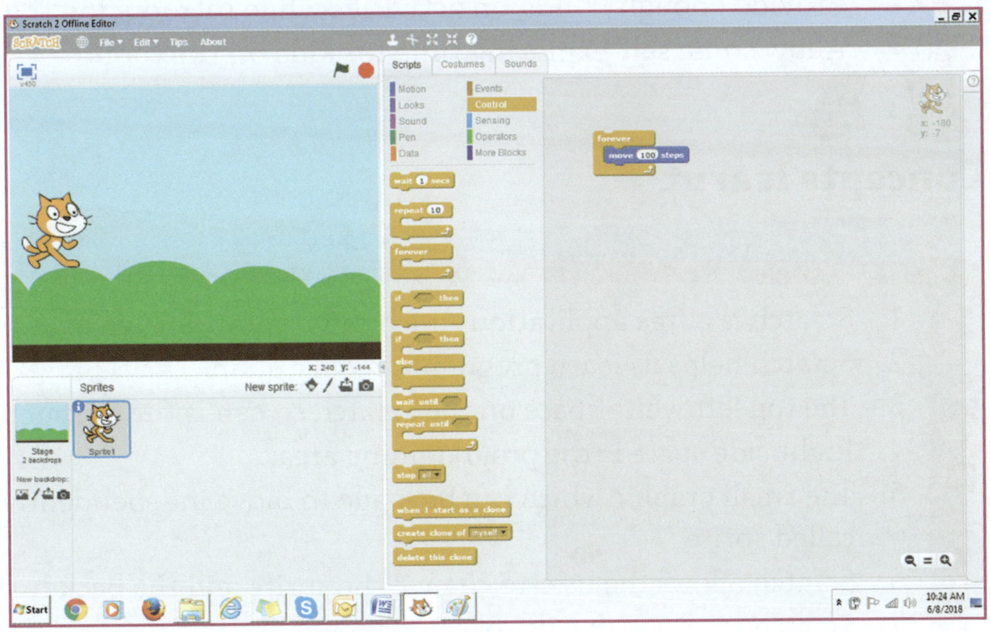

Fig. 9.19: Moving the sprite using the forever code

6. Go to Events and select the code 'when clicked'. Bring it to right hand side of the screen and place it over forever code. This code is needed to start a motion (Fig. 9.20).
7. Click on full screen mode and then click the green flag to start the program.

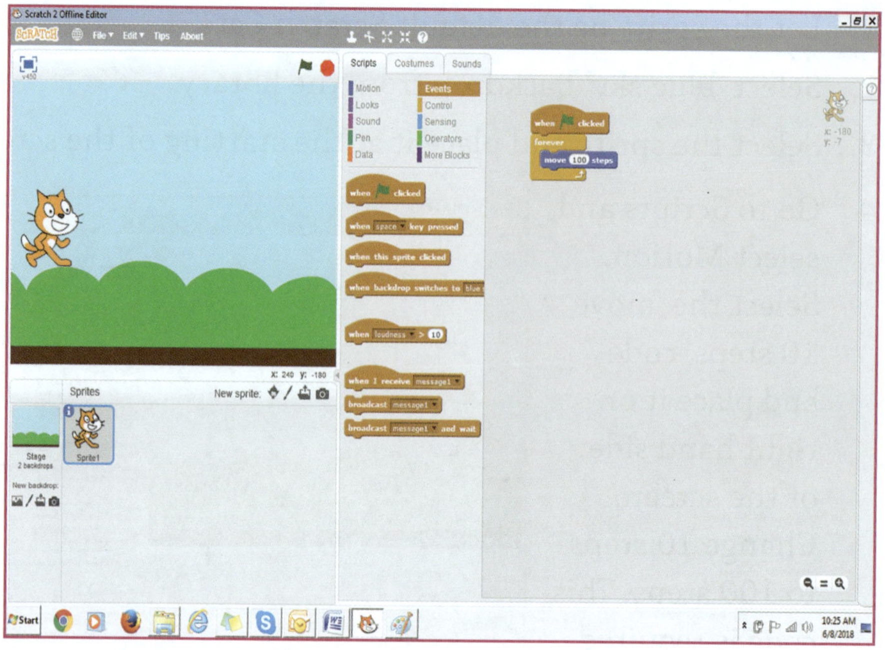

Fig. 9.20: Move on click

Teacher's note

- Always keep the Scratch screen open while introducing the students to the features.
- Provide enough hands-on activities while introducing the features.
- Allow some self-exploring time for kids on the tool.

Concepts learnt

1. Scratch is a free application which can be downloaded over the Internet.
2. Scratch helps us learn programming in a simple way.
3. The top left white space on the Scratch screen is the output screen.
4. Right side space is the programming area.
5. The small graphic which can be made to move independently on the screen is called sprite.
6. Scratch allows the user to change the sprite and the backdrop.
7. Scratch comes with control components like full screen mode, start and stop.
8. Scratch provides support tools like Shrink, Grow, Delete and Duplicate.
9. Scratch provides access to certain functions of programming like Sounds, Costumes and Scripts.

Exercise

A Fill in the blanks.

1. ______________ (Programming codes/Sprite) are a set of instructions which determine the behaviour of an object.
2. The small graphic characters used in Scratch are called______________ (cats/sprites).
3. The default backdrop in Scratch is a ______________ (grey/white) screen.
4. The control tool used to start an animation is a ____________ (Green flag/Red dot).
5. The tool that is used to increase the size of the sprite is the ______________ (Grow/Shrink) tool.

B Write T for True or F for False.

1. The default sprite in Scratch is a cat. ☐
2. A sprite selected cannot be changed later. ☐
3. Scratch does not provide the flexibility to add self -recorded sounds. ☐
4. Scratch comes with a default library of images for backdrop. ☐
5. In Scripts, pre-set programming codes are categorized under various heads. ☐

C Choose the correct option.

1. Scratch does not allow you to ______________.
   - (a) be creative
   - (b) use your own graphics
   - (c) write your own code
   - (d) modify values in a code
2. Which of the following is not a part of Scripts in Scratch?
   - (a) Motion
   - (b) Costumes
   - (c) Looks
   - (d) Sound
3. ______________ is the tool used to reduce the size of a sprite.
   - (a) Shrink Tool
   - (b) Grow Tool
   - (c) Delete Tool
   - (d) Duplicate Tool

4. Which of the given category under Scripts remains selected by default?
   (a) Pen (b) Motion
   (c) Control (d) Sensing
5. Which one of the following is not a control tool?
   (a) Start (b) Stop
   (c) Full Screen (d) Delete tool

D Answer these questions briefly.

1. What is Scratch and how is it useful?
2. Which feature in Scratch helps us to access the programming codes? Under what heads are the programming codes categorized?
3. Explain the flexibility provided by Scratch in changing the default sprite.
4. Explain the flexibility provided by Scratch to add sound effects.
5. Write the steps by which you can make the default sprite to move from one end of the screen to another.

E Application-based questions.

1. List the steps to be followed to change the body colour of the default sprite to red.
2. Is it possible to have more than one sprite on a screen?
3. "Move 10 steps" is a default code available in Scratch. Is it possible to change the value 10?
4. A programmer wants to duplicate his available sprite on screen. Kindly help the programmer with the steps to be followed.
5. John wants to program an animation with the background of your school. What are the steps he should follow to get the same?

Computer is my mentor!

Aim: To create a birthday message

Procedure:

1. Open the Scratch application.
2. Remove default sprite using the Delete tool.
3. Go to 'Choose backdrop from library' and select the theme party.
4. Go to 'Choose sprite from library' and select the first letter of your name. Repeat the steps and select all the letters of your name as sprites.
5. Drag and put the alphabet sprites in the correct order.
6. Select the first alphabet sprite. Go to Sounds. Remove default sound. Click on 'Choose sound from library'. In the sound library go to music loops and select the second sound 'birthday'.
7. Keep the first alphabet sprite selected. Go to Scripts and select Looks. Under Looks select 'Change colour effect by 25'. Go to controls, select the forever code and wrap the first code under that. Go to Events and select 'When flag clicked' and place it over the forever code. Repeat this for all the sprites.

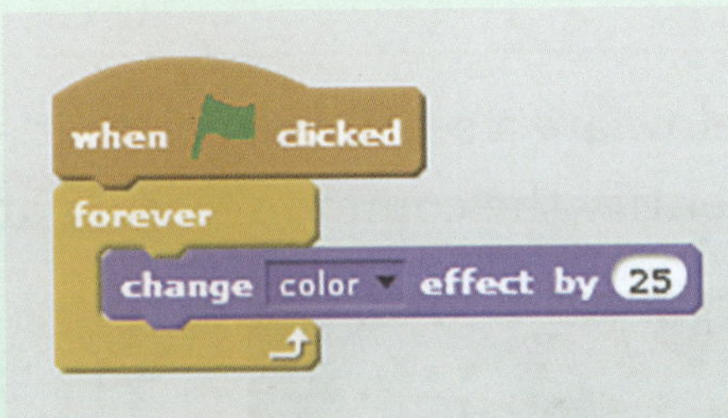

8. Go back to the first alphabet sprite. Create a separate set of codes for sound just below previous codes. Go to sounds and select 'Play sound birthday until done'. Go to control. Select forever code and wrap the previous code under it. Go to Events and select 'When flag clicked' and place it over the forever code.

9. Go to full screen mode and click on the green flag to see the output. Click on red dot to stop.
10. Go to files. Select 'Save as'; select the location on your system to save it. Give your project a name and click on Save.

Output: The screen should have the background of balloons with your name written in the centre. As the green flag is clicked the birthday music should start and the letters should change colour.

10 Entertainment and Multimedia

Learning log

- Multimedia
- Multimedia in entertainment
- Use of multimedia

Introduction

Below are a set of images that are the creation of the digital media. Can you identify the common feature among all these images?

Yes, the graphics, animations, movies and games that we watch, from which these images are taken, are the result of an effective combination of not only different computer applications but multiple sources of information or varieties of media. Multimedia is mostly used in the field of entertainment. In this chapter, we shall learn the basics of multimedia and the application of the same in the field of entertainment.

Multimedia

Multimedia can be defined as any computer application that integrates text, graphics, animation, video, audio or any other method of communication.

Multimedia programs used for learning are completely different from books or television as they present learning information to both students and teachers in a more meaningful and engaging manner than either books or television can singularly.

Multimedia devices are electronic devices that are used to store and experience multimedia content. Personal computers use multimedia devices like webcams, digital cameras, microphones, etc.

Fig. 10.1 Multimedia devices

Elements of multimedia

The different building blocks of multimedia are discussed below. Any multimedia application consists any or all of them.

- Text—In any language that may be processed by the computer

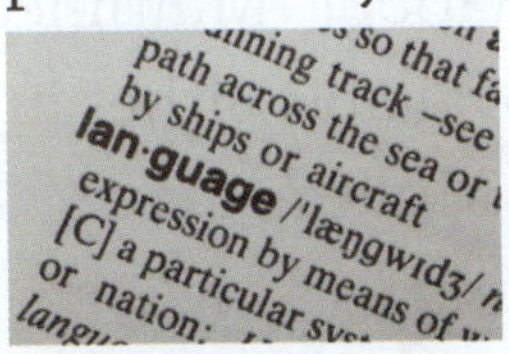

- Audio—Sound, music, speech, structured audio

- Still Image—Scanned image, photographs, drawings, maps and slides

- Video—Movie, a sequence of pictures

- Graphics—Computer generated image

- Animation—A sequence of graphics images

Categorization of multimedia

Multimedia may be broadly divided into linear and non-linear categories.

- Linear active content is one that progresses without any navigational control. For example, a cinema presentation.
- Non-linear content uses interactivity to control the progress. For example, a video game or computer-based training.

Multimedia presentations can be of two types, namely live and recorded.

- A recorded presentation may allow interactivity through a navigation system.
- A live presentation may allow interactivity between the presenter and the participant.

Multimedia in Entertainment

Entertainment is a form of activity that holds the attention and interest of an audience or gives pleasure and delight. Multimedia is being extensively used in the entertainment industry, to develop special effects in movies and animations. Multimedia games are a popular pastime for children and are software programs available either in CD-ROMs or online. Some video games also use multimedia features. Multimedia applications that allow users to actively participate instead of just sitting by as passive recipients of information are called **Interactive Multimedia.**

Multimedia is basic to creating content in the entertainment industry. Some of the uses of multimedia in the field of entertainment are:

Photo editing

Photo editing software is quite popular these days. From photo corrections to removing unwanted marks and scratches, these software help save the precious time of the user.

Few examples of software used to tweak, organize, edit photos are

Fig. 10.2: Photo editing software

Adobe Photoshop, PixBuilder Studio, Dreamweaver, Windows Live Photo Gallery, Google Picasa, etc.

Word web

interactivity: it is the way communication takes place between human beings and computer software, for instance, in video games

navigation: the actions of moving through computer menus, files, folders, webpage or the Internet

passive recipients: receiving information passively

Video editing

Video editing software is used to edit videos. Using this software, you can add captions, subtitles and special effects to get the output as a movie on a DVD, pen drive or any external device. Whether you use your phone, digital camera or camcorder to capture any memorable moments, the video editing software lets you stitch together and trim your clips into one film.

Few examples of software used for professional editing purpose are CyberLink PowerDirector, Windows Live Movie Maker, OpenShot Video Editor (Fig. 10.3).

Fig.: 10.3: Video editing software

Games

One of the best areas of entertainment where one can see the usage of multimedia is games. Games serve as recreation to every individual. They are nowadays available in both offline and online mode. We find many games online that focus on developing individuals. Educational games, racing games, puzzles, adventure games and so on, are available for free and paid usage.

Fig. 10.4: Games

Use of multimedia

Multimedia can be defined as an interface used to present information in various formats like characters, numbers, symbols, audio, video, graphic and animation. Multimedia has its use in various sectors like business, education, research, entertainment etc. It is used in business for making presentations, training, advertising and networking.

netsearch

For additional information, visit:
https://videoscribe.co/
http://focusky.com/
http://torchbrowser.com/

Multimedia is used in education to develop applications which can be shared by various people simultaneously. For example dictionaries, e-books, newspaper, etc. Multimedia makes information more comprehensive as lot of variety may be instilled in learning or research. By going beyond text it not only makes things easier for the trainee but is a lifting experience for the trainer as well. Today multimedia is being used in all sectors of life like space, health care and not just cartoon and animation. Multimedia is mainly used in the field of entertainment. Different types of animation and cartoon effects can be applied. Effects on audio and video can also be given using multimedia.

Concepts learnt

1. Multimedia is described as the field that deals with computer-controlled integration of text, graphics, drawings, videos and any other media.
2. The different building blocks of Multimedia are Text, Audio, Image, Video, Graphics and Animation.
3. Multimedia is used in the entertainment industry, to develop special effects in movies and animations.
4. Adobe Photoshop and Dreamweaver are examples of Photo editing software.
5. Windows Live Movie Maker is an example of Video editing software.
6. Multimedia finds its roots in every sector from education to industry.

Exercise

A Fill in the blanks.

1. An application that uses a collection of multiple media sources is _____________ (multimedia/entertainment) application.
2. Multimedia applications that allow the users to actively participate in a session are called _____________ (entertainment/interactive) application.
3. A sequence of graphics images is _____________ (a graphic/an animation).
4. PowerDirector is an example of software used for _____________ (video editing/games).
5. _____________ (Photo/Graphics) is a computer generated image.

B Write T for True or F for False.

1. A sequence of picture can be converted into video. ☐
2. Photo editing software can be used to cut and crop video files. ☐
3. Multimedia games are available as software programs online. ☐
4. PixBuilder is a photo editing software. ☐
5. Multimedia is used only in business sector. ☐

C Choose the correct option.

1. Which among the following is not a building block of multimedia?
   (a) Text (b) Audio
   (c) Table (d) Video
2. Identify the false statement.
   (a) We use video editing software to tweak and edit photos.
   (b) Digital camera or camcorder is used to capture memorable moments as video.
   (c) One can add captions, subtitles, special effects using video editing software.
   (d) PixBuilder Studio is an example of video editing software.
3. Which of the following is not an example of still image?
   (a) Scanned image (b) Slides
   (c) Videos (d) Maps

4. Which among the following is a photo editing software?
   (a) Picasa (b) Cyberlink
   (c) Windows live Movie Maker (d) Windows Movie Maker

D Answer these questions briefly.

1. What do you mean by multimedia?
2. How is multimedia categorized?
3. What are the two kinds of multimedia presentations?
4. Write a short note on how multimedia is used in gaming.
5. Write a short note on the various uses of multimedia today.

E Application-based questions.

1. Mention few online dictionaries and newspapers available on the web.
2. Choose any character of your liking from any novel or book that is made into a movie. Share your opinion about the difference in their presentability.
3. Write a short note on Windows Live Movie Maker.

Computer is my mentor!

Create a multimedia work that you can present to the class using any software. The work can be on a topic and in a format of your choice, but all group members must agree on both the topic and format. Include at least two of the following forms of media: images, video, sound, animation, text or graphics. Be sure that your presentation lasts between 1 and 5 minutes.

Worksheet I

A Choose the correct option.

1 Which of these uses beads and string device for mathematical calculation?

a. Abacus
b. Tally stick
c. Harvard Mark 1
d. EDVAC

2. Electronic transmitters were used in which of the following generation computers?

a. First-generation computers
b. Second-generation computers
c. Third-generation computers
d. Fourth-generation computers

3. Which of the following is the correct expansion of LSIC?

a. Large Speed Integrated Communication
b. Light Speed Integrated Communication
c. Large Scale Integrated Circuits
d. Light Speed Integrated Circuits

4. Which of the following options can be used to change the overall appearance of the computer screen?

a. Color
b. Theme
c. Background
d. Screensaver

5. What is a suitable command to extract primary color from the Background?

a. Automatically pick an Accent Color from my background
b. Recent colors
c. Windows colors
d. Extract the primary colors from my background

6. Which of the following options is not available in 'Choose a fit' menu?

a. Stretch
b. Tile
c. Center
d. Rotate

7. What are folders present inside a folder called?

a. Micro folders
b. Sub-folders
c. Mini folders
d. Inside folders

8. Temporarily deleted files is found in which of the following folders?

a. Documents
b. Downloads
c. Recycle Bin
d. My Computer

9. Which of the following is a shortcut key to select all the files in a folder?
   a. Ctrl + A b. Ctrl + C
   c. Ctrl + V d. Ctrl + X
10. Ctrl + Shift + N command is used to perform one of these operations.
   a. Cut the files b. Move the files
   c. Create a new folder d. Renaming of files

B Fill in the blanks.

1. The ____________________ (Pascaline/Arithmometer) device was able to do all the four basic mathematical calculations.
2. The first stored program computer was developed by ____________________ (Von Neumann/John Presper Eckert).
3. Mouse cursor setting is available on ____________________ (Theme/Start) setting screen.
4. ________________ (Address bar/Taskbar) is not a personalized setting.
5. Option that can be used to change the mode of the files from extra-large icons to small icons is ____________________ (Current View/Layout).

C Write T for True or F for False.

1. Third-generation computers could form a network. ☐
2. Background option provides a quick check on the weather report. ☐
3. Windows Spotlight is a feature available in the Lock Screen option. ☐
4. Rename option helps to provide the desired name for the files. ☐
5. Home tab has the option to select all the files at a time. ☐

Worksheet II

A **Choose the correct option.**

1. Which of the following options reverses an operation performed in MS Word document?

    a. Undo b. Redo

    c. Save d. Save As

2. Which of the following is the representation of contents in a table aligned to the top and center?

    a. 

    b. 

    c. 

    d. 

3. Text effects option cannot be used to perform which of the following operations?

    a. Shadow b. Reflection

    c. Glow d. Strikethrough

4. Which of the following is a shortcut to increase the font size?

    a. Alt + Shift + < b. Alt + Shift + >

    c. Ctrl + Shift + < d. Ctrl + Shift + >

5. One of the following terms is suitable for a combination of different formatting options for tables available by default in MS Word.

    a. Borders b. Quick Style

    c. Justification d. Alignment

B **Fill in the blanks.**

1. The operation command that aligns the text both left and right is ________________ (Justification/Align center).
2. ________________ (Font Color/Highlighter) option is used to apply color over text in MS Word.
3. Tables can be added from ________________ (Home/Insert) tab.

4. Tables that have a standard format of calendars are known as ________________ (Quick Tables/Instant Tables).
5. ________________ (Merge/Split) option combines two or more cells.

C Write T for True or F for False.

1. View tab is a contextual tab. ☐
2. Italics command changes the features of the text. ☐
3. Font Color option is present in Font group of View tab. ☐
4. Borders are the two thin lines crossing at right angles, used as a marker. ☐
5. Cell Size option belongs to Layout tab. ☐

Worksheet III

A Choose the correct option.

1. Which of these has the shortcuts for the Comments pane?
   a. Status bar
   b. Notes pane
   c. Slide pane
   d. Title bar
2. Which of the following tabs are used to add themes and colour scheme to the presentation?
   a. Transition
   b. Animation
   c. Design
   d. Insert
3. Features from which of the following tabs can be used to choreograph the movement of things on the slides.
   a. SLIDE SHOW
   b. Transitions
   c. Review
   d. Animations
4. Which of the following is not available in the form of an E-newspaper?
   a. Times of India
   b. Darbar festival
   c. Hindustan Times
   d. Deccan Herald
5. Which of the following is the most advanced news media?
   a. Newspaper
   b. Radio
   c. Television
   d. Computer
6. In the digital world, which of the following serves as an easy medium to stay updated with the news?
   a. Computer and Newspaper
   b. Newspaper and Radio
   c. Television and Computer
   d. Computer and Internet
7. Which of the following is not correct with respect to Emails?
   a. Emails can be sent to multiple recipients.
   b. It is the fastest means of communication.
   c. Only text messages can be sent through mails.
   d. It is cheaper than post or courier services.
8. Which of the following is a perfect example for a password to an Email account?
   a. Ch!ntu10
   b. CH!NTU13
   c. ch!ntu12
   d. Chintu23

9. Which of the following is not an Email domain name?
   a. myworld b. google
   c. icloud d. outlook
10. Which of these provides description of the Email?
   a. Inbox b. Outbox
   c. To d. Subject

B Fill in the blanks.

1. ______________ (OpenOffice Impress/LibreOffice) is a presentation software.
2. Color or Greyscale feature is available in ______________ (Design/View) tab of MS PowerPoint.
3. ______________ (Newsstand/Flipboard) is a place that sells newspapers and periodicals.
4. News from various websites can be accessed through ______________ (Google Play Newsstand/Flipboard) in the form of a magazine.
5. The unsent scripted messages are stored in the ______________ (Draft/Inbox) folder.

C Write T for True or F for False.

1. The Slide pane is used to add content to each slide. ☐
2. Flipboard is a news aggregator operated by Google. ☐
3. News connects an individual only to the feature. ☐
4. Privacy and terms need not be accepted to create an Email account. ☐
5. Unwanted advertising mails from unknown recipients are placed in the Spam folder. ☐

Worksheet IV

A Choose the correct option.

1. In Scratch Programming, which among the following is a default sprite?
   a. Cat
   b. Boy
   c. Girl
   d. Bat
2. Which of the following icons is used to choose sprite from the Scratch library?
   a. 
   b. 
   c. 
   d. 
3. Which of the following options is not available under sound effects in Scratch Program?
   a. Upload sound from file
   b. Record new sound
   c. Choose sound from library
   d. Pause sound recording
4. Which of the following is a sequence of graphic images?
   a. Graphics
   b. Animation
   c. Video
   d. Still images
5. Which of the following is not an element of multimedia?
   a. Animation
   b. Video
   c. Audio
   d. Scanner

B Fill in the blanks.

1. ________________ (Pen/Motion) category under Scripts remains selected by default.
2. To switch between normal view to full screen view the user can use ________________ (Control/Support) tools.
3. ____________________ (Adobe Photoshop/CyberLink) application can be used to remove unwanted marks and scratches from the photos.
4. PowerDirector is an example for software used in ___________ (photo/video) editing.

5. _______________ (Dictionaries/Educational games) belong to the category of education applications used to share information by various people simultaneously.

C Write T for True or F for False.

1. Scratch provides the user with an option to change the colour of the sprite. ☐
2. Scratch does not allow the user to modify values in a code. ☐
3. Computer-based training is a non-linear content category of multimedia. ☐
4. Multimedia applications that allow users to just sit as a passive recipient for information are called Interactive Multimedia. ☐
5. Multimedia games serve as recreation tool for every individual. ☐

Worksheet V

Answer these questions.

1. Write a note on third-generation computers.

____

____

____

____

2. What are the options available from 'Choose a fit' menu from the Background settings?

____

____

____

____

3. Write the steps to change the theme of a computer screen.

____

____

____

____

4. Label the components of the File Explorer.

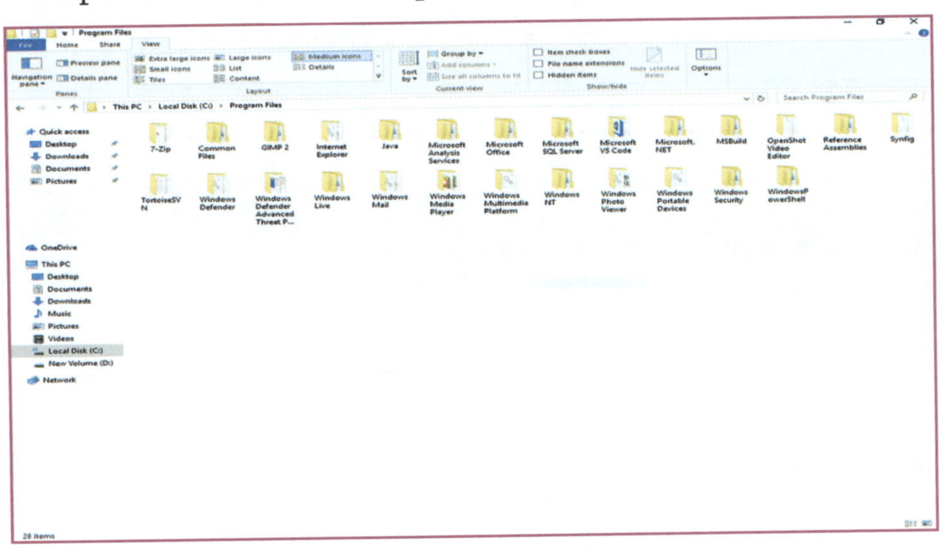

5. What are the different ways to rename a folder?

6. Write the steps to save a Word document.

7. Differentiate between text colour and font highlighter colour.

8. What are the different groups in Design tab? Explain them in one line.

9. Write a note on merging cells.

10. Write the steps to create a new item.

Worksheet VI

Answer these questions.

1. What are the uses of MS PowerPoint 2013?

2. Write a short note on the following:
   a. Transition tab
   b. Animation tab
   c. SLIDE SHOW tab

3. Write a note on E-newspapers.

4. Write a note on Flipboard.

5. List the features of an Email account and explain how to sign out from the account.

6. List the steps to attach a document in an Email.

7. List the steps to choose a stage background in Scratch programming.

8. Explain scripts in Scratch programming.

9. What are the different elements of multimedia?

10. Write a note on use of multimedia in video editing.

Revision Worksheet 1

Maximum Marks: 50

A Choose the correct option. (5 x 1 = 5)

1. The vacuum tube device belongs to ______________ computers.
   a. first-generation b. second-generation
   c. third-generation d. fourth-generation
2. Which among the following options does not belong to personalization of computer?
   a. Taskbar b. Screen saver
   c. Address bar d. Wallpaper
3. Which of the following option can be used to change the name to a file?
   a. Create b. Rename
   c. Copy d. Paste
4. Shadow effect can be given using ______________.
   a. Text effect b. Heading effect
   c. Copy and Paste d. Line spacing
5. Small units in a table are called ______________.
   a. columns b. rows
   c. cells d. plates

B Fill in the blanks. (5 x 1 = 5)

1. The difference and analytical engine was invented by ___________. (Charles Babbage/Alan Turing)
2. Undo is a tool that ___________ (deletes/reverses) the previous action.
3. The temporarily deleted files are moved to __________ (Recycle bin/ Documents) folder in the computer.
4. Highlighter option is used to apply ___________ (colour/movement) over text.
5. Tables that have standard formats like calendars and tabular columns are called ______________ (Quick tables/Fast tables).

C Write T for True or F for False. (5 x 1 = 5)

1. IBM ASCC was the first programmable computer. ☐
2. Lock screen is a part of personalization. ☐

3. We can create sub-folders inside a folder. ☐
4. Cut option removes the text from the original document. ☐
5. Merge option is used to combine two or more cells. ☐

D Answer these questions briefly. **(10 x 2 = 20)**

1. Differentiate between second and third generation computers.
2. Write a note on the artificial intelligence technology in fifth generation of computers.
3. What is meant by personalization of a computer?
4. List the changes that can be made using Taskbar option.
5. How do you create a new folder and a sub-folder inside it?
6. Differentiate between Undo and Redo options.
7. What is the function of Find and Replace options?
8. How to insert a table in MS Word?
9. Explain Table Style options in MS Word.
10. Write the steps to copy and paste a document.

E Answer these questions in detail. **(5 x 3 = 15)**

1. Write the steps to organize the files in descending order.
2. Write a note on different panes in File Explorer.
3. Explain the Line Spacing operation in MS Word.
4. What are the three options using which the Background menu can be changed in Windows 10?
5. Explain the steps to delete a row or column in MS Word.

Revision Worksheet 2

Maximum Marks: 50

A Choose the correct option. (5 x 1 = 5)

1. Which of the following is a commonly used presentation program?
   a. MS PowerPoint b. MS Excel
   c. MS Word d. Apple Keynote
2. Which among the following is a news aggregator?
   a. Blog b. Flipboard
   c. Email d. E-newspaper
3. Pictures or documents can be sent through Email as
   a. Attachments b. Spam
   c. Draft d. Card
4. The default stage backdrop of Scratch is a _____ screen.
   a. white b. grey
   c. pale blue d. yellow
5. The sequence of graphic images is known as _____
   a. animation b. audio
   c. graphics d. None of these

B Fill in the blanks. (5 x 1 = 5)

1. The bar that is present at the top of the program window is ______________ (Title bar/Quick Access toolbar).
2. ________________ (Flipboard/Blog) aggregates content from other websites in the form of text, images and videos.
3. The mails that we send will be in the ________________ (Outbox/Sent) until it is sent.
4. The default sprite in the Scratch is a ________________ (cat/mouse).
5. ____________________ (Adobe Photoshop/Cyber Link) is an example of video editing software.

C Write T for True or F for False. (5 x 1 = 5)

1. Animation tab is used to change the design of the presentation. ☐
2. One who creates blogs is known as a blogger. ☐

3. Cc recipients of an Email are not visible to other recipients. ☐
4. A sprite selected once cannot be changed again. ☐
5. Interactive multimedia allows users to actively participate in the sessions. ☐

D Answer these questions briefly. **(10 x 2 = 20)**

1. What is presentation software? Give two examples.
2. How are features in Transition and Animation tab different in MS PowerPoint?
3. Write a short note on Tool tab in MS PowerPoint.
4. Latest news around the world is important for every individual and needs to be updated. Why?
5. Write a short note on blogs.
6. Briefly explain E-newspaper, Blog and Flipboard.
7. What is an Email? Mention the precautions to be taken while using an Email account?
8. What are the basic fields that need to be filled in while sending message through an Email?
9. Name the feature in Scratch that helps us to access the programming codes.
10. How is multimedia used in gaming?

E Answer these questions in detail. **(5 x 3 = 15)**

1. What are the steps to fill in a registration form to create an Email account?
2. What is a stage background? Explain the steps to add a stage background in Scratch programming.
3. Explain the Scripts option available in Scratch programming.
4. How is multimedia categorized?
5. Write a short note on how multimedia is used in photo editing.

CLASS 4

QUESTION PAPER SET A

KSHITIJ IIT Kharagpur

NCO

SOF NATIONAL CYBER OLYMPIAD 2017-18

DO NOT OPEN THIS BOOKLET UNTIL ASKED TO DO SO

Total Questions: 35 | Time: 1 hr.

Guidelines for the Candidate

1. You will get additional ten minutes to fill up information about yourself on the OMR Sheet, before the start of the exam.
2. Write your **Name, School Code, Class, Section, Roll No.** and **Mobile Number** clearly on the **OMR Sheet** and do not forget to sign it. We will share with you your marks / result on your mobile number.
3. The Question Paper comprises three sections:
   Logical Reasoning (5 Questions), **Computers and Information Technology** (25 Questions) and **Achievers Section** (5 Questions).
   Each question in Achievers Section carries 2 marks, whereas all other questions carry one mark each.
4. All questions are compulsory. There is no negative marking. Use of calculator is not permitted.
5. There is only ONE correct answer. Choose only ONE option for an answer.
6. To mark your choice of answers by darkening the circles on the OMR Sheet, use **HB Pencil** or **Blue / Black ball point pen** only. E.g.
   Q.16: _____ means to hold down the left mouse button while you move the mouse pointer to a new place.
   A. Single click B. Double click C. Dragging D. Left click
   As the correct answer is option C, you must darken the circle corresponding to option C in the OMR Sheet. 16. Ⓐ Ⓑ ● Ⓓ
7. Rough work should be done in the blank space provided in this booklet.
8. Return the OMR Sheet to the invigilator at the end of the exam.
9. Please fill in your personal details in the space provided on this page before attempting the paper.
10. *For classes 8, 9, 10, 11 & 12 "TEENAGE PRODIGY" is being conducted by KSHITIJ IIT Kharagpur in association with SOF. For details, please visit : www.sofworld.org/iit-kharagpur-teenage-prodigy.*

SOF
SCIENCE OLYMPIAD FOUNDATION
Inspiring Young Minds Through Knowledge Olympiads

Name:..

Section:.............. SOF Olympiad Roll No.:......................... Contact No.:..

1. Some letters are given which are numbered 1, 2, 3, 4, 5 and 6. Find the combination of numbers so that letters are arranged accordingly to form a meaningful word.

O N W R E D
1 2 3 4 5 6

A. 3, 2, 1, 4, 5, 6 B. 2, 3, 1, 4, 5, 6 C. 3, 1, 2, 6, 5, 4 D. 3, 1, 4, 2, 6, 5

---

2. Priya is facing the Temple. She makes a 1/4 turn to her right and then 3/4 turn to her left. What will she be facing now?

A. Market

B. College

C. Airport

D. Church

---

3. Find the missing number, if a certain rule is followed either row-wise or column-wise.

63	40	?
9	5	11
7	8	6

A. 98 B. 66 C. 70 D. 82

---

4. If in a certain code language, 'FAVOUR' is written as '5#2@3∗' and 'DANGER' is written as '6#1$7∗', then how will 'FOUNDER' be written in that code language?

A. 5@3167∗ B. 521∗6@2 C. 5@7∗6$2 D. 5#3@6$1

---

5. Select the correct mirror image of Fig. (X), if the mirror is placed along MN.

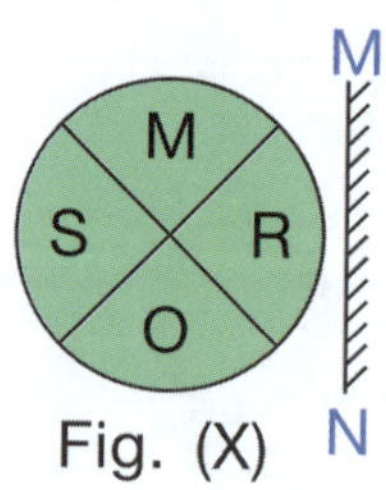

Fig. (X)

A. 

B. 

C. 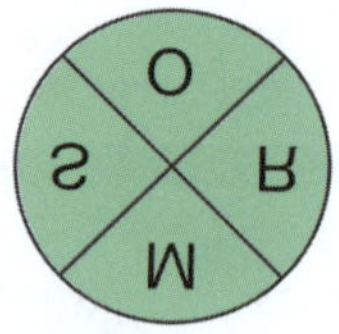

D. 

SPACE FOR ROUGH WORK

6. What would be the result if you perform the given steps for the following text in MS-Word 2010?

Computer helps in storing information.

(i) Select the word 'information'. (ii) Press Ctrl + }] key.

A. Selected word will get underlined.
B. Selected word will become bold.
C. The size of the font of the selected word will get increased.
D. Selected word will get converted in uppercase letters.

---

7. Identify the following:
- It is an input device.
- It is more commonly used device to capture live pictures.

A.  B.  C.  D. 

---

8. Sudha's teacher has asked her to paste the image of an input device which has the following characteristics:
- It is a pointing device that provides direct input.
- It can be lifted and repositioned.

Which of the following devices has the above characteristics?

A. Touchpad B. Stylus C. Scanner D. Microphone

---

9. Which of the following statements hold(s) true about the command button given here with respect to MS-Word 2010?

Statement 1 : It increases the font size of selected text.
Statement 2 : It changes all the letters of selected text to lowercase.

A. Only Statement 1 B. Only Statement 2
C. Both Statement 1 and Statement 2 D. Neither Statement 1 nor Statement 2

---

10. Which of the following statements is/are CORRECT about the program whose icon is shown here with respect to Windows 7?

(i) It organizes and controls the working of all the peripherals attached to a system.
(ii) It protects your system from untrusted sources.
(iii) It is a kind of utility software.

A. Only (i) B. Only (ii) C. Only (iii) D. All (i), (ii) and (iii)

SPACE FOR ROUGH WORK

11. Which of the following is the function of the disk drive available in CPU cabinet?
   A. To read and write data to/from a USB flash drive.
   B. To read and write data to/from a Compact or Digital Versatile Discs.
   C. To format the hard disk.
   D. To calculate the storage space available on hard disk.

---

12. Megha wanted to type the sentence – She wants to call her friend immediately, but instead she typed – She wants too call here friend immediatdly. Which of the following set of words will be highlighted by the Spelling and Grammar feature of MS-Word 2010?
   A. too, wants
   B. here, friend
   C. here, call
   D. too, here, immediatdly

---

13. Select the odd one out.
   A. 
   B. 
   C. 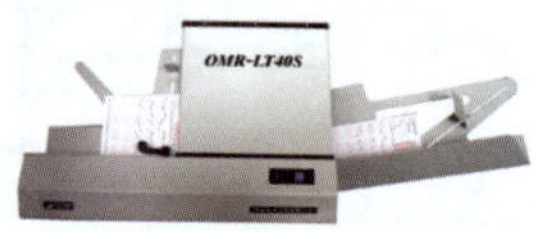

   D. 

---

14. Select the CORRECT match with respect to Windows 7.
   A. Alt + Tab - Used to switch from one application window to another.
   B. Alt + F4 - Displays the fourth item on taskbar.
   C. Ctrl + Esc - Show/hide the notification area icons.
   D.  + L - Enlarges the desktop icons.

---

15. Which of the following statements hold(s) true about the icon marked as (X) in given screenshot of MS-Paint?

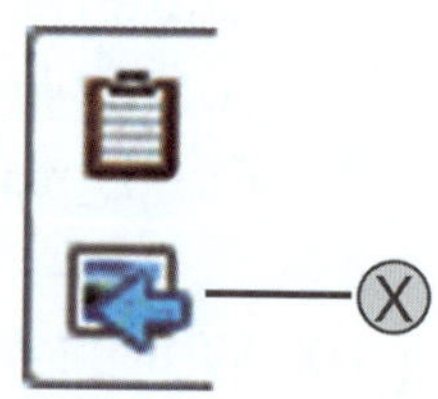

   Statement 1 : It lets you insert existing images in your system.
   Statement 2 : The name of this icon is "Insert Picture".
   A. Only Statement 1
   B. Only Statement 2
   C. Both Statement 1 and Statement 2
   D. Neither Statement 1 nor Statement 2

---

16. Which of the following command button's task is performed when you press F11 key on keyboard while working in MS-Paint?
   A. 
   B. 
   C. 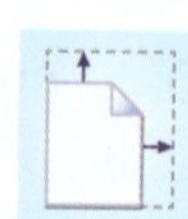
   D. 

SPACE FOR ROUGH WORK

17. Which of the following is/are system software?

(i) 

(ii) 

(iii) 

(iv) 

A. Only (i)
B. Both (i) and (iii)
C. Both (ii) and (iv)
D. Both (ii) and (iii)

---

18. Which of the following is the name of a removable thin card, used in smartphones and digital cameras to store data?

A. SD card
B. Disk card
C. Memory bar
D. Media disk

---

19. __________ generation of computers have the ability to speak and understand human languages, analyse situations and think logically. Thus, these computers are based on __________.

A. Fifth, Artificial intelligence
B. Fourth, Integrated intelligence
C. Fifth, Integrated intelligence
D. Fourth, Sufficient intelligence

---

20. You frequently use Spelling and Grammar feature available in MS-Word 2010. You want that this feature shall always be visible to you no matter which tab is open. Which of the following actions when performed will do so?

A. Click and drag it to the title bar.
B. Right click on it and select "Add to Quick Access Toolbar".
C. Minimize the ribbon.
D. All of these

---

21. Which of the following Shape outline medium has been applied in making shape 1 and shape 2 (as shown here) in MS-Paint?

	Shape 1	Shape 2
A.	Watercolor	Natural pencil
B.	Natural pencil	Watercolor
C.	Natural pencil	Natural pencil
D.	Watercolor	Watercolor

Shape 1

Shape 2

---

22. Which of the following devices can be connected to other device (directly/indirectly) via given port?

A. Only (i)
B. Both (i) and (ii)
C. Both (ii) and (iii)
D. (i), (ii) and (iii)

Port

(i)

(ii)

(iii)

SPACE FOR ROUGH WORK

23. Today's computers typically come with this device, that contains several billion bytes (GB, TB) of storage. It is a secondary storage device that provides relatively quick access to large amount of data. Identify it.

A. 

B. 

C. 

D. 

---

24. Utilities are the programs that assist in the smooth functioning of a computer. Some utilities help you to :

1. Avoid virus attack
2. Take backup of data
3. Recover data that has been accidentally erased

Which of the following is a utility software?

A.

B. Norton by Symantec

C.

D.

---

25. What does the icons 1 and 2 represent in the given snapshot of Internet Explorer?

A. (1) – Display most recently-entered web addresses in the address bar
   (2) – Refresh

B. (1) – Review
   (2) – Display most recently-entered web addresses in the address bar

C. (1) – Display most recently-entered web addresses in the address bar
   (2) – Review

D. (1) – Refresh
   (2) – Review

---

26. Which of the following options of File tab/Paint button displays the given pop-up menu in MS-Paint?

A. 

B. 

C. 

D. 

SPACE FOR ROUGH WORK

27. Which of the following prevents unauthorized access in a network?

A. Firewall B. Infrared C. Bluetooth D. Screen saver

---

28. Complete the following sentences.

_______ is internet service that translates websites names into _________ . The company or organization that provides services for accessing and using the internet is called ______.

A. DNS, Symbols, URL
B. URL, Code, DNS
C. DNS, Numbers, ISP
D. URL, Symbols, Wireless Fidelity

---

29. Google Glasses are an interactive pair of eyeglasses. They provide smartphone like display and natural language voice command support, Bluetooth and Wi-Fi connectivity. They are examples of ________ technology.

A. Fixed B. Handheld C. Hidden D. Wearable

---

30. Which of the following software directly interacts with the user and does not perform the maintenance and management tasks of the computer system?

A. Word Processing Software
B. Antivirus Software
C. Disk Defragmenter
D. Device Driver

ACHIEVERS SECTION

31. Which of the following statements hold(s) true about plotters ?

Statement 1 : They can work on very large sheets of paper.

Statement 2 : They can print on flat materials like plywood, cardboard and plastic.

A. Only Statement 1
B. Only Statement 2
C. Both Statement 1 and Statement 2
D. Neither Statement 1 nor Statement 2

---

32. Which of the following statements is CORRECT about Icon-1 and Icon 2 with respect to Windows 7?

Icon-1

Icon-2

A. Icon-1 displays desktop backgrounds and Icon-2 displays local drives.

B. Icon-1 displays options for screen brightness and resolutions and Icon-2 is used for changing the system time.

C. Icon-1 displays various desktop gadgets available in the system and Icon-2 shows the list of computers and other devices available on the network.

D. Icon-1 displays the options to change taskbar appearance and Icon- 2 displays the options to change the appearance of Start menu.

SPACE FOR ROUGH WORK

33. What would be displayed on screen if you perform the following steps for the given text in MS-Word 2010 ?

Be good for something.

Be thankful for everything.

(i) Select the first sentence.

(ii) Click on  icon.

(iii) Drag the mouse from first letter of sentence 2 to the last letter.

A. Be good for something.
Be thankful for everything.

B. Be good for something.
Be thankful for everything.

C. Be good for something.
Be thankful for everything.

D. Be good for something.
Be thankful for everything.

34. Which of the following statements is/are CORRECT ?

(i) Abacus is believed to be the first automated device.

(ii) Charles Babbage invented the Difference Engine.

(iii) The first generation computers were massive structures that provided large storage capacity.

A. Only (i) B. Only (ii) C. Both (i) and (iii) D. Both (ii) and (iii)

35. Which of the following options best describes the network technologies shown in Image-1 and Image-2?

Image-1

Image-2

A. 1- Wireless technology that provides internet access.
2- Wireless technology that is used for data exchange over short distances.

B. 1-Wired technology that provides internet access.
2- Wired technology that is used for data exchange over short distances.

C. 1- A mode of connecting to internet by paying some fee.
2- It represents untrusted networks.

D. 1- It represents untrusted networks.
2- It represents data transmission technology.

ANSWER KEYS

1.	(C)	**2.**	(A)	**3.**	(B)	**4.**	(A)	**5.**	(B)	**6.**	(C)	**7.**	(C)
8.	(B)	**9.**	(D)	**10.**	(C)	**11.**	(B)	**12.**	(D)	**13.**	(A)	**14.**	(A)
15.	(A)	**16.**	(B)	**17.**	(B)	**18.**	(A)	**19.**	(A)	**20.**	(B)	**21.**	(A)
22.	(D)	**23.**	(D)	**24.**	(B)	**25.**	(A)	**26.**	(B)	**27.**	(A)	**28.**	(C)
29.	(D)	**30.**	(A)	**31.**	(C)	**32.**	(C)	**33.**	(B)	**34.**	(B)	**35.**	(A)

Updates on Open Office

You have studied the applications like MS Word, MS PowerPoint which comes as the package MS Office. There are many free open sources available using which we can perform the same tasks that we do in MS Word and MS PowerPoint. Libre Office is one such package which allows you to create documents similar to that of MS Word and presentations similar to that of MS PowerPoint.

Opening Libre Office Writer Document

Libre Office Writer Document allows you create a document similar to that of MS Word. You can open a Writer Document by clicking the mouse on the Writer Document button on the Libre Office window as shown below.

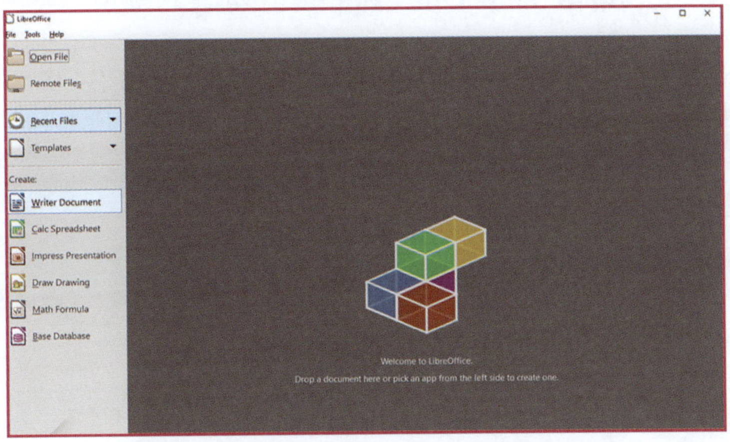

Fig. 1: Libre Office Writer Document

When you open the Libre Office Writer Document, the options that appear on the ribbon is shown in the image below. The options similar to that of MS Word are available here also.

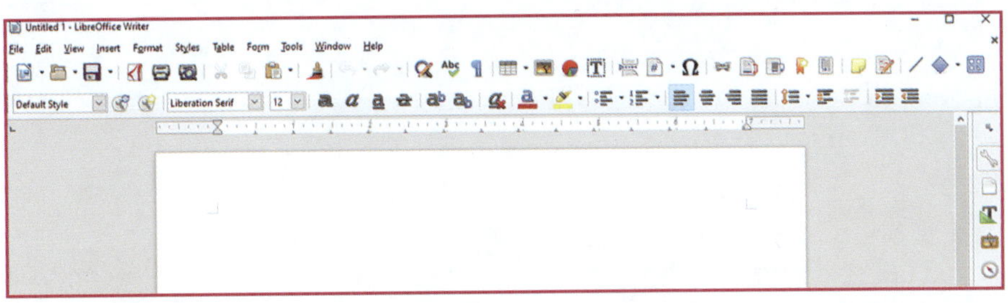

Fig. 2: Components of Libre Office Writer Document

Opening Libre Office Impress Presentation

Libre Office Impress Presentation allows you to create a presentation similar to that of MS PowerPoint. You can open Impress Presentation by clicking the mouse on the Impress Presentation button on the Libre Office window as shown below.

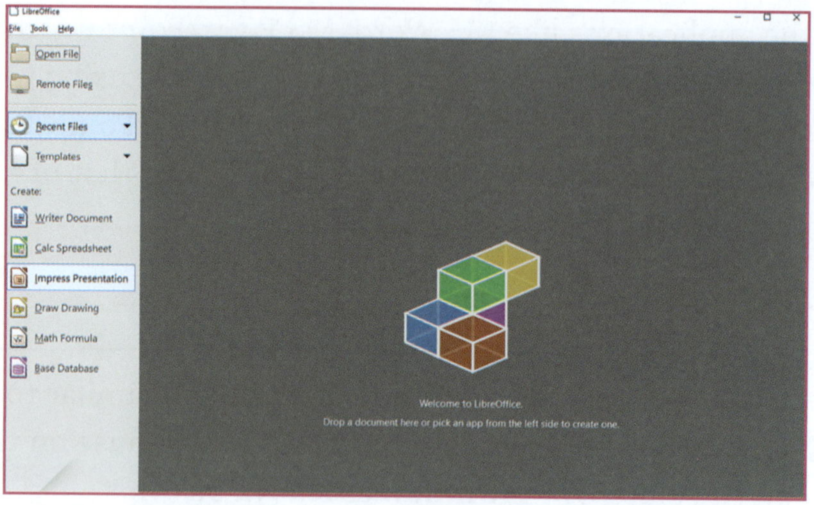

Fig. 3: Libre Office Impress Presentation

When you open an Impress Presentation, the options that appear in the ribbon are shown in the image below. The options similar to that of MS PowerPoint are available here also.

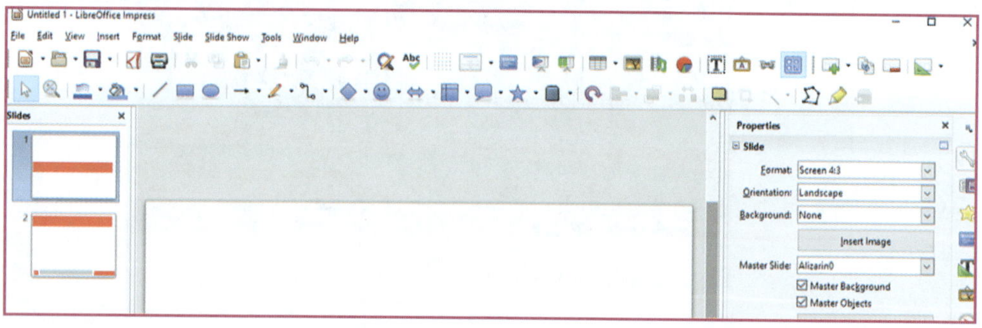

Fig. 4: Components of Libre Office Impress Presentation

Windows 8 Pointers

Windows 8 is an operating system launched by Microsoft in the year 2012 which was released after Windows 7.

Windows 8 has a start screen, which is a feature that replaced the start menu. It displays all the applications as tiles. The start screen also has live tiles, which provide information and show notifications. It requires staying connected to the internet for live tiles to function.

There is a toolbar on the Windows 8 known as Charms bar that appears on the right side of the screen. The Charms bar can be accessed from any application or from the desktop by sliding from the right edge of a touchscreen or compatible trackpad to the left. It can also be accessed by moving the cursor to one of the right corners of the screen or pressing ⊞ + C. The Charms bar has tools to search the computer, access PC settings and start screen and devices connected to the PC.

Another new addition to Windows 8 is an in-built application store known as the Windows Store which has several applications that can be downloaded to run on the Windows.

There is a new toolbar in Windows 8 known as Hot Corners. When the cursor is moved to the top left corner, a small window appears. This is the window of the previous opened application. Hot Corners are useful in switching between the applications.

Windows Explorer in previous versions of Windows has been named as File Explorer in Windows 8. It has a ribbon toolbar that gives easy access to commonly used commands. The File Explorer has several useful sections that allows the user to navigate through files and folders on the computer.

Fig. 1: Windows Start screen

Fig. 2: Charms Bar

Fig 3: Hot Corners

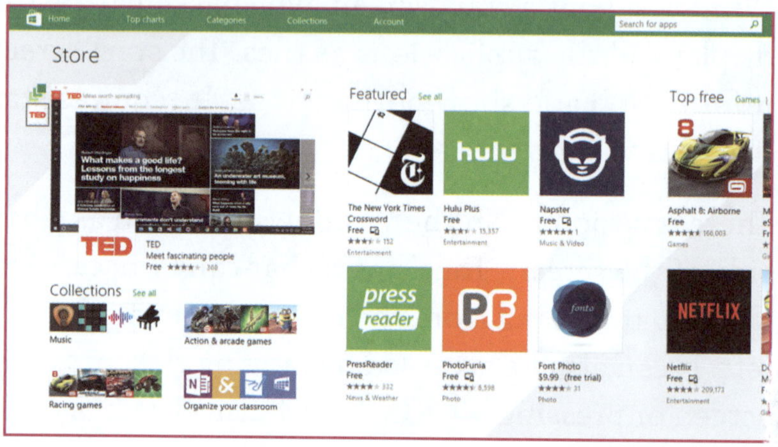

Fig 4: Windows Store

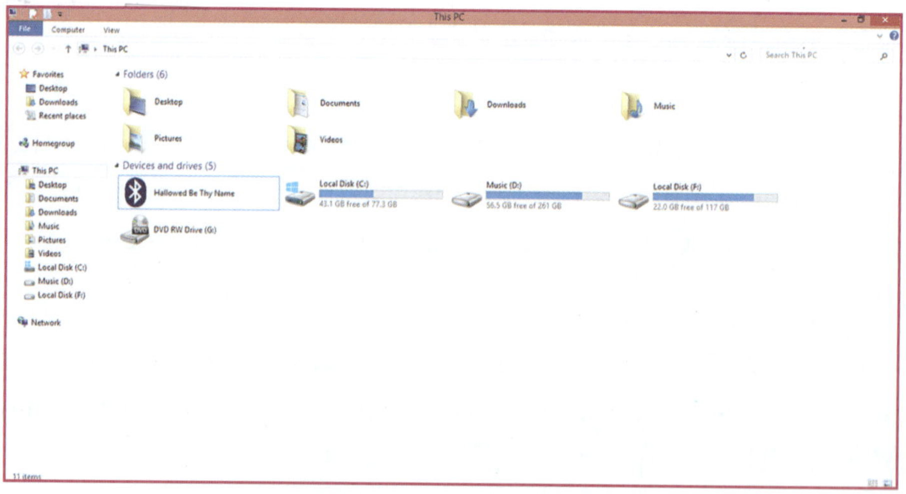

Fig 5: File Explorer